Five Seventeenth-Century Poets

DONNE ● HERBERT ● CRASHAW ●

VAUGHAN ● MARVELL

Five Seventeenth-Century Poets

DONNE ● HERBERT ● CRASHAW ●

VAUGHAN ● MARVELL

Edited, with an Introduction, Commentaries and Notes
by
BRIJRAJ SINGH
Formerly Professor of English, University of Delhi

OXFORD
UNIVERSITY PRESS

OXFORD
UNIVERSITY PRESS

YMCA Library Building, Jai Singh Road, New Delhi 110001

Oxford University Press is a department of the University of Oxford.
It furthers the University's objective of excellence in research, scholarship
and education by publishing worldwide in

Oxford   New York

Auckland Bangkok Buenos Aires Cape Town Chennai
Dar es Salaam Delhi Hong Kong Istanbul Karachi Kolkata
Kuala Lumpur Madrid Melbourne Mexico City Mumbai Nairobi
São Paulo Shanghai Singapore Taipei Tokyo Toronto

with an associated company in Berlin

Oxford is a registered trade mark of Oxford University Press
in the UK and in certain other countries.

Published in India
by Oxford University Press

First published 1992
Sixth impression 2002

ISBN 0-19-562800-4

Printed in India by Chaman Offset Press, New Delhi 110002
and published by Manzar Khan, Oxford University Press
YMCA Library Building, Jai Singh Road, New Delhi 110001

For my son Viru
"A box where sweets compacted lie"
who I hope will one day learn to read this book

and for all my former students
now teaching the seventeenth century: Heroes all

PREFACE

For more than three decades Indian students have used Helen Gardner's anthology *The Metaphysical Poets* to study the poets of the first half of the seventeenth century. Admirable though the book is, its paucity of annotations has always been a major hurdle in the way of students who are not very familiar with Biblical allusions and seventeenth-century British history. A replacement more suited to the needs of Indian students of seventeenth-century English poetry seems to be required, and this anthology hopes to perform that function.

Its limitation compared to Gardner's book is its narrower range: it offers selections from the work of five poets of the period. On the other had, it annotates each of the poems much more fully, and in both the annotations and its critical commentaries takes into account the significant scholarship that has proliferated on the seventeenth century since Gardner's anthology was published. The bibliography, too, is more extensive and up-to-date. I hope that those who teach as well as study the seventeenth century in India will find my book both useful and uncompromising in its standard of scholarship.

Work for this book was done at the new, beautiful and congenial Benjamin Rosenthal Library of Queens College, New York. The City University of New York has a wonderfully generous policy of allowing all its members to make full use of the academic facilities of any of its constituent colleges. This fact should not remain unacknowledged.

My wife Frances was supportive as ever, and Dolcy Suting freed both of us from domestic chores so we could devote all the time we needed to our work.

Brijraj Singh

Republic Day, 1990 Hostos Community College, New York

CONTENTS

INTRODUCTION

METAPHYSICAL POETRY

The poets represented in this book have been called 'Metaphysical' for so long that it may be best to start with a consideration of that term.

Its earliest uses were pejorative. William Drummond of Hawthornden (1585-1649) spoke, in an undated letter, of poets who use 'Metaphysical *Ideas* and *Scholastical Quiddities*'; and Dryden, in 1693, accused Donne of affecting 'the metaphysics where nature only should reign', and perplexing the 'minds of the fair sex with nice speculations of philosophy, when he should engage their hearts...with the softnesses of love'. Samuel Johnson, who made the first systematic study of Donne and some of his contemporaries in his *Life of Cowley*, followed suit when he defined these poets' wit as 'Metaphysical', by which he meant a heterogeneous yoking together of ideas by violence. His rhetorical question: 'Who but Donne would have thought of a good man as a telescope?' was meant to suggest something unnatural in these poets' quest after novelty.

In the twentieth century it has been pointed out that Johnson was criticizing only the worst excesses of poets like Cowley, that there is much genuine praise for Donne in his critique, that he was well read in the 'Metaphysicals' and included several quotations from them in his *Dictionary*. While this is true, it needs to be emphasized that the new understanding of Johnson's purposes has resulted as much from a changed attitude towards the 'Metaphysicals' as from more careful Johnson scholarship. For in the early years of this century a Donne revival took place, and the word 'Metaphysical', which was hitherto a term of criticism, consequently became a badge of distinction.

T.S. Eliot had much to do with this revival. Looking for models for the kind of poetry he wanted to write, he found none more suitable than the French *Symbolistes* and Donne, the latter having then been recently edited by Herbert Grierson. Eliot's essays on Donne, Herbert and Marvell had as an aim the creation of a sensibility that could better understand his own poetic purposes. But he was already becoming so respected that whatever he said about these poets came to be received as the truth. The age was responding to what it saw mirrored of itself in Donne no less than in Eliot.

Though Eliot corrected many misapprehensions about the poets of the seventeenth century, in one respect he helped to solidify an older tradition: he retained the term 'Metaphysical' for these poets, though as a term of praise. He even spoke about a 'school of Donne'. The result was that readers came to think of seventeenth-century poets as forming a continuum, a poetic tradition, where each found his voice in learning from the others. And since Donne was chronologically the earliest, the poet with whom Eliot himself had the greatest affinities and whom he had singled out for special consideration, it came to be believed not only that he was the greatest poet of this group but also that the other poets who followed shared essential qualities in common with him.

Much of the critical effort of Eliot and his followers was directed at defining what these qualities were, a task rendered harder by the fact that none of these poets had left behind a theory of poetry which could help to explain what they were doing. Critics pointed out that the term 'Metaphysical' did not necessarily refer to a metaphysical quality in Donne's poems; indeed, though he and the others wrote some poems that could be truly described as metaphysical, on the whole their work was not transcendental. Instead, the term was meant to describe the vivid recreation of palpable, immediate reality in vigorous colloquial rhythms which were part of a sixteenth-century fashion found on the Continent and also in the verse of some late Elizabethan dramatists. F.R. Leavis argued that Donne was superior to Milton because his verse enacted his meaning. Eliot himself popularized the view that Donne possessed a unified sensibility and that for him every thought was an experience. Many commentators focused upon Donne's imagery', in which they saw the clearest embodiment of his 'Metaphysical' qualities. It became a commonplace of criticism that Donne's images were original and striking, that they represented the fusion of the intellectual with the emotional, that they were recondite, that they were put to argumentative use, and that they were either piled up one on the other in breathtaking succession or else were elaborated almost to the breaking point of ingenuity.

Of course, not all readers were convinced. Rosemund Tuve argued that what appeared to be striking or original in Donne or Herbert was, in fact, rooted in medieval and Renaissance traditions which modern readers had failed to recognize. These poets' imagery, far from being 'Metaphysical' in the sense described above, was borrowed from the Liturgy, commentaries by Church Fathers, emblem books, stained glass windows in churches, and other sources with which all people of the sixteenth and seventeenth centuries were familiar. Tuve did much to correct an unhistorical approach to these poets. But in maintaining that poets like Donne could be explained entirely in terms of tradition she denied them the very originality that has caught every reader's attention down the centuries.

Another significant approach was that suggested by Louis Martz. In seeing the poets as poets of meditation rather than 'Metaphysical' he tried to focus attention away from their style to their content. By stressing their shared techniques, aims and traditions, he corrected the misconception that Donne was somehow the founder of a school to which his less talented contemporaries belonged. So long as the word 'Metaphysical' was in vogue it had conferred a primacy upon Donne, but its replacement by 'Metaphysical' came to suggest a prior tradition from which Donne as well as the others drew in different ways.

The scholarship with which Martz establishes his theory is matched by his sensitivity in reading the poems. He shows that in the seventeenth century there was not the cleavage between Roman Catholicism and various forms of Protestantism that became characteristic in later ages. Protestants might denounce Catholic doctrine, yet they drew upon common devotional materials and manuals of meditation. The truth is that there was a remarkable intellectual openness about the age which terms like Protestant and Catholic conceal: the divisions were real, but there was much interflow of literature and thought from one side to the other. Martz brings out this aspect of the age well by placing the Protestant poets in a catholic tradition of meditation.

However, the fact remains that there was also a Protestant tradition that had developed by now, based upon a poetics derived from the Bible; and to ignore it as a major influence upon poets like Herbert and Marvell would be to deny something of the richness and complexity of the age. Barbara Lewalski has provided a corrective to Martz by studying this Protestant tradition out of which so much of sixteenth- and seventeenth-century religious verse in England grows.

Persuasive as Lewalski is, she and Martz raise certain problems. First, to see the poets represented here as being in the meditative tradition, whether Catholic or Protestant, is to give less than due consideration to their secular poetry. It is true that all these poets wrote religious verse; it is equally true that much of their secular verse is shot through with religious images or can be said to have a larger religious purpose. We may even grant that the structure of this secular verse recalls the structure of meditation. But there is also a substantial core of secular verse—some of Donne's elegies and *Songs and Sonnets*, for example, or Marvell's love lyrics and Horatian Ode—which cannot be explained in terms of religious meditation.

Second, to emphasize an intellectual tradition from which poets draw is inevitably to flatten out somewhat the differences which they exhibit, even when we acknowledge that they draw upon it in different ways. It is to stress commonality at the expense of individuality, even uniqueness. There can be no doubt of the myriad links which bind the poets in this anthology together. Donne and Herbert were friends; Herbert's *The Temple* was an inspiration for Crashaw's *Steps to the Temple* and Vaughan's *Silex Scintillans;* Marvell was conscious that in his poems he was summing up his predecessors' achievements and taking them to new limits. But the dominant impression we get on reading these poets is not one of similarities but of differences. One can never mistake a poem by one for another's. Neither the term 'Metaphysical' nor the term 'meditation' underlines this differentiating quality. That is why I have avoided these terms in the title, preferring to see the poets as belonging to no school, adhering to no one master, and bound together essentially by an interest in religion and by history, by the fact that they wrote largely in the first half of the seventeenth century. To view their meaning as the outcome of their different encounters with their times may be a better approach than that provided by labels such as 'Metaphysical poets' or 'poets of meditation'.

DONNE

In order to understand Donne's negotiations with history it is worth remembering that he stood at the meeting point of the medieval and modern periods. Tuve has pointed out his debt to medieval emblems and symbols, and the hair-splitting logic and quality of argument we encounter in his verse and sermons owe more to the scholastic tradition than is the case with his later contemporaries. At the same time, in his restless quest for experience and a desire to make sense of it, and in his sceptical, questioning attitude he is modern rather than medieval.

To the medieval man the universe was God's book that could be read at different levels and in different ways. According to this view God has built subtle and hidden correspondences and relationships between all objects in the universe and between man and these objects. These correspondences show the 'wit' of God; and the task of man, in the words of S.L. Bethell, is to use his own divinely derived wit not only to appreciate the conceits already fully written in the book of nature but also to form conceits of his own from what is present in nature only potentially, 'piecing together the scattered letters into meaningful phrases'. Using the sixteenth-century Italian theorist Tesauro as his source, Bethell goes on to say that for the medieval poet the highest kind of wit took the form of arguments which were daring and fallacious and playful. They were witty not because the poet saw his task as the creation of fictions but because he wanted to reveal the truths that God had hidden in His works. Since he wanted to open men's eyes to the wit of God, he created the most outrageous arguments and relationships in order to teach us that even the most remote and unusual relationships that man could conceive of had been ordained by God. Through the poet's outrageous fallacies God's truth was revealed; indeed, the more surprising the poet's wit, the better it revealed the surprises that God Himself had hidden in the universe. The less promising the poet's subject, the more triumphantly was he able to express God's order, for no one would suspect the presence of order there. In Donne an example of this kind of wit is to be found in 'The Flea', where the flea, blood and sex are linked to the sacrament of marriage. According to Bethell, in this conceit Donne displays an order which is revealed through and in the least promising material: 'jewels among the mud'

Bethell's explanation of Donne's wit is more convincing because better grounded in history than that provided by critics who see Donne merely as outrageous and learned and argumentative and dramatic: in one word, a 'Metaphysical' poet. But while it accounts for the sense of triumph that accompanies Donne's forceful and victorious arguments, it leaves unexplained the note of desperation which, too, is so characteristic of his poetry. This desperation comes from a feeling that the certainties of the medieval world are no longer available. The Renaissance gave to early Elizabethan poets like Marlowe a sense of the unrestricted powers of man which we find expressed in a work like the first part of *Tamburlaine;* but by Donne's time a feeling of questioning and doubt had set in. Critics have pointed to the first *Anniversary* (1611) as an example of the shattering impact that the disintegration of the medieval word view, the new scientific discoveries and the growing political tensions had on Donne's mind:

> The new philosophy calls all in doubt,
> The element of fire is quite put out;
> The sun is lost, and th' earth, and no man's wit
> Can well direct him where to look for it.
> And freely men confess that this world's spent (205-9)

What Donne is referring to here are the various astronomical discoveries that took place as he was beginning his poetic career or just before that, and which can be said to mark the end of the medieval worldview and the ushering in of the modern by profoundly altering man's understanding of the universe. Copernicus' overthrow in the 1540s of the geocentric in favour of the heliocentric theory of the universe—that is, his discovery that the earth, instead of being the fixed centre of the solar system, revolved around the sun—led men to question the Biblical account of the Creation. In the early 1600s Kepler laid the foundations of scientific astronomy that replaced conjectures and hypotheses sanctioned by the Bible, and around the same time Galileo's invention of the telescope not only confirmed Copernicus' theories but also led to a discovery of truths about the heavenly bodies which were at odds with scriptural teaching.

Coexistent with unsettling astronomical discoveries were the great debates in matters of religion. In the early sixteenth century Martin Luther challenged the teachings of the Catholic Church, and shortly thereafter John Calvin propounded his doctrines of predestination, the importance of faith as against good works, and of the salvation of the elect. In England Luther's thought contributed to the establishment of Calvin, gave a fillip to Puritanism which, though not the strong force in Donne's youth that it was shortly thereafter to become, introduced new ferment in religion and politics. The theory of the divine right of kings began to be challenged. A sense that the world was adrift started gaining ground.

Donne's poetry makes it clear these developments and discover-
ies created a doubt in his mind about what to believe. The phrase
'round world's imagin'd corners', which he uses in one of his Holy
Sonnets, shows how the old and the new jostle in his understanding
of the world: the world is round, as the new geographers maintain,
but its flatness, which was earlier believed in, is not totally rejected.
His third Satire expresses a sense of confusion as to which truth he
should adhere to, that preached by the Catholics, or by the Luther-
ans, or the Calvinists.

Donne's desperation comes, then, from a frantic effort to hold
together the pieces of a world that threaten to fragment. He seeks in
love a glue that will hold his universe together, or else allow him to
create a unified alternative to a universe that is collapsing. Mortality
threatens, not only in the form of impending physical dissolution but
also in the larger metaphorical meaning of the end of a settled,
known vision of the world. How to guard against it? Maybe a 'bracelet
of bright hair around the bone' will serve as a charm; maybe the now
discredited phoenix riddle will get a new lease of life from the
example of his love: 'We two, being one, are it'. Perhaps sex will serve
as bonding between the body and the soul which might otherwise
remain dualities. Love may turn a breach into an 'expansion, / Like
gold to airy thinness beat'. The urgent need to persuade, a feeling
that more is at stake in uniting with the mistress than the gratification
of uncontrollable desire, and the consequent willingness to use
whatever twists and turns of argument the situation provides—qualities
that have drawn readers to Donne's love poetry again and again—are
best explained not by invoking his 'Metaphysical' conceits, or even
by seeing him against the background of medieval or meditative
thought, but through a realization of his strong need to hold fast to
something that would survive the dissolution of the old world order
and the uncertainties of the new.

Earthly love could provide only temporary holding power against
history, even though through the strength of his argument Donne
sought to invest it with a power that would last beyond the grave. So
he turned to God as the antidote to history and transience and
change, and did so with the same clamour for immediate attention
with which he had addressed his mistresses. There is, in his religious
verse, the same dramatic immediacy of appeal, the same insistence
on being heard and receiving a promise, that characterizes his love
poetry. His fear that tonight might be the world's last night brings
home the intensity of his fear at the imminent collapse of old

certainties in all directions; his fear that he might perish on the shore is not only a fear of death and damnation but a terror of being abandoned in a world without direction. If Donne's wit grows out of the medieval worldview that saw the artist as a subtle and expert reader of God's witty book of the world, his drama, passion and desperation arise from a sense that perhaps this book has become impossible to decipher. Donne's poetry has its roots, then, in the burdens and uncertainties of history. They confer upon him, as they confer upon all who experience them, the gifts of irony and scepticism. But unlike some later poets who, too, have felt these uncertainties, Donne does not revel and glory in them. Rather, to be free from them by means of a woman's or God's love is a desire that underlies a good deal of his poetry.

This is an appropriate moment for taking notice of two recent studies of Donne which arrive at very different conclusions from that suggested above. John Carey agrees that there is a strong presence in Donne's poetry of the sense of change and of a desire for certainty. But instead of seeking an explanation for these qualities in the history of the period, he ascribes them to a biographical fact about the poet: Donne's having renounced Catholicism. The argument goes that Donne always felt guilty about having ceased to be a Catholic, and his vehemence and restlessness are attempts to 'cauterize' that guilt. In all people, events and things that embody flux, inconstancy or change he finds mirrored images of his own apostasy, and his search for constancy in woman or faith in religion are but the obverse of the feeling that he has betrayed his faith. When he asks to be martyred in love or be subjected to the same scourges that Christ suffered on the cross, he is reliving his guilt at having escaped religious persecution and death—which was the fate of so many Catholics when he was young. Other major themes in his poetry—his egotism, his self-absorption, the frequent use of images of kingship—derive from his worldly ambition which his imprudent marriage frustrated. Ambition made him grovel before the great, and as compensation he sets himself up as a king in his poetry. Carey argues that in the elegy on his mistress going to bed Donne is less interested in the girl than in the rich clothes she is wearing; this proves that his concerns are not so much sexual as material and worldly.

If Carey tries to replace the historical by the biographical, Thomas Docherty reinstates the importance of history in Donne criticism. He argues that the Copernican revolution caused a 'fall' of man into temporality, into a sense of being trapped in time, of being decentred. Donne experiences this 'fall' and tries to regain the sense of wholeness that existed before Copernicus. But his struggle *against* history, as in 'The Sunne Rising', itself takes place *in* history. Analysis of 'The Flea' leads Docherty to the conclusion that the fact that Donne has constantly to make and remake himself in his poetry means that there is no such thing as a coherent, centralized, unified Donne: the poem questions the sense of self that the poet is trying to build up, and each succeeding poem questions what has been built up already. Insofar as this subversive quality is identified as the Other, or Woman, Donne's very masculinity, the power by which he tries to create and control, is seen to be allied to its opposite. Such a self becomes not only impossible to represent in poetry but is finally seen not to exist at all. In 'The Shadow' the fact of trying to hold time still is doomed, for the lovers are themselves nothing but shadows, that is to say, not there at all. For presence cannot be created: at the very moment of realization it evaporates, renders itself absent.

This summary of Docherty does scant justice to his book. So much of his argument is based upon puns, word play and detailed reading from the inside out that the only way to represent it would be through elaborate quotation, which is not possible here. Instead, what can be said here is that if Docherty's book rejects the biographical method of Carey in favour of the historical, the historical method that he uses is itself of a highly abstract kind. For Docherty is a poststructuralist, and history for him is less a matter of the intellectual and cultural currents of the times than a sense of temporality itself. By decentring, relativizing, and bringing forth concealed meanings which explode those on the surface, he reveals how temporality makes it impossible for the subject to constitute itself; indeed, makes the subject so problematic that it disappears altogether in the very act of inscribing itself. Docherty's approach is not easy of access, but it offers a complex, subtle and a radically different way of explaining Donne's work as the outcome of encounters with history. If Carey's work represents the best of conventional critical approaches, Docherty suggests the excitements and difficulties of newer modes of critical inquiry.

HERBERT

Herbert is a different case. A scion of the nobility, and a man utterly honest with himself and possessed of high ideals, he sought the fulfilment of these ideals in the service of God. Had James I lived, Herbert may well have followed a court career. But James died in 1625, and Herbert does not seem to have found Charles I to be the kind of figure to whom he could offer total dedication. Evidence for this is slight, but the oration he made on the occasion of Charles's visit to Cambridge lacks the fulsomeness that a public address on such an occasion generally produced. A year-long stint as an MP at a time when relations between the king and Parliament were becoming tense convinced him that the only king in whose court he could serve was the King of Heaven. His retreat to his church at Bemerton is the retreat of one who rejects the temporal and the worldly in the knowledge that their service inevitably demands a sacrifice of one's highest self.

Some readers find Herbert's range too limited and his effects too tame and bland when compared to Donne. The truth is that Herbert's efforts come from having seen beyond Donne. Donne uses his poetry to work out his dilemmas; Herbert has worked them out already and the poems are written from a position of achieved resolution. Though all his poems are religious, and though he uses a number of Christian symbols, it is not necessary to share his religious beliefs in order to read him with pleasure. Indeed, as Helen Vendler says, he is better served when read by readers who do not share his religious beliefs. For his subject is primarily the workings of his own mind and heart rather than the expression of Christian doctrine. Herbert's God represents the highest and finest ideal of his own moral and aesthetic nature. In Vendler's words:

> From the rebuking yet forgiving irony which Herbert felt for his own lapses from candor springs his conception of Christ, always his better self commenting on his more specious moments...For Herbert, pleasing God meant not playing himself false, and [he] must have noted that his best poems were the result of his most stringent moments with himself, those times in which he asked himself for the greatest clarity and the most unflinching self-examination. That honesty, so pleasing to God, seemed as well pleasing to the Muse; it is no wonder that Herbert thought the two one.

It is out of Herbert's scrupulous honesty with himself, a desire to get his own feelings and the equation between God and himself exactly right, that the drama of his poems springs. Because this drama is more subdued than that of Donne, some readers have failed to note its presence at all. But he is constantly making and dismantling his poems. He starts off by claiming that he has a story to tell, only to end up by disclaiming any story ('Affliction I'); he begins with an observation, only to subject it to criticism which finally ends in its rejection ('The Temper I'). Poems of rebellion end in acquiescence ('The Collar'): the voice of God superimposes upon that of the poet, thus giving the poet's metaphors an altered significance. The poet makes statements and strikes attitudes which are then revised ('The Flower'). A sudden awareness that God is watching causes him to change direction ('Jordan II'). Flowers of rhetoric wilt ('Jordan I'). Elaboration is simplified. Broken music is mended ('Deniall').

Several recent critics have commented on this feature in Herbert, with the result that his poems have become a *locus* of contemporary criticism, in a way that Donne's were a generation ago. Thus, Stanley Fish calls his poems 'self-consuming artifacts'. Helen Vendler labels them 'reinvented' poems, saying that their most characteristic quality is their provisional nature. Barbara Leah Harman sees them as 'collapsing' poems. All three are useful terms. Their applicability to specific poems of Herbert is examined later in this book. Here a more general discussion of these characterizations is offered.

Fish sees most of Herbert's poems as dissolving in the very act of being constituted; those that don't dissolve (e.g. 'Jordan I') Fish regards as failures. They dissolve because, according to Fish, Herbert is successful in his endeavour to have his voice merged into or appropriated by God so that the poet has no voice left. But Fish also has a theoretical reason for explaining why Herbert's poems dissolve. He is a reader-response critic, which is to say that he transfers the question of the validity of the text from the text itself to the reader who reads it. As he acknowledges, to practice this kind of criticism is necessarily to destabilize the text, to make it more flickering and uncertain. According to this view, *all* works of art are self-consuming or dissolving, Herbert's poems no less than any others. But if all poems are self-consuming, the dissolution of Herbert's poems is a foregone conclusion even before they come to be written, and so it can hardly be said that they dissolve because the poet has successfully merged his voice into that of God. The presence of two contrary views with which to explain the phenomenon of Herbert's poetry results in Fish's failure to explain exactly *why* these poems are self-consuming. Also, as Barbara Harman points out, his theory of self-consuming artifacts fails to account for the difference between one poem of Herbert and another, or indeed between one poet and another. If all works of art are self-consuming, how can one be distinguished from another?

Vendler argues that Herbert's are 'reinvented poems' because of their persistent and self-critical attempt to revise what they are saying and bring it to perfection. The self-critical dialectic finally issues in a truth to which the poet can give assent because he feels it to be a part of his deepest being. Herbert's poems, according to this view, are both aesthetic and moral victories. Vendler's reading emphasizes the self-questioning nature of Herbert's. But it also dehistoricizes him. A critical temper and a quest for perfection have characterized other ages than his; so in what way do his 'reinventions' differ, say, from Swift's or Yeats's? Is Herbert's mental and moral make-up unique to him as an individual? Could he have flourished in any other age and written the same kind of poetry? Her readings illuminate the individual poems of Herbert, but do not explain him as a poet.

The same can be said for Harman's view that Herbert's are 'collapsing' poems, by which she means that when he begins a narration he knows *from the start* that what he is saying isn't so, even though he does not disclose this knowledge at the start. It is only at the end that it is disclosed, with the result that the poem has the rug pulled away from underneath its feet, as it were: it 'collapses' Because Harman does not explain *why* Herbert wrote collapsing poems, her reading becomes just another reading, another way of interpreting poems, without necessarily being undergirded by a theory of how meaning is made which will turn her readings into a discourse on the nature of poetry.

Yet an attempt must be made to explain why Herbert's poems consume themselves, are reinvented, or collapse. The answer may lie in the nature of his encounter with his times.

Harman provides a clue when, summing up the debate between Fish and Vendler, she says that whereas the former argues that Herbert has no story to tell beyond that of the Bible as understood by the Anglicans of his age, the latter argues that he has a story to tell that appears in his transformation of this Biblical material through the interjection of the self. Harman asks to what extent one can go beyond the framework of the historical consciousness one inhabits. For Fish such moving out beyond history is not possible; for Vendler it is.

Clearly the problem is one of the ability of the individual to go beyond or against the assumptions of the age, of the individual's ability to be unique. The question of individuality is a modern one and dates essentially from the Renaissance. This is not to say that people did not possess a sense of individuality in the middle ages, but with the Renaissance it became possible for man to assert his individuality by denying the dominant assumptions of his age: the possibility of a critical attitude towards history had dawned. And as the individual began to stand against and apart from the dominant culture in the Renaissance—literature offers many such examples, like the satirist and malcontent in Elizabethan drama or characters like Edmund in *King Lear*—a myth got created that in medieval times man always had an ordered role in society, that of the servant/master, or courtier/king, or landtiller/landholder. Herbert frequently invokes these relationships when talking about himself and God.

What does this say about his poetry in relation to the prevailing consciousness of his times? Or, to put the question differently, what is the nature of the embodiment in his poetry of the history of his times? As a Renaissance man he has a very strong sense of the self. He 'aspire[s] to a full consent' with God, but not through a process of self-denial or self-annihilation. 'Aaron' shows that his voice is not silenced by God but rather made an instrument for God while retaining its own quality. His problem, then, is to yield full consent to God while being fully himself.

The matter may be expressed in different terms. Herbert wanted to establish a relationship with God in which he and God were in full and equal partnership. There is nothing in this view of God to which the most scrupulous Anglican theologian would not give assent. But because Herbert was a highly intelligent, honest and self-aware man, his notion of the man—God relationship is more subtle and searching than is commonly found in Anglican theology. For him God is love, of course, and also occasionally the tormenting, unresponsive Being who sends afflictions to the poet. But Herbert's God is also a witty and humorous God. He plays little jokes on the poet: He conceals His order and purposes and then takes delight in seeing the poet first fumble towards and then recognize them with a flash of joy. Indeed, if God hides His purposes, He also leads man to their discovery, sometimes through tortuous, complex or unusual paths. He causes His servant, at the same time, to yearn for and rebel against Him; and when the servant is at his most rebellious the recognition comes that he is also closest to God. The servant's acquiescence to the will of his

Master proves to be otherwise than what it seemed, for the Master is now revealed not as lord but friend.

In fact, God engages in a constant cat-and-mouse game with Herbert, and though Herbert finds it tormenting, frustrating or baffling, his cry of despair or rejection turns suddenly and often into a sometimes delighted, sometimes quiet note of acceptance as the realization dawns that God's game is motivated by love. To serve God better Herbert wants to change himself, only to discover that God loves him best as he is. Sensing that God prefers not complex subtleties of thought and expression but unaffected simplicity and directness, Herbert decides to shed all his wit and learning. But he realizes that these qualities, too, are God's gift, and that purity is to be had not through a simplistic rejection of one's intellectual faculties but rather by using them so fully that one is enabled to go beyond them. God teaches, that is, that man's wit is to be transcended by being fully utilized.

It was this understanding of God that Herbert wanted to express in his poetry. But while the poetic traditions of the Renaissance made it possible for man to experience a sense of his unique identity (e.g. the Elizabethan satirist), or for him to find satisfaction in serving an idea or an institution bigger than himself (e.g. Donne's 'Thou hast done, I have no more'), they provided few models for the kind of meaning Herbert wanted to express. The best of Anglican theology in the early seventeenth century allowed for, indeed fostered, Herbert's aims, but no English poet before him with the possible exception of Donne had achieved quite what he wanted to do. In Herbert we therefore have the spectacle of a man belonging very much to his age in terms of his theology, his daring experiments in versification, and in the unaffected purity of his language, but also making extensive use of medieval methods and devices in his poetry. Tuve has shown how so much of his imagery is derived from medieval emblem books and stained glass windows; we may add that his frequent use of allegory and the creation of the persona of the *naif* who speaks so many of the poems are medieval also.

The medieval element in Herbert is not to be mistaken for nostalgia on his part, for it does not attempt a revival of those aspects of the medieval world which the Renaissance had displaced. Rather, it consists of those aspects which still retained vitality in the early seventeenth century, and may be said to represent his critical stance towards his age, a stance made possible by the questioning attitude that the Renaissance fostered. That Herbert turned his back on his age is clear. He knew it well and was steeped in its culture, yet in his poetry there is hardly, if any, reference to it—to the momentous social and political events of the day, to the many writers contemporary with him or to the intellectual and theological currents of the time. Instead, he withdrew from a secular career to bury himself in Bemerton—the actions of a man who sees the limitations of the modern world with its flux and change and emphasis on the self, and commits himself to a service in which he will find permanence and values larger than the self, without, at the same time, losing a sense of the self.

We are now in a position to account for the fact that his poems collapse, or are reinvented, or self-consumed. Herbert is a man of his age and also at war with it; or rather, a man whose roots in his age are seen precisely in his being able to turn his back on it. For it must be emphasized that the critical attitude towards his times that Herbert has is itself part of the total culture of his age. Underneath the deep and genuine religious feelings that his poems express is latent a jostling between a man with a strong sense of self and a desire for something larger than the self. The superimposition of this latter desire upon a full realization of what he is causes his poems to collapse or become self-consuming. It causes him to start the poem by saying one thing only to revise or repudiate it. In his poems we see Herbert self-consciously writing poems that embody a criticism of his self-consciousness. In the enactment of this very modern drama lies part of his appeal to the non-Christian reader.

CRASHAW

Unlike the other poets represented here, Crashaw was a Roman Catholic. Eliot has called him 'primarily a European'. There is no doubt of his debt to Continental intellectual and religious traditions. Apart from the fact that he fled England to live first in Holland and then in Italy, and may also have travelled to Spain, there is the influence of the Italian poet Marino on his early work, his fascination with saints like Teresa which was not shared by his English contemporaries, and the contribution of St Francis de Sales to his thought. Recently R.V. Young has studied his poetry against the background of the literary traditions and religious thought of the Spanish Golden Age, which, according to Young, provides the best framework for

Crashaw. As against all this is the undeniable fact that though adept at writing poetry in Latin and Greek, he chose English for his best work. However much virtue there may be in seeing Crashaw in terms of Continental and Counter-Reformation, as opposed to English traditions, his English roots cannot be ignored. It should not be forgotten that he was a regular visitor to Little Gidding and acknowledged his debt to Herbert by entitling his book *Steps to the Temple*.

An understanding of two terms will help us to appreciate Crashaw better: *emblems* and *baroque*. Emblem books were very popular in England and on the Continent in the sixteenth and seventeenth centuries. Often used as aids to private meditation, they consisted of pictorial representations of Christian ideas and symbols. Though the symbol or idea which they represented was abstract, the emblems themselves tended to be vividly visual and literal. Thus the symbolical idea of the soul being nourished by the blood of Christ was depicted literally as a prone woman gathering in a heart-shaped cup the liquid that is spouting from Christ who is being crushed in a winepress. The modern student may find some of these emblems bizarre or shocking, but the original audience would have focused upon the symbolical meanings sought to be conveyed rather than upon their literalness, however vivid.

Emblem books are sometimes associated with Roman Catholicism since it is believed that the Protestants, and especially Puritans, with their opposition to idol worship and icons, would have frowned upon them. In fact, they were in use among Catholics and Protestants alike, and among the most popular emblem makers were the Protestant Francis Quarles and the Puritan George Wither. These books provided a source for the imagery of Donne, Herbert and Crashaw. Many of Donne's images that strike the modern reader as outrageous and elaborate were drawn from the popular emblems of the day. A number of Herbert's images, including that of the winepress in 'The Agonie', have the same source. Emblem books also help us to understand better Crashaw's vivid and sensuous images. His emphasis on the tactile and the olfactory, his occasionally extravagant embellishments, his detailed and elaborate descriptions are all qualities which can be traced back to the influence of emblem books.

If Donne and Crashaw go to the same sources for some of their imagery, how can we explain the obvious differences between them? For while Donne uses images to further an argument and to explore a feeling, a mood or an attitude, Crashaw's use tends to be more ritualistic and celebratory. Instead of moving rapidly from image to image like Donne, Crashaw often repeats an image in different ways, so that his poems seems to be far more static than Donne's. Donne's images can be elaborate and extended, but Crashaw's are far more exaggerated and extravagant. One reason for this difference lies in the fact that Crashaw is a more baroque poet than Donne.

Baroque is an art form associated with Bernini in sculpture and Marino in poetry. While it is generally believed that the baroque developed essentially in Catholic countries on the Continent and has few adherents in Protestant England, there are more examples of baroque art in England than is commonly recognized. In fact, the poetry of Donne is not without some baroque features: the elaborate conceits of tears in 'A Valediction: Of Weeping' are baroque in their wealth of detail. The baroque has been criticized as a structureless, grotesque art form lacking in restraint and shape. At its worst it can be characterized by excessive ornamentation for its own sake, the presence of a breathless, hothouse atmosphere, ludicrous juxtapositions of imagery, and a lack of control. Though Crashaw is sometimes guilty of these excesses, often his poems show features which have made the baroque so attractive an art form to so many artists. For one thing, his poems possess the intellectual control which good baroque exhibits. His complex verse paragraphs, which are marked by ingenious rhymes, intricate metrical patterns and images that seem to have strayed far from the main theme, often come to a conclusion in a cool and pointed couplet, showing that the poet has always been in control of his material. We see this kind of control exhibited in the hymn on the Epiphany sung by the three kings. The conceits of this poem, and the hymn on the name of Jesus, are prevented from getting out of hand also by the strong theological content of these poems. At other times humour tempers the excesses of Crashaw's baroque. Thus the early part of the hymn on St Teresa and the first part of 'The Flaming Heart' are cool and witty, and this enables the reader to keep the later raptures and abstractions in perspective. Indeed, in the hymn to St Teresa the tight expression of a paradox contained in the opening lines links and validates the detailed images which follow. The figure of Mary Magdalen, who washed Christ's feet with her tears and wiped them with her hair and kissed them (Luke 7:38) was popular with baroque artists because it combined the erotic with the love of the divine, and Crashaw uses it in 'The Weeper'. The conceits may seem to verge perilously close to the grotesque when Mary's tears are said to flow heavenwards from eyes that are called portable oceans. But these excesses reveal the ecstasy that humankind can feel in the worship of God. For a final point to be made about Crashaw's baroque is that, unlike Donne, who focused upon sin, death and damnation, and whose poems are marked by intense self-introspection and a sense of the self's unworthiness, Crashaw is concerned essentially with a celebration of God's love. His poetry does not describe his own religious experiences; rather, his baroque tends towards an annihilation of the self, making the practitioner an anonymous figure, celebrating together with other celebrants.

While it may be unwise to seek a link between an artist's commitment to an aesthetic movement and the details of his biography, it is tempting to hazard the guess that Crashaw's predilection for the baroque may have a relationship to the facts of his own life. Bereaved of his mother, a loving stepmother and his father when he was yet a boy, he was motivated throughout his life by a search for a sense of security such as he experienced for a while at Peterhouse in Cambridge, only to lose it as a result of the political upheavals in England. A desire for security may account for the attraction he felt towards mother figures like Mary Collet, Nicholas Ferrar's niece and 'mother' to the Little Gidding community, and later towards Queen Henrietta Maria and Susan, Countess of Denbigh. Perhaps a similar impulse may account for his conversion to Roman Catholicism: the mother church provided the shelter and security which the turmoil of British politics had snatched from him. The desire for a safe haven where he can worship in peace is what the baroque also provided him. In the mystical raptures of the baroque all questions and fears could be stilled and the self could be forgotten, absorbed in adoration and rendered undistinguishable from the other adorers. But Crashaw's use of the baroque goes beyond providing psychological security. It contains also his political comment upon England. Through the use of an aesthetic which was more widely prevalent on the Continent than in England and was, moreover, associated with the Counter-Reformation, he is signalling his rejection of Puritan politics and religion in England.

MARVELL

Marvell is a very difficult poet to write about. In one sense he is conventional: the genres he used were not of his invention but borrowed from previous poets. Lyrics, religious meditations, odes, dialogues, *carpe diem* poems were all forms which had been used before. But while deliberately recalling the lessons of the masters he also used these forms in ways that departed from the masters' methods. Rosalie Colie has shown how Marvell exhausts the possibilities of the genres that he uses, and yet maintains a critical, mocking distance towards them so that we can never be sure how seriously he takes the forms he uses so well. Always so poised, elegant and polished, he seems transparently clear, yet his very clarity conceals depths we can only sense. Critics call attention to an elusive quality in his work which creates a feeling that even when he seems to be revealing all, something is being held back, something which for him is utterly inviolate.

The difficulty of pinning him down is a major quality of his life as well as his work. At a time when Milton cut short his European tour in order to be in England and participate in the politics of his country, Marvell was content to spend the Civil War years abroad. Though he seems to have been a monarchist he was happy to enter Cromwell's service. In spite of his loyalty to the Republic he continued to serve Charles II, yet he maintained a critical attitude towards his policies. Similarly in his best poems, all dating prior to the Restoration, there is a refusal to commit himself to any one cause, though the attraction of each is fully examined. His 'Dialogue' poems end inconclusively, or if they seem to arrive at a conclusion, that conclusion is effectively undercut by a pervasive irony. He obviously favours a life of retirement, but even in such a state as described in 'The Garden' he is aware of the Fall and the consequent exile from paradise. There is in him the realization that the values of retirement can be preserved only if people are willing to give up this kind of life and engage in action. But action itself is of value to the extent that it is informed by the attitudes that retirement alone fosters. He respects Cromwell, but his admiration for him is tempered by that for Charles I. He recognizes that Charles's execution was necessary; yet it makes Cromwell a bloody man in his eyes.

Critics like Cleanth Brooks have seen in these stances an example of Marvell's irony, paradox and ambiguity. This is a valid insight. But though it describes an important phenomenon, it does not account for it. Recently Louis Martz has attempted such an explanation. He calls Marvell a Mannerist poet. Mannered art comes into being towards the end of periods of great achievement. The Mannerism that Martz associates with Marvell was a style in painting and sculpture which came into being in Italy in the sixteenth century and is associated with the names of artists like Parmigianino and Bronzino. It was introduced into England early in the seventeenth century by Inigo Jones. Among its characteristics are polish and elegance, a sense of cool distancing from the subject, the presence of conflicting elements held together in uneasy and precarious tension, and a certain deliberateness of posing. This description of Mannerism is a description of the effects of Marvell's poems as well.

To call Marvell a Mannerist is not only to describe the effect of his poetry but also to place him in the context of an artistic tradition. But Mannerism is a style, and Martz raises the question whether there is any substance behind Marvell's exquisitely elegant style. By subtitling his essay 'The Masks of Mannerism' Martz implies that Marvell is not all style and no substance but that the style is a cover for a meaning that, because of his temperament, he did not or could not openly reveal. This point of view needs examination.

In Marvell's poetry we encounter a few images and ideas that seem to have been close to his deepest self. One is that of music, the fair singer entrapping his mind and heart with a song. Another is that of the soul seeing itself as being in this world but not of it and yearning to return to Heaven, an image which, in its quality of detachment, critics have seen as autobiographical. A third is a strong desire for solitude. But together with these intensely private concerns there is also a desire to prevent the social consensus from breaking down.

This last concern is of some importance in understanding Marvell. The Civil War era and its aftermath saw the collapse of the status quo in politics, government, religion and other institutions that had been built over a period of time. Party feelings ran high; men lost their jobs and sometimes lives because of the opinions they held. Marvell was an exception in that his commitments were never such as to prevent his being able to work with people of opposite persuasions. Though a Cromwellian, he continued to hold his membership of Parliament even after the Restoration. Yet he was not afraid to criticize the new rulers when he thought that there was a danger of Charles II assuming arbitrary powers and later collaborating with Catholic France against a Protestant Holland. His poems *The Second Advice to a Painter* (1665) and *The Third Advice to a Painter* (1666) blame England's rulers for having provoked an unnecessary naval war with Holland, the prose pamphlet *The Rehearsal Transpros'd* (1672) makes a plea for maintaining the liberty of conscience, and his other prose work *The Growth of Popery and Arbitrary Government* (1677) expresses fear that the actions of the English government are going to lead to Britain's capitulation to France both politically and in matters of religion. The remarkable thing is that though the positions expressed in these works were strongly held, Marvell expressed himself throughout with moderation and an absence of bitterness or invective. It is as though he were playing the part of a member of the loyal opposition—with the emphasis falling as much upon 'loyal' as upon 'opposition'. As he said in *The Growth of Popery*, the salvation of England lay in the honest application to their work of the small group of people who 'can neither flatter, nor betray their king or country: but being conscious of their own loyalty and integrity, proceed through good and bad report, to acquit themselves in their duty...' Opposition to what he thought was good or right did not make him abandon his position as M.P., as happened to so many other Cromwellians. He fought for his beliefs. Sometimes he won, as when he was able to have England's policies towards Holland reversed. But losing did not cause him to quit.

These qualities, so evident in Marvell's public life after the Restoration, may help us to gain a proper approach to his pre-Restoration poems. For his life and work was of one piece, and his later career may be seen as a gloss on his earlier writings. His Mannerism masks—or perhaps it may be more accurate to say that it expresses—Marvell's wish to make consensus, moderation, tolerance and balance prevail in life, public as well as private. His irony and detachment are not signs of indifference; quite the reverse. He may have a desire, deep down, to retreat, to listen to music, to contemplate the condition of his soul. But his political position is not to be seen as a necessary means to create conditions that will make it possible to pursue his interests. Rather, it is part and parcel of the interests he wishes to pursue. He may have stopped writing great poetry after the Restoration, but the life he led in post-Restoration England, far from being an expression of new-found commitment, is merely the expression in politics of the temper of mind that created his incomparable early poetry. Thus his Mannerism is best seen not as a mask but as the thing itself, a poised sophistication that is able to hold opposites in perfect balance. In Marvell's case the style *is* the man. It enacts his view of life, the meditative, the contemplative, the retired, the erotic, the political and the active.

VAUGHAN

Only in the last few decades has criticism shed the misconceptions about Henry Vaughan that limited a proper perception of his achievement and relegated him to a minor talent. These misconceptions were that Vaughan is a forerunner of Wordsworth, that he is mystical, that he is an imitator of Herbert, and that there is a sharp break between his earlier secular poetry and the religious poetry of *Silex Scintillans* written after his Christian conversion. If it is necessary here once again to challenge these misconceptions, it is not so much because they still enjoy currency as because by seeing how limiting they are we may come to see Vaughan's achievement better.

It is true that Vaughan, like Wordsworth, wrote on a number of natural objects like flowers and waterfalls and trees; he seems, moreover, to have kept his eye on these objects more completely than other poets of the seventeenth century, with the result that quite often in his poetry it is not simply any flowers or hills or sunsets that he describes but particular and specific ones. This gives to his natural description a directness and freshness not often found in Donne or Herbert or Marvell or Crashaw. It is also true that Vaughan seems to have had an interest in childhood, and the opening lines of 'The Retreate', which describe a vision of the purity that he possessed as a child but which he has lost as he has grown older, have an obvious similarity with Wordsworth's *Intimations* Ode. But there seems to be no evidence that Wordsworth knew or had this poem in mind when he was writing his Ode. Indeed, Vaughan and Wordsworth had very different purposes in writing about childhood. Wordsworth wants to glorify the child as a seer and a philosopher and is concerned with the question: given that the 'visionary gleam' of childhood is lost, in what can the poet find consolation? Vaughan, on the other hand, uses childhood as a symbol to suggest a contrast between the past, when the soul existed in a condition of spiritual unity, and the present state of disorder, and as Simmonds points out he 'forces us to contemplate both states simultaneously.'

There is also little in common between Vaughan's view of Nature and Wordsworth's. If for Wordsworth nature was a manifestation of God, something in and through which His presence could be sensed, for Vaughan the apprehension of God was possible only through the grace of Christ and could also require a turning away from the phenomenal world. Though in 'Regeneration' the pilgrim-poet has to learn to see and hear the works of God, it is not as a result of this discipline of the senses that he is finally enabled to hear the voice of God. And when he does hear it, his wish is 'to die before my death'—a wish that shows that the apprehension of God requires a rejection of the world of nature. Similarly, 'The Night' rejects daylight in favour of the night, for it is only in total darkness, when sense perceptions are laid aside, that communion with God becomes possible.

The view that Vaughan was a mystic whose poetry was influenced by Hermetic philosophy restricts his achievement as drastically as does the view that his importance lies in being a precursor of Wordsworth. If mysticism means a supra-sensory and immediate apprehension of God, the opening lines of a poem like 'The World' may be adduced as an example, for they express a vision which the poet seems to have reached in a mystic flash. But if the whole poem is held up as an example of his mysticism, one would be hard put to explain they intensely worldly concerns of the rest of the work, including what may well be a critical reference to Cromwell in the second stanza. Moreover, at the end Vaughan suggests that though he has had a vision of eternity, it cannot belong to him for he partakes of the nature of fallen mankind. Indeed, the view that Vaughan is a mystic poet concerned with eternity and immortality and a transcendent world of light has always to confront the uncomfortable fact that there is also in his work a great deal of criticism, condemnation and satire. The 'otherworldly' poet proves to be surprisingly worldly in his concerns. He may feel that the here and now is somehow incomplete and that it represents the shadow of an unseen but more complete world; but instead of dismissing the here and now as a true mystic would, Vaughan possesses a very strong sense of it.

Often a perception of Vaughan as a mystic has gone hand in hand with an emphasis on Hermetic influences on his thought. Hermeticism had its roots in neoplatonism and in the Jewish mystical tradition of the Cabbala. It has tended to be viewed negatively by commentators because one of its branches—alchemy—was seen as little more than futile and foolish attempts to find ways of transmuting base metals into gold. But alchemy laid the foundations of modern chemistry, and Hermeticism may be regarded as man's attempts in a prescientific world to find a scientific explanation for the universe, notwithstanding all its emphasis on hidden significances and secret codes.

Vaughan's twin brother Thomas was a Hermetic philosopher, and Thomas' influence on the poet is difficult to deny. Hermeticism provided Vaughan with a number of terms which he uses in his poetry, like balsam, hatch, exhalation and glance, as also with certain image clusters, such as those dealing with water and light. Above all, it gave him an interest in seeking a meaning hidden below the surface of things, in studying natural phenomena so as to reach a significance which is imperceptible to the senses. But to see Vaughan essentially as a hermetic poet is to deny his accessibility to the uninitiated reader. It is to transform him from a poet of genius into some sort of a secretive, mysterious figure who fills his verse with arcane references to dead sciences, when the truth is that even when the reader does not understand the full significance of Vaughan's references, the general tenor of his meaning is within grasp.

Indeed, an overmuch concentration on Hermetic ideas shifts the attention away from Vaughan's poetry. It becomes possible for the reader to ascribe all the puzzles and obscurities in the poems to some sort of a vague philosophy when in fact these difficulties may have been caused by the poet's own inability to write well. For Vaughan was an unequal writer: if he was capable of brilliant and memorable lines, he could also be obscure or limp at times. To see him as a Hermetic philosopher is to level the highs and lows of his writing. Finally, the Hermetic approach to Vaughan does what the other approaches—the Wordsworthian and the mystical—do: they focus only upon a limited body of Vaughan's poetry (essentially *Silex Scintillans*) to the exclusion of the whole.

The same happens when he is approached in terms of Herbert. There is no denying that *Silex Scintillans* would not have been possible had Vaughan not read Herbert. *Silex* is full of quotations, half quotations and echoes of Herbert. From Herbert Vaughan learned to experiment with verse forms, vary the length of his lines, and make his stanzas firmer more self-contained, and more logical. Several poems in *Silex* start off as Herbert's do, though Vaughan often reaches a different conclusion. It would be no exaggeration to say that Herbert's influence on Vaughan was so great that it made Vaughan abandon all other earlier influences like those of Carew and Jonson, whose presence can scarcely be sensed in *Silex*. But for all that, it would be a mistake to think that Vaughan's poems are a mere rewriting of Herbert's. Herbert's influence, instead of swamping Vaughan's individuality, helped it to come into its own. Whereas Herbert emphasizes the eucharistic elements in Christianity such as the crucifixion and communion, in Vaughan there is a greater emphasis upon the private and visionary experience. Nor should it be a surprise that this is so, for Herbert and Vaughan inherited different histories. In the older poet there is a strong sense of the church as a building and as an institution, for he was a parish priest of the Church of England. In Vaughan this sense is absent, for in his time the Church of England was proscribed by the Puritans in Wales and had to go underground. Rectors, vicars and curates, including the poet's twin brother, were expelled from their benefices; the only Christian doctrine that was allowed to be preached was that of the Puritans. In these circumstances Vaughan could not have remained a passive imitator of Herbert; instead, we find him placing greater emphasis on Biblical texts, on external nature, and on the inner nature of man than Herbert did.

If Herbert's influence is strong but not dominant in *Silex* Part One, it is less strong in Part Two, and not at all present in the earlier works. This fact brings us to the last misconception about Vaughan, a misconception which is also basic since the other misconceptions are based upon and flow from it. This last misconception consists of the view that around 1648 Vaughan experienced a spiritual conversion, that a reading of Herbert played a part in this conversion, and that the poetry he wrote after his conversion (namely, the two parts of *Silex*), is totally different from the kind of poetry he had written so far; it is also infinitely superior.

Frank Kermode was the first to maintain that there is little evidence that Vaughan underwent a conversion, and he argued that the changes in Vaughan's poetry have aesthetic rather than biographical causes. Since then other critics like Simmonds have accepted the view that the conversion theory is suspect. A strong case exists today for claiming that whether or not there was a conversion in Vaughan's life, the changes in his poetry can be explained in other terms, and furthermore that these changes were not as drastic as they were once considered to be. The proponents of the conversion theory like Thomas Hutchinson and E.C. Pettet maintain that whereas in *Poems* (1646) and *Olor Iscanus* (published 1651, but probably completed by 1649) Vaughan is amatory, satirical, Cavalier and, at best, mediocre, in *Silex Scintillans* (1650 and 1655) he is religious, mystical, other worldly and inspired. This view grows out of a neglect of Vaughan's early work and also serves to fuel this neglect. As critics like Simmonds and Jonathan Post have taken a fresh look at the early poems, this view has begun to appear more and more fallacious. Their work makes it clear that attempting to see the links between

Vaughan's early and late achievement can help us to understand the nature of *Silex Scintillans* better than if we were to focus on that work to the exclusion of his early poems.

Vaughan's 1646 *Poems* described him as 'Gent.', and his use of this term seems to have been motivated by a desire to signal his affinity with the Court or Cavalier poets of the age like Thomas Carew, Robert Herrick, Richard Lovelace and Sir John Suckling. Like them he writes love poetry in the mode of Ben Jonson, though his achievement in this mode is inferior to theirs. But unlike the Cavaliers he also had a strong vein of satire, and half of his first book consists of a versification of Juvenal's Tenth Satire. This work forms the obverse of his love poems, for if in them he celebrates Amoret, in the satire he lashes out against the Puritans whose dominance of England has made amorous dallying increasingly impossible.

Vaughan's second work, *Olor Iscanus,* extends the scope of his first. There are a number of pastoral poems which seek to create an ideal world in which the pleasures of love can be enjoyed. But alternating with them are elegies, many addressed to people who were killed while fighting for the Royalist cause in the Civil War, and they provide a commentary on the troubled nature of contemporary history which made the pastoral world an unattainable ideal. The Vigorous and powerful 'Charnel-house' describes the carnage of war. In it Vaughan seems to have an obsession with death and destruction, but a contemplation of these horrors does not prevent him from chiding, mocking, satirizing and being ironical and witty at the expense of his Puritan enemies. All these visions—the pastoral, the elegiac, the ironic—are sought to be mediated in the verse letters that form an important part of *Olor.* Written in imitation of Jonson, they put forward an ideal of judiciousness and reason and ethical behaviour. If they do not succeed in describing concretely or in detail how this ideal can be brought to fruition, it is because in the troubled history of the period no such concrete realization is possible. What was an achievable ideal for Jonson has been transformed by contemporary politics into the merely desirable.

When Vaughan turned, under the influence of Herbert, from secular to sacred poetry in *Silex Scintillans,* he abandoned both the themes and the style of the Sons of Ben, but the break was not as great as it might seem. For one thing, for Jonson the intellectual order and structure of poetry were reflective of a moral order in the poet's mind. Vaughan, in turning from Jonsonian or secular to Herbertian or religious poetry, was only moving from an ethical to a specifically

Christian point of view. Secondly, if the early poems of Vaughan are a response to the history of the times, this kind of response is not absent from *Silex* but may be said to underline it. Critics sometimes talk of *Silex* as though it marked Vaughan's 'escape' from history and politics. The truth would seem to be that the choice of religious poetry was itself partly a political act. By the time *Silex* came to be written, the King had been beheaded, Cromwell was in firm control of England, and the Church of England had been proscribed in Wales. A Royalist and an Anglican, Vaughan, when faced with this situation, took recourse to the writing of religious poetry as his way of combating Puritanism and keeping the Anglican Church alive. If the mystical elements in this poetry are 'escapist' or give the impression that Vaughan is rejecting the world, it is not the world as such that he rejects but the world of the Puritans: as Simmonds says, his turning inwards to his soul is motivated in part by his contemplation of his enemies. And if, though he was never ordained, Vaughan turns, in Part Two of *Silex*, to liturgical and theological themes, it is because now that Anglican worship has been banned, Vaughan feels obliged to take on the role of a priest and make his poetry the Church in which he can worship with his readers.

Jonathan Post points out that there is a very strong sense, in *Silex*, of beginnings, an emphasis upon the beauty of the morning, or of childhood, or of early times in history, and a suggestion that thereafter there has been a falling off. There is also a sense of looking forward, a longing for the time in future when man may be reconnected to God. Vaughan may owe this notion that there was a perfection in the past which may perhaps be recaptured in the future, but that the present is degenerate, to Herbert and to a Christian vision of history generally, with its belief in the Fall and its looking forward to the Second Coming of Christ. But his powerful and frequent recounting of this version of history in his religious poetry is also expressive of his actual condition and that of the Anglican Church and the Royalist cause.

That religious poetry for Vaughan is not a refuge from history but at least in part a cloak for engaging covertly with history can be seen also in the satirical elements which several poems in *Silex* contain. He started his poetic career with a translation of Juvenal, and though the inspiration in *Silex* was religious, he did not abandon satire in this work. Satirical features in 'The Proffer' may be adduced as further examples of religious poems that contain satire on the Puritans. But as Jonathan Post has pointed out, it is not so much in individual poems that we have to seek the satirical as in the tones of voice that Vaughan employs. *Silex* contains at least two tones, the clear, precise, 'still, soft call' of the voice of Christ and the rude, cacophonous, clumsy and shrill accents of the world's babble. If 'Peace', which describes the world of the elect, is written in the soft voice which Vaughan associates with Christ, this voice has only transcended, not conquered, the 'noise and danger' of the world. For the hubbub of the world can be heard clearly in 'The Night', and it is only through struggle, pain and suffering that the sinner can learn, in 'Regeneration', to hear the voice of God in the wind. there were times when Vaughan saw himself as the sinner in need of God's grace. But there are also other times when he writes from the position of one of the elect; on these occasions the fallen world represents not the poet but Puritans.

It is only when the political substratum of Vaughan's religious achievement in *Silex Scintillans* is realized that we will be able to appreciate the sobriquet of 'Silurist' that he gave to himself. Commentators have tended to view Vaughan's self-assumed title, based on the name of an old British tribe in Wales (*Silures*) as little more than antiquarian attitudinizing. But the Silures were a warlike tribe, and in the seventeenth century the Anglican Church saw them as defenders of the original English church which was supposed to have flourished in the third and fourth centuries before being destroyed by the Saxons who also pushed the Silures into Wales. By calling himself 'Silurist' the author of *Silex* is indicating that he, too, is a defender of the faith and though forced to retreat to Wales will carry on the fight against the destroyers of the Anglican Church. Vaughan's assumption of the sobriquet is an act of political and religious defiance.

If *Silex Scintillans* represents the highest achievement of Vaughan, it is not, then, because the work marks a clean break from his past but because it grows out of it. *Silex* may represent an abandonment of several of the early themes, techniques and poetic influences. But other themes—those of satire, for instance, or a moral outlook on life, or a concern with death—are extended and rendered more complex by being brought within the matrix of Christian thought rather than repudiated. Above all, *Silex* continues Vaughan's engagement with the history of his times; the only question is how history is to be regarded by a Christian whose church has been driven underground. it is this changed context—and the influence of Herbert—that accounts in large measure for the differences between Vaughan's earlier secular poetry and his religious work. To recognize this is to recognize how religious poetry draws its strength not from a rejection of the world but from a critical engagement with it.

Finally, can any generalizations be offered about the five poets represented here that will serve as a conclusion to the discussion and help the reader both to take a unified view of their achievements and to recognize their range and variety? Clearly a term like 'Metaphysical' Will not suffice, for though it emphasizes similarities, it conceals how these poets differ from one another; and the same can be said, though to a lesser degree, about other terms like 'poets of meditation.' But focusing upon some other concepts that have been implicit in this Introduction may help us to achieve a more satisfactory angle of vision. First, all our poets are, to a greater or lesser extent, in line with contemporary Continental poetic, artistic and religious traditions. The affinities of Donne's poetic practices both to the artistic theories of Tesauro and to the Ignatian practice of meditation have already been noted; and the latter is present, too, in Herbert, though he is perhaps the most home-grown, the most 'English' of the five. Certainly the medieval element in Herbert and his use of allegory and emblem books links him to a tradition which, though strong in England, had its roots and reached a high level of development on the Continent. The Mannerism of Marvell and even more so the Baroque of Crashaw can be fully appreciated only in relation to the prevalence of these artistic styles in Italy and Spain. To see these two poets as only English would be to make their achievement appear strange and somewhat incomprehensible. And though Vaughan, like Herbert, was home-grown and never travelled abroad, he was the recipient through his twin brother Thomas of Hermetic ideas which flourished more on the Continent than in England.

Second, though four of the five poets (Herbert is an exception) wrote secular verse, all five of them were deeply involved in religion and greatly concerned with the religious life and with the condition of their souls, though in different ways. Donne is very anxious to find out what true religion is and demands a promise of salvation with compelling urgency. Herbert works out an equal partnership with a personal God in which his full individuality—his scrupulous honesty, delicacy, tact and intelligence—remain inviolate even as he surrenders himself totally to God's will. Crashaw focuses intently on scenes from the life of Christ or His saints—the Nativity, the coming of the magi, St Teresa's resolve to be a martyr—and engages in an intense and rapt adoration or celebrates the occasion with skilful and subtle music. Vaughan tells the story of his soul's pilgrimage, sees a transcendental power immanent in the beauties of nature, or expresses a wish for a mystical communion with God. As for Marvell, though his religious output is small, and though his meditative exercises in 'On a Drop of Dew' may seem stylized, he also produced in 'The Coronet' one of the most haunting accounts of the fact that no articulation of the love of God in human language can be free from selfish motivations, and showed how the devotee can overcome this limitation.

The close and complex relationship between religion and politics in the seventeenth century leads to the final point: the poetry of each of the five poets is best approached in terms of the history of the period defined in the broadest sense of the term. Not that they were political poets, but they were all, with the exception of Marvell (and he is an ambiguous case at best) Royalist supporters; and the cataclysmic history of their times is a major determinant of their work. Nor is this simply a matter of the presence of political allusions in their writing or of politics providing a context for what they wrote. Rather, politics (broadly understood) determined the kind of poetry they would write and made their highly individual achievements possible. The web of socio-political and intellectual conditions of the period—what we call the culture of the age, and of which the political struggle between king and Parliament was only the most visible and significant manifestation—is as responsible for turning Herbert to religious poetry as it is for turning Crashaw to the Baroque, as responsible for making Vaughan's work a combination of the mystical and satirical as it is for forcing upon Marvell the need to maintain a sense of cool distance from both the Royalist and Puritan parties and making Donne experience with desperation a sense of the imminent collapse of coherence, order and life itself. The poetry of the five poets represented here powerfully demonstrates the astonishing range of accomplishment which the culture of the first half of the seventeenth century produced. Inhabiting the same historical period, they shared qualities in common. But each man's different involvement with the history of his time differentiated his work from that of the others and gave him his particular identity and individuality. Only a constant attention to the determination of their writing by the historical possibilities offered by the age—and by historical is here meant the intellectual, the social, the political and the cultural as well—will enable us to understand the myriad links that join the five poets together and also their uniqueness.

SUGGESTED FURTHER READING
(INCLUDING LIST OF WORKS CITED)

Aubrey, John. *Brief Lives*. London: Secker and Warburg. 1949.

Benet, Diana. *Secretary of Praise: The Poetic Vocation of George Herbert*. Columbia, MO: University of Missouri Press. 1984.

Berthoff, Ann E. *The Resolved Soul: A Study of Marvell's Major Poems*. Princeton, NJ: Princeton University Press. 1970.

Bertonasco, Mark F. *Crashaw and the Baroque*. Tuscaloosa, AL: University of Alabama Press. 1971.

Bethell, S.L. 'The Nature of Metaphysical Wit.' *Discussions of John Donne*. Ed. John Frank Kermode. Boston: Heath. 1962.

Brooks, Cleanth. *The Well Wrought Urn*. New York: Harcourt, Brace. 1947.

Calhoun, Thomas O. *Henry Vaughan: The Achievement of Silex Scintillans*. Newark, DE: University of Delaware Press. 1981.

Carey, John. *John Donne: Life, Mind and Art*. New York: Oxford University Press. 1981.

Charles, Amy M. *A Life of George Herbert*. Ithaca, NY: Cornell University Press. 1977.

Colie, Rosalie Littell. *'My ecchoing song': Andrew Marvell's Poetry of Criticism*. Princeton, NJ: Princeton University Press. 1970.

Cooper, Robert M. *An Essay on the Art of Richard Crashaw*. Salzburg: Institut für Anglistik und Amerikanistic, Universitat Salzburg. 1982.

Crashaw, Richard. *The Complete Poetry*. Ed. L.C. Martin. 2nd. ed. Oxford: Oxford University Press. 1957.

——. *The Complete Poetry*. Ed. Walton Williams. New York: Anchor. 1972.

Datta, Kitty Scoular. 'Marvell's Prose and Poetry: More Notes.' *Modern Philology* 63. 1966: 319-21.

——. *Natural Magic: Studies in the Presentation of Nature in English Poetry from Spenser to Marvell*. Oxford: Oxford University Press. 1965.

——. 'New Light on Marvell's "Dialogue between the Soul and Body".' *Renaissance Quarterly* 22. 1969: 242-55.

Docherty, Thomas. *John Donne, Undone*. London: Methuen. 1986.

Donne, John. *The Complete English Poems of John Donne*. Ed. C.A. Patrides. London: Dent. 1985.

——. *The Complete Poetry of John Donne*. Ed. John T. Shawcross. Garden City, NY: Anchor. 1967.

——. *John Donne The Complete English Poems*. Ed. A.J. Smith. Harmondsworth, Middlesex: Penguin. 1986.

——. *John Donne: The Divine Poems*. 2nd ed. Ed. Helen Gardner. Oxford: Clarendon Press. 1978.

——. *John Donne: The Elegies and The Songs and Sonnets*. Ed. Helen Gardner. Oxford: Clarendon Press. 1967.

Donne, John. *The Poems of John Donne*. 2 vols. Ed. H.J.C. Grierson. Oxford: Oxford University Press. 1912.

———. *The Songs and Sonnets of John Donne*. Ed. Theodore Redpath. London: Methuen. 1956.

Durr, R.A. *On the Mystical Poetry of Henry Vaughan*. Cambridge, MA: Harvard University Press. 1962.

Eliot, T.S. 'Andrew Marvell.' *Selected Essays*. 1932. New York: Harcourt, Brace. 1950.

———. 'Donne in our Time.' In *A Garland for John Donne*. Ed. Theodore Spencer. Cambridge, MA: Harvard University Press. 1931.

———. 'Metaphysical Poets.' *Selected Essays*.

Empson, William. *Seven Types of Ambiguity*. London: Chatto and Windus. 1930.

Fish, Stanley Eugene. *The Self-Consuming Artifacts: The Experience of Seventeenth-Century Literature*. Berkeley, CA: University of California Press. 1972.

Freeman, Rosemary. *English Emblem Books*. London: Chatto and Windus. 1948

Gardner, Helen, ed. *The Metaphysical Poets*. 1957. 2nd. ed. London: Oxford UP. 1967.

Harman, Barbara Leah. *Costly Monuments: Representations of the Self in George Herbert's Poetry*. Cambridge, MA: Harvard UP. 1982.

Herbert, George. *The Works of George Herbert*. Ed. F.E. Hutchinson. Oxford: Clarendon Press. 1941.

Hunt, John Dixon. *Andrew Marvell: His Life and Writings*. Ithaca, NY. Cornell University Press. 1978.

Hutchinson, F.E. *Henry Vaughan: A Life and Interpretation*. Oxford: Clarendon Press. 1947

Johnson, Samuel. 'Life of Cowley.' In *Lives of the English Poets*. 2 vols. London: Dent. 1925.

Kermode, Frank. 'The Private Imagery of Henry Vaughan.' *Review of English Studies*. n.s. 1. 1950: 206-25.

Leavis, F.R. 'The Line of Wit.' In *Revaluations*. London: Chatto and Windus. 1936.

Lewalski, Barbara. *Protestant Poetics and the Seventeenth-Century Religious Lyric*. Princeton, NJ: Princeton University Press. 1979.

Lord, George de Forest, ed. *Andrew Marvell: A Collection of Critical Essays*. Englewood Cliffs, NJ: Prentice-Hall. 1968.

Martz, Louis L. 'Marvell and the Masks of Mannerism.' In *Approaches to Marvell: The York Tercentenary Lectures*. Ed. C.A. Patrides. London: Routledge. 1978.

———. *The Paradise Within: Studies in Vaughan, Traherne and Milton*. New Haven, CT: Yale University Press. 1964.

———. *The Poetry of Meditation*. New Haven, CT: Yale University Press. 1954.

Martz, Louis L. *The Wit of Love: Donne, Carew, Crashaw, Marvell*. Notre Dame, IN: University of Notre Dame Press. 1969.

Marvell, Andrew. *Complete Poetry*. Ed. George de Forest Lord. New York: Modern Library. 1968.

———. *The Poems and Letters of Andrew Marvell*. 3rd. rev. ed. Ed. H.M. Margoliouth and revised and corrected by Pierre Legouis with the help of E.E. Duncan-Jones. Oxford: Clarendon Press. 1971.

Palmer, George Herbert, ed. *The English Works of George Herbert*. 6 vols. Boston and New York: Houghton. 1905.

Pettet. E.C. *Of Paradise and Light: A Study of Vaughan's* Silex Scintillans. Cambridge: Cambridge University Press. 1960.

Post, Jonathan F.S. *Henry Vaughan: The Unfolding Vision*. Princeton, NJ: Princeton University Press. 1982.

Rajan, Balachandra. 'Andrew Marvell: The Aesthetics of Inconclusiveness.' *Approaches of Marvell: York Tercentenary Lectures*. Ed. C.A. Patrides. London: Routledge. 1978.

Rickey, Mary Ellen. *Utmost Art: Complexity in the Verse of George Herbert*. Lexington, KY: University of Kentucky Press. (1966).

Rostvig, Maren-Sophie. *The Happy Man: Studies in the Metamorphosis of a Classical Ideal 1600-1700*. 2 vols. Oslo. 1954.

Roston, Murray. *The Soul of Wit*. London: Oxford University Press. 1974.

Sanders, Wilbur. *John Donne's Poetry*. Cambridge: Cambridge University Press. 1971.

Simmonds, James D. *Masques of God: Form and Theme in the Poetry of Henry Vaughan*. Pittsburgh, PA: University of Pittsburgh Press. 1972.

Summers, Joseph H. *George Herbert: His Religion and Art*. Cambridge, MA: Harvard University Press. 1954.

Tuve, Rosamund. *Elizabethan and Metaphysical Imagery*. Chicago: University of Chicago Press. 1947.

Vaughan, Henry. *The Complete Poetry*. Ed. French Fogle. Garden City, NY: Anchor. 1964.

———. *Poetry and Selected Prose*. Ed. L.C. Martin. London: Oxford University Press. 1963.

———. *The Secular Poems of Henry Vaughan*. Ed. E.L. Marilla. Uppsala: A.B. Lundequistoka Bokhandeln. 1958.

Vendler, Helen. *The Poetry of George Herbert*. Cambridge, MA: Harvard University Press. 1975.

Wallerstein, Ruth. *Richard Crashaw: A Study in Style and Poetic Development*. Madison, WI: University of Wisconsin Press. 1959

Walton, Izaac. *Lives*. 1670. London: Oxford University Press. 1927.

White, Helen C. *The Metaphysical Poets: A Study in Religious Experience*. 1936. New York: Collier. 1962.

Young, R.V. *Richard Crashaw and the Spanish Golden Age*. New Haven, CT: Yale University Press. 1982.

JOHN DONNE

John Donne (1572-1631) was born to a prosperous London mer-
chant. His mother and uncles were devoted Roman Catholics. He
matriculated from Hart Hall, Oxford and may have spent some time
at Cambridge and travelled abroad before studying law at Lincoln's
Inn. He joined expeditions to Cadiz and the Azores, and in 1597
became secretary to Sir Thomas Egerton, the Lord Keeper. A secret
marriage in 1601 with Anne More, the niece of Egerton's wife,
resulted in his dismissal from service. The next decade, part of which
was spent at Mitcham, was marked by poverty, the birth of several
children, his own ill health, and several unsuccessful attempts to get
a job. To this period belong a number of his *Songs and Sonnets*, the
'Holy Sonnets', and the prose works *Pseudo-Martyr* (1610) and
Ignatius his Conclave (1611) in which he discussed his faith as an
Anglican and took issue with aspects of Roman Catholic beliefs.
Around this time he also found a patron in Sir Richard Drury, went
abroad with him, and in 1611 wrote the first *Anniversary* on the
death of the young daughter of his new patron; the second *Anniver-
sary* appeared the following year. By now Donne's fortunes were on
the mend. He served as an M.P., in 1615 was ordained into the
Church of England, and the same year was awarded a D.D. from
Cambridge at the King's command. His wife died in 1617. In 1621 he
became Dean of St. Paul's Cathedral in London. From then up to the
end of his life he travelled abroad, was engaged in numerous affairs
of the Church, and preached many eloquent sermons which were
published and helped to define the nature of the Anglican Church.

Donne's poems circulated in manuscript form during his lifetime
among a small coterie of courtiers and wits but, apart from a few
shorter pieces and the two *Anniversaries*, remained unpublished till
two years after his death. The first edition, based on several manu-
scripts, was published in 1633. The second edition of 1635 changed
their order of appearance and added a few more poems. The
compilers of some manuscripts had given titles to the poems and also

to the various sections under which they were arranged (e.g. 'Elegies', 'Sonnets and Songs', 'Holy Sonnets', etc). While the first edition did not use these latter headings, the second did, with one important change: it transposed the words in 'Sonnets and Songs' to read 'Songs and Sonnets', thus recalling the title of Tottel's Miscellany. Since then the label has stuck though commentators have noted that there are only a few songs in the sequence and no sonnet properly so called, the term being applied loosely to denote short love lyrics.

SATIRES

If our appreciation of the poised urbanity, polished and smooth versification, and subtle wit of Augustan satirists leads to a depreciation of Donne's achievement as a satirist, it may help to remember that Pope himself was one of Donne's admirers and commended his satires as among 'his best things'. He 'versified' two of Donne's five satires, the second and fourth, but the harsh jaggedness that he smoothed out was probably intentional on Donne's part. C.S. Lewis suggested that Elizabethan satirists deliberately cultivated a roughness because they wrongly saw satire as connected to the mythical satyr, half man and half goat, who was portrayed as being shaggy and wild. Donne's harshness would seem to have been due more to the fact that he was imitating Roman models like Juvenal and Persius. Though it is not possible to identify any lines in Donne as imitations of Roman models, his satires may be said to revive their tone and technique in the social context of late Elizabethan England. There is the same vehement lashing of vices combined with shifting allusiveness, narration, snatches of conversation, moralizing, and terse observation. Milgate points to their urban settings and uncompromising realism as yet other features that they share in common with their Roman models. He also notes that Donne's world is not only corrupt but also crowded, and, like Ben Jonson the poet, captures the unceasing go-getting of the city.

While it is impossible to date Donne's satires accurately, commentators agree that they are among his very early poems and were probably written between 1593 and 1596 while he was also writing his elegies. They were first published in 1633 and arranged under the heading 'Satires' in 1635.

SATIRE III (of Religion)

Donne's mother was a Roman Catholic and one of his brothers was
imprisoned for sheltering a Roman Catholic priest. Inevitably he felt
an attraction for this Church. Though he had accepted Anglicanism
by 1597, when he entered Egerton's service, or even earlier, in the
period immediately preceding he seems to have been in doubt as to
which Church to embrace. 'Satire III', which Milgate dates around
1594 or 1595, belongs to this period. There is in it an insistence on
the need to decide, but there is equally an open-ended and inquiring
outlook which refuses to allow temporal or spiritual authority to
dictate faith to him, and which sees honest doubt as being more
valuable than unthinking acceptance. He is convinced that there is
a truth and it can be found. What is questioned is the facile or
dogmatic claims that various churches make of being its sole reposi-
tory.

The text given here is the modernized version in A.J. Smith.

Satire 3

            Kind pity chokes my spleen; brave scorn forbids
            Those tears to issue which swell my eye-lids,
            I must not laugh, nor weep sins, and be wise,
            Can railing then cure these worn maladies?
            Is not our mistress fair religion,
            As worthy of all our soul's devotion,
            As virtue was to the first blinded age?
            Are not heaven's joys as valiant to assuage
            Lusts, as earth's honour was to them? Alas,
10   As we do them in means, shall they surpass
            Us in the end, and shall they father's spirit
            Meet blind philosophers in heaven, whose merit
            Of strict life may be imputed faith, and hear
            Thee, whom he taught so easy ways and near
            To follow, damned? O if thou dar'st, fear this;
            This fear great courage, and high valour is.
            Dar'st thou aid mutinous Dutch, and dar'st thou lay
            Thee in ships' wooden sepulchres, a prey
            To leaders' rage, to storms, to shot, to dearth?
20   Dar'st thou dive seas, and dungeons of the earth?

Hast thou courageous fire to thaw the ice
Of frozen north discoveries? and thrice
Colder than salamanders, like divine
Children in th'oven, fires of Spain, and the line,
Whose countries limbecks to our bodies be,
Canst thou for gain bear? and must every he
Which cries not, 'Goddess!' to thy mistress, draw,
Or eat thy poisonous words? courage of straw!
O desperate coward, wilt thou seem bold, and
30 To thy foes and his (who made thee to stand
Sentinel in his world's garrison) thus yield,
And for forbidden wars, leave th'appointed field?
Know thy foes: the foul Devil, he, whom thou
Strivest to please, for hate, not love, would allow
Thee fain, his whole realm to be quit; and as
The world's all parts wither away and pass,
So the world's self, thy other loved foe, is
In her decrepit wane, and thou loving this,
Dost love a withered and worn strumpet; last,
40 Flesh (itself's death) and joys which flesh can taste,
Thou lovest; and thy fair goodly soul, which doth
Give this flesh power to taste joy, thou dost loathe.
Seek true religion. O where? Mirreus
Thinking her unhoused here, and fled from us,
Seeks her at Rome, there, because he doth know
That she was there a thousand years ago,
He loves her rags so, as we here obey
The statecloth where the Prince sate yesterday.
Crants to such brave loves will not be enthralled,
50 But loves her only, who at Geneva is called
Religion, plain, simple, sullen, young,
Contemptuous, yet unhandsome; as among
Lecherous humours, there is one that judges
No wenches wholesome, but coarse country drudges.
Graius stays still at home here, and because
Some preachers, vile ambitious bawds, and laws
Still new like fashions, bid him think that she
Which dwells with us, is only perfect, he
Embraceth her, whom his godfathers will
60 Tender to him, being tender, as wards still

Take such wives as their guardians offer, or
Pay values. Careless Phrygius doth abhor
All, because all cannot be good, as one
Knowing some women whores, dares marry none.
Gracchus loves all as one, and thinks that so
As women do in divers countries go
In divers habits, yet are still one kind,
So doth, so is religion; and this blind-. .
ness too much light breeds; but unmoved thou
70   Of force must one, and forced but one allow;
And the right; ask thy father which is she,
Let him ask his; though truth and falsehood be
Near twins, yet truth a little elder is;
Be busy to seek her, believe me this,
He's not of none, nor worst, that seeks the best.
To adore, or scorn an image, or protest,
May all be bad; doubt wisely, in strange way
To stand inquiring right, is not to stray;
To sleep, or run wrong is. On a huge hill,
80   Cragged, and steep, Truth stands, and he that will
Reach her, about must, and about must go;
And what the hill's suddenness resists, win so;
Yet strive so, that before age, death's twilight,
Thy soul rest, for none can work in that night.
To will, implies delay, therefore now do.
Hard deeds, the body's pains; hard knowledge too
The mind's endeavours reach, and mysteries
Are like the sun, dazzling, yet plain to all eyes.
Keep the truth which thou hast found; men do not stand
90   In so ill case here, that God hath with his hand
Signed kings blank-charters to kill whom they hate,
Nor are they vicars; but hangmen to Fate.
Fool and wretch, wilt thou let thy soul be tied
To man's laws, by which she shall not be tried
At the last day? Or will it then boot thee
To say a Philip, or a Gregory,
A Harry, or a Martin taught thee this?
Is not this excuse for mere contraries,
Equally strong; cannot both sides say so?
100 That thou mayest rightly obey power, her bounds know;

Those past, her nature, and name is changed; to be
Then humble to her is idolatry.
As streams are, power is; those blessed flowers that dwell
At the rough stream's calm head, thrive and prove well,
But having left their roots, and themselves given
To the stream's tyrannous rage, alas are driven
Through mills, and rocks, and woods, and at last, almost
Consumed in going, in the sea are lost:
So perish souls, which more choose men's unjust
110   Power from God claimed, than God himself to trust.

NOTES

1   *spleen*. Milgate says that the spleen was regarded as the seat of both laughter and melancholy; hence the word here implies bitter or satirical laughter. Donne's meaning is that his scornful laughter at men's follies is restrained ('choked') by the pity he feels for them.

1-2   *scorn...lids*. My scornful feelings check my natural impulse to cry.

3   I must neither laugh nor weep at men's sins; at the same time I must show wisdom.

4   *railing*. Deriding, uttering a vehement complaint against.
    worn. Old, longstanding.

5   *mistress fair religion*. The search for a true church will be described in the poem in terms of a man's search for a good woman. The use of sexual metaphors to characterize religious pursuits is characteristic of Donne, but it receives sanction from the Bible where the Church is described as the Bride of Christ.

7   'The first blinded age' is the period of pre-Christian antiquity which was 'blinded' (i.e. blind) because it lacked the light of Christianity. In the absence of a knowledge of Christian teaching that age made virtue its highest good in life.

8-9   The thought of a Christian heaven should be as powerful a motivation in helping us to overcome the lures of the world as the desire of earthly fame was to the ancients.

10-11   *means...end*. Though Christianity provides us a better means for salvation than the concept of earthly virtue did to the ancients, their stricter adherence to it may have enabled them to attain heaven more easily than might be possible for us, given our lax practice of Christianity.

12-13   *whose merit...imputed faith*. Martin Luther taught that salvation could be achieved not through meritorious living but through faith alone because God would 'impute' (i.e. bestow or credit) the merits of Christ to the faithful. Donne reverses the idea and says that the ancients necessarily lacked Christian faith but possessed merit, nevertheless God may have granted them salvation by imputing faith to them. The Bible allows the possibility that meritorious ancients could have been saved though they were not Christian: see Romans 2:14-15. For another example of Donne's daring reversal of the concept of imputation see 'To his Mistress Going to Bed' l.42.

14-15   *easy ways and near/To follow.* i.e. follow the Christian way.

17   *mutinous Dutch.* The Dutch had revolted against their Spanish occupiers and Englishmen were unofficially going to their help.

20   *dungeons.* Caves.

22   *frozen north discoveries.* The Cabots, Martin Frobisher and John Davis had tried to find a north-west passage to the Pacific during the previous hundred years.

23   *salamanders.* The salamander, a lizard-like creature, was thought to be so cold that it preferred to live in the fire.

23-4   *divine...oven.* Shadrach, Mesach and Abednego were thrown into the fire by Nebuchadnezzar for refusing to follow his religious practices but God miraculously preserved them. In ll. 89 ff. Donne returns to the idea of kings trying to force a particular religion on their people.

24   *fires of...line.* 'Fires of Spain' may refer both to the fact that Spain is a much warmer country than England and also to the fire to which heretics were consigned during the Inquisition. 'The line' is the Equator. Countries on the Equator have a hot climate.

25   *limbecks.* Alembics. These countries are like alembics in which Englishmen's bodies are heated up.

27-8   *draw/words.* i.e. must everyone who refuses to call your mistress 'goddess' be compelled either to fight you ('draw' = to draw one's sword) or suffer your verbal abuse?

30   *thy foes and his.* Your and God's enemies, identified in ll. 33 ff. as the devil, the world and the flesh.

30-2   *who made thee.../field?* i.e. will you leave your post of duty as a sentry on the moral battlefield to which God appointed you and engage instead in worldly wars which are forbidden to you?

34-5   i.e. the devil will give your his whole kingdom (hell) because he hates, not loves, you.

35   *to be quit.* Obscure. It may mean that the devil will give you his kingdom to be rid of your importunities, or 'in full discharge of what he owes you' (Milgate).

38   *In her...wane.* It was a common Elizabethan belief that the world was running down. Donne expresses the same idea at some length in the first *Anniversary.*

40   Flesh itself is mortal, and the joys of the flesh bring on death.

43   *Mirreus.* An imaginary name for a Roman Catholic. It is built upon *myrrh*, a sweet-smelling substance, and may therefore refer to the use of incense in Roman Catholic worship.

47   *rags.* Contemptuous description of the ceremonial trappings of Roman Catholicism.

48   *statecloth.* Canopy over the throne.

49   *Crants.* The Dutch or German-sounding name represents the followers of John Calvin (1509-1564) who inaugurated a Reformed Church characterized by strict discipline and a plain, even austere form of worship. Calvin's Swiss origins are referred to in 1. 50 ('Geneva') and the austerity of his doctrine in 11. 51-52.

53   *lecherous humours.* The lecher's tastes.

55   *Graius.* A Greek name used for one who embraces the religion of his forefathers unthinkingly. No special significance attaches to the choice of this name.

56   *bawds.* Pandars or pimps. Some priests try to win converts for their Church as pimps try to find customers for the prostitutes in their keeping.

56-7   *laws...fashions.* A comment on the proliferating laws in Elizabethan England that sought to regulate religious practices.

59   *Godfathers.* Spiritual mentors.

60   *Tender...tender.* Note the wordplay. The first *Tender* means to offer, the second, young.

62   *Pay values.* A ward who refused an arranged marriage had to pay a fine to his guardian. The idea is that if a man accepts a religion simply because he was born into it, he must pay a fine if he subsequently refuses to attend his parish church.
        Phrygius. Smith suggests that the name, used here as the type of man who cannot make up his mind between religions and therefore accepts none, recalls the Phrygians who were confronted by a multiplicity of gods as a consequence of foreign invasions by people of numerous different religions.

65   *Gracchus.* Those who find all religions of equal worth are typified by Gracchus, a name reminiscent of the Gracchi, a liberal and enlightened Roman family.

67   *habits.* Dresses.

68-9   *blind-/...breeds.* Too much light causes blindness.

71   *ask thy father.* Cf Deuteronomy 30:7: 'ask thy father, and he will show thee; thy elders, and they will tell thee.'

75   'He is not of no religion or of the worst religion who seeks the best religion' (Smith).

76   The line refers to various Churches: the Roman Catholics who worship images, the Puritans who scorn these practices, and the other Protestants.

77   *in strange way.* 'On an unfamiliar road.' (Milgate).

81   The repetition of 'about must' suggests the effort involved in reaching the top. F.R. Leavis praised this passage as an example of versification that enacts the meaning.

82   i.e. 'overcome in this way the resistance that the hill's steepness offers to your ascent.' (Smith).

83   *death's twilight.* Twilight is the period just before darkness falls; old age is therefore the twilight of death.

84   *for none can...night.* Cf. John 9:4: 'the night cometh, when no man can work.'

86-7   i.e. just as the body's hard and painful labour can accomplish difficult tasks, so can the mind's labours achieve hard knowledge.

87   *mysteries.* The central truths of religion.

89-91   *men...they hate.* i.e., it is not as if men are in a desperate situation because God has given kings a free hand to kill whoever they wish to. To sign a blank charter is to sign a blank warrant of execution that gives the bearer permission to execute whosoever's name he chooses to fill in.

92   The meaning is that kings who do kill those people who differ from them are not the agents of fate but only its executioners: they cannot kill anyone except him whom fate has marked for death.

95   *last day.* Day of Judgement.
        boot thee. Help you.

96-97   *Philip, or a Gregory,/A Harry, or a Martin.* Philip II of Spain, Pope Gregory XIV, Pope when the poem was written, Henry VIII, who founded the English Church, or Martin Luther, who started the Reformation.

100   *power.* Power of kings.

101·   *Those past.* Beyond those limits.

103-10 Power is compared in this extended image to a stream. The true source of power is God, and those who draw their sustenance from His commands thrive, just as those flowers do best that grow close to a stream's source. The further away a king's power is from the authority of God, the more violent and turbulent it becomes, and those people who depend upon this power are bound to perish like those flowers that are carried away by stormy rivers into the sea.

ELEGIES

Elegies are generally thought of as poems lamenting someone's death, and that is what the earliest elegies were. But there is another tradition of love elegies going back to Ovid's *Amores.* Though Donne wrote a funeral elegy, the other poems in this genre are Ovidian love elegies, though they also show the influence of the Italian Paradox and of Elizabethan comedy. Ovid's elegies, so called because they were written in the elegiac metre (a couplet in which an alexandrine is followed by a pentameter), aim to outrage the Roman sense of propriety and use social realism and satire. These qualities are characteristic of Donne, too, except that his couplets, though displaying extraordinary flexibility, are in the pentameter, and he goes well beyond his classical models by grafting on to them perverse paradoxes learnt from the Italians and what Gardner calls 'the logic-chopping of Elizabethan comedy.' The result is that some of his finest elegies hardly recall Ovid to mind.

The world of several of Donne's elegies is materialistic, cynical and bourgeois. Though some like 'On his Mistress' express tenderness and concern, there is no attempt to idealize love, nor is it ever regarded as a mystical union transcending boundaries of the flesh and sex. What we get instead is assertive argumentation, a conviction of male superiority, or, as in 'To his Mistress Going to Bed', frank lust. Often, as in 'The Perfume', women are treated as objects for sexual or material gratification, and images of disease or physical abnormalities abound. Indeed, the world of some of Donne's elegies like 'The Perfume' is so similar to the corrupt world of Ben Jonson's comedies or some of his satirical poems that it comes as no surprise that the latter knew Donne's elegy 'The Bracelet' by heart.

Though the elegies are impossible to date accurately it is generally agreed that they are among his early works and were probably written between 1593 and 1596 while he was a law student at Lincoln's Inn. The only exception is 'The Autumnal', which Gardner dates around 1600. During his lifetime they circulated in manuscript like most of his other poems. The 1633 edition planned to include thirteen of them but only eight were printed, the licensor having objected to the printing of five others. The 1635 edition grouped seventeen poems under the heading 'Elegies' and the 1699 edition added two more. Grierson included twenty poems in his edition under the head 'Elegies'. The authenticity of several has been questioned by Helen Gardner who allows only thirteen to stand, rejecting most of the rest as dubious and printing 'The Autumnal' separately because of its later composition.

The ordering of the poems in the present edition follows Gardner but the text as given here is the modernized version of A.J. Smith.

THE PERFUME

'This vigorous monologue, addressed by a young dandy to his partner in an amorous misadventure, translates the tone and spirit of Ovid's elegies into Elizabethan terms.' (Gardner). The poem is a satire in which Donne treats everybody except himself with scorn or contempt, but the comic tone keeps the denunciation at the level of a joke and the poet obviously enjoys his discomfiture even as he rues it.

The Perfume

    Once, and but once found in thy company,
    All thy supposed escapes are laid on me;
    And as a thief at bar, is questioned there
    By all the men, that have been robbed that year,
    So am I, (by this traitorous means surprised)
    By thy hydroptic father catechized.
    Though he had wont to search with glazed eyes,
    As though he came to kill a cockatrice,
    Though he have oft sworn, that he would remove
10 Thy beauty's beauty, and food of our love,
    Hope of his goods, if I with thee were seen,
    Yet close and secret, as our souls, we have been.
    Though thy immortal mother which doth lie
    Still buried in her bed, yet will not die,
    Takes this advantage to sleep out day-light,
    And watch thy entries, and returns all night,
    And, when she takes thy hand, and would seem kind,
    Doth search what rings, and armlets she can find,
    And kissing notes the colour of thy face,
20 And fearing lest thou art swoll'n, doth thee embrace;
    To try if thou long, doth name strange meats,
    And notes thy paleness, blushing, sighs, and sweats;
    And politicly will to thee confess
    The sins of her own youth's rank lustiness;
    Yet love these sorceries did remove, and move
    Thee to gull thine own mother for my love.
    Thy little brethren, which like faery sprites

Oft skipped into our chamber, those sweet nights,
And kissed, and ingled on thy father's knee,
30   Were bribed next day, to tell what they did see:
The grim eight-foot-high iron-bound serving-man,
That oft names God in oaths, and only then,
He that to bar the first gate, doth as wide
As the great Rhodian Colossus stride,
Which, if in hell no other pains there were,
Makes me fear hell, because he must be there:
Though by thy father he were hired to this,
Could never witness any touch or kiss.
But Oh, too common ill, I brought with me
40   That, which betrayed me to mine enemy:
A loud perfume, which at my entrance cried
Even at thy father's nose, so we were spied.
When, like a tyrant king, that in his bed
Smelt gunpowder, the pale wretch shivered.
Had it been some bad smell, he would have thought
That his own feet, or breath, that smell had wrought.
But as we in our isle imprisoned,
Where cattle only, and diverse dogs are bred,
The precious unicorns, strange monsters call,
50   So thought he good, strange, that had none at all.
I taught my silks, their whistling to forbear,
Even my oppressed shoes, dumb and speechless were,
Only, thou bitter sweet, whom I had laid
Next me, me traitorously hast betrayed,
And unsuspected hast invisibly
At once fled unto him, and stayed with me.
Base excrement of earth, which dost confound
Sense, from distinguishing the sick from sound;
By thee the silly amorous sucks his death
60   By drawing in a leprous harlot's breath;
By thee, the greatest stain to man's estate
Falls on us, to be called effeminate;
Though you be much loved in the prince's hall,
There, things that seem, exceed substantial.
Gods, when ye fumed on altars, were pleased well,
Because you were burnt, not that they liked your smell;
You are loathsome all, being taken simply alone,

Shall we love ill things joined, and hate each one?
If you were good, your good doth soon decay;
70   And you are rare, that takes the good away.
All my perfumes, I give most willingly
To embalm thy father's corse; What? will he die?

NOTES

2   *escapes.* Escapades.
5   *traitorous means surprised.* Betrayed by the perfume.
6   *Hydroptic.* Suffering from dropsy.
8   *cockatrice.* A mythical animal whose glance was supposed to kill. The
      joke lies in the fact that the father thinks that his gaze is so powerful
      that it can kill even a cockatrice, while in fact his eyes are 'glazed' (1.
      7), i.e. bleary through sickness or old age, or possibly peering
      through spectacles.
11   Hope of inheriting the father's money is what the lover finds truly
      attractive in his mistress ('beauty's beauty', 1. 10); it is this hope that
      fans his passion for her.
15   *this.* i.e. of the fact that being a hypochondriac she spends all her time
      in bed.
20   *Swoll'n.* Swollen, pregnant.
21   She names exotic foods to find out if you crave any of them. This is
      her way of trying to find out if you are pregnant.
25   Your love for me helped you to escape these practices of sorcerers.
      The parents are like sorcerers because they use enchantments and
      spells for their daughter.
      remove, and move. Notice the wordplay.
27   *brethren.* Brothers.
27-8 *like faery sprites...chamber.* Gardner thinks that the simile may have
      been suggested by *A Midsummer Night's Dream* where fairies trip
      through the house at the end of the play. If so, the poem may have
      been written shortly after the play was first staged in 1595-96.
29   *ingled.* Fondled.
31   The comic exaggeration of the servant's size is Ovidian.
34   *Rhodian Colossus.* The statue of Apollo in the harbour of Rhodes was
      one of the seven wonders of the world. It was said to be so huge that
      ships could sail between its legs.
41   *loud.* Strong. Here and in 'cried' the perfume is described as though
      it were a sound.
43   *When.* Then.
47   *our isle.* Our island, i.e. England.

49-50 Just as we call precious unicorns monsters because they are not
       found in England, so your father, who has no good in him, thought
       that the sweet ('good') perfume was strange. The unicorn was a
       mythical one-horned creature and used for a variety of symbolic
       meanings in medieval poetry.

52   i.e. my shoes did not squeak. The line playfully alludes to the fact that
       people charged with felony who refused to plead ('dumb and speech-
       less') were punished by having their feet pressed ('oppressed').

53   *bitter sweet.* The oxymoron refers to the perfume.

57   *Base excrement of earth.* perfume. Cf. Touchstone in *As You Like It*
       on civet: 'the very uncleanly flux of a cat' (III. 2. 60). Some perfumes
       were made from excrement.

57-8   *confound...sound.* Which confuses the senses so that they cannot dis-
       tinguish the healthy from the sick.

59   *silly amorous.* Foolish lover. The idea is that the lover does not
       recognize that the prostitute is diseased since she has used perfume
       to conceal her bad breath.

64   i.e. appearances are valued more than the substance.

65-6   The lines refer to the Roman custom of burning incense on altars as
       a form of worship.

67   *being taken simply alone.* If each of your ingredients is considered
       separately. See note on 1. 57 above.

68   i.e. should we love a produce which is a compound of bad things
       when we hate each of its ingredients?

69-70 The lines refer to the fact that perfume evaporates as also to its
       scarcity.

TO HIS MISTRESS GOING TO BED

In *Amores* I.v. Ovid describes how Corinna came one afternoon to
his room, and how, having undressed her and admired her naked-
ness, he took her to bed. Ovid's erotic reverie becomes in Donne an
insistent demand for satisfaction in the present.

To his Mistress Going to Bed

       Come, Madam, come, all rest my powers defy,
       Until I labour, I in labour lie.
       The foe oft-times having the foe in sight,
       Is tired with standing though they never fight.

Off with that girdle, like heaven's zone glistering,
But a far fairer world encompassing.
Unpin that spangled breastplate which you wear,
That th' eyes of busy fools may be stopped there.
Unlace yourself, for that harmonious chime
10 Tells me from you, that now 'tis your bed time.
Off with that happy busk, which I envy,
That still can be, and still can stand so nigh
Your gown going off, such beauteous state reveals,
As when from flowery meads th' hill's shadow steals.
Off with that wiry coronet and show
The hairy diadem which on you doth grow;
Now off with those shoes, and then safely tread
In this love's hallowed temple, this soft bed.
In such white robes heaven's angels used to be
20 Received by men; thou angel bring'st with thee
A heaven like Mahomet's paradise; and though
Ill spirits walk in white, we easily know
By this these angels from an evil sprite
Those set our hairs, but these our flesh upright.
    Licence my roving hands, and let them go
Before, behind, between, above, below.
O my America, my new found land,
My kingdom, safeliest when with one man manned,
My mine of precious stones, my empery,
30 How blessed am I in this discovering thee!
To enter in these bonds, is to be free;
Then where my hand is set, my seal shall be
    Full nakedness, all joys are due to thee.
As souls unbodied, bodies unclothed must be,
To taste whole joys. Gems which you women use
Are like Atlanta's balls, cast in men's views,
That when a fool's eye lighteth on a gem,
His earthly soul may covet theirs, not them.
Like pictures, or like books' gay coverings made
40 For laymen, are all women thus arrayed;
Themselves are mystic books, which only we
Whom their imputed grace will dignify
Must see revealed. Then since I may know,
As liberally, as to a midwife, show

Thyself: cast all, yea, this white linen hence,
Here is no penance, much less innocence.
   To teach thee, I am naked first, why then
What needst thou have more covering than a man.

NOTES

2   *labour...labour.* Until I exert myself in sexual intercourse I remain
     in an agony of anticipation.
4   *standing.* A *double entendre.* Refers both to the army waiting to fight
     and to his erection.
5   *zone.* The reference is to the outermost sphere of the universe in
     Ptolemaic astronomy.
7   *breastplate.* The stomacher, an item of women's clothing which cov-
     ered the chest. *Breastplate* is also a piece of armour; as such the word
     picks up the war metaphor from 1. 3.
9   *harmonious chime.* The mistress is wearing a chiming watch.
11   *busk.* Corset, an inner garment.
12   i.e. that can retain its shape and consciousness though it is so close
     to your body.
15   *wiry coronet.* A headdress made out of intricately interwoven, possi-
     bly golden, wires.
16   *hairy diadem.* Crown of hair.
24   *the flesh upright.* Another reference to his erection.
27   *new found land.* Not necessarily the Canadian province but any
     newly discovered country. The Elizabethan age was one of many
     such discoveries.
29   *empery.* Empire.
32   *seal.* Impression signifying my possession; but also penis. Cf. 'The
     Relic' 11. 29-30.
34   *souls unbodied.* Souls must be liberated from bodies before they can
     experience heavenly bliss.
36   *Atlanta's balls.* Atlanta vowed to marry only that man who could
     defeat her in a race. Hippomenes threw golden balls in her path to
     distract her in her race against him and so caused her to lose. Donne
     reverses the use of the legend by making women use their jewels to
     distract men from their goal.
39-43 The idea is that only men who have been initiated into the mysteries
     of love may see women naked. Women are compared to books
     dealing with esoteric subjects. Ordinary men ('laymen', 1. 40) only
     admire their covers ('gay coverings', 1. 39) without being able to read
     them.

42   *imputed grace*. In Calvinist theology salvation requires the bestowal
      ('imputation') of divine grace on men. Donne transfers the concept
      to sexual relationships by saying that women impute grace only to a
      few elect men. See also 'Satire III' 11. 12-13 and note.
45.   *white*. The colour of penance. As the next line makes clear, there is
      nothing to be repented in their love making.
46   *Here is*. i.e. there is no place here for.

ON HIS MISTRESS

The poem attempts to dissuade the poet's mistress from accompany-
ing him disguised as a page on his foreign travels. The theme is
common enough; what is remarkable is the dramatic intensity with
which it is treated. This has led some critics to surmise that it was
addressed to Donne's wife, Anne, but autobiographical truth is not
necessary for the creation of intensity. The poem was admired by
Hazlitt, and Lamb used it to refute the charge that Donne is obscure.

On his Mistress

        By our first strange and fatal interview,
        By all desires which thereof did ensue,
        By our long starving hopes, by that remorse
        Which my words' masculine persuasive force
        Begot in thee, and by the memory
        Of hurts, which spies and rivals threatened me,
        I calmly beg: but by thy father's wrath,
        By all pains, which want and divorcement hath,
        I conjure thee; and all the oaths which I
10   And thou have sworn to seal joint constancy,
        Here I unswear, and overswear them thus,
        Thou shalt not love by ways so dangerous.
        Temper, O fair love, love's impetuous rage,
        Be my true mistress still, not my feigned page;
        I'll go, and, by thy kind leave, leave behind
        Thee, only worthy to nurse in my mind
        Thirst to come back; oh, if thou die before,
        From other lands my soul towards thee shall soar,

Thy (else almighty) beauty cannot move
20   Rage from the seas, nor thy love teach them love,
Nor tame wild Boreas' harshness; thou hast read
How roughly he in pieces shivered
Fair Orithea, whom he swore he loved.
Fall ill or good, 'tis madness to have proved
Dangers unurged; feed on this flattery,
That absent lovers one in th' other be.
Dissemble nothing, not a boy, nor change
Thy body's habit, nor mind's; be not strange
To thy self only; all will spy in thy face
30   A blushing womanly discovering grace;
Richly clothed apes, are called apes, and as soon
Eclipsed as bright we call the moon the moon.
Men of France, changeable chameleons,
Spitals of diseases, shops of fashions,
Love's fuellers, and the rightest company
Of players, which upon the world's stage be,
Will quickly know thee, and know thee; and alas
Th' indifferent Italian, as we pass
His warm land, well content to think thee page,
40   Will hunt thee with such lust, and hideous rage,
As Lot's fair guests were vexed. But none of these
Nor spongy hydroptic Dutch shall thee displease,
If thou stay here. Oh stay here, for, for thee
England is only a worthy gallery,
To walk in expectation, till from thence
Our greatest King call thee to his presence.
When I am gone, dream me some happiness,
Nor let thy looks our long-hid love confess,
Nor praise, nor dispraise me, nor bless nor curse
50   Openly love's force, nor in bed fright thy nurse
With midnight's startings, crying out, 'Oh, oh
Nurse, O my love is slain, I saw him go
O'er the white Alps alone; I saw him, I,
Assailed, fight, taken, stabbed, bleed, fall, and die.
Augur me better chance, except dread Jove
Think it enough for me to have had thy love.

NOTES

1   *fatal interview*. Fateful meeting.
3   *remorse*. Pity
4   *words' masculine persuasive force*. An accurate and pithy description of much of Donne's love poetry.
8   *divorcement*. Separation.
9   *conjure*. Solemnly demand.
15-17 *leave...back*. i.e. you are the only one able to sustain in me a desire to return.
19   *move*. Remove.
21-3   Boreas, the north wind, carried off Orithea to Thrace. Donne here seems to be confusing this story, told in Ovid's *Metamorphoses*, with another recounted in Burton's *Anatomy of Melancholy* about a pine tree, once a woman who was killed by Boreas in a jealous fit.
24   *proved*. Tried, experienced.
27   *Dissemble*. Donne uses the word in the sense of to hide as well as in the now obsolete sense of to simulate or pretend.
28   *habit*. Dress.
28-9   *be not...only*. Your disguise will deceive no one but yourself.
30   *discovering grace*. Grace that will dis-cover, i.e. reveal the truth.
31   *apes*. Fools, boors.
31-2   *as soon...moon*. i.e. we call the moon by that name whether it is eclipsed or not. The idea is that truth cannot be hidden.
33   Frenchmen were stereotyped in Elizabethan England as changeable.
34   *Spitals*. Hospitals. Spital-houses treated venereal diseases.
       shops of fashions. French love of fashion was a common subject of satire.
35   *Love's fuellers*. They fuel or serve to increase love. The reference could be to French pedlars of aphrodisiacs.
37   *know thee, and know thee*. Discover your identity and rape you. 'To know' in the sexual sense is to have carnal knowledge of.
38   *indifferent*. Bisexual.
41   *Lot's fair guests*. Genesis 19 tells the story of the men of Sodom who surrounded Lot's house and demanded that he hand over two men (really angels in disguise) who were staying there as guests so that they could have sex with them. God destroyed Sodom for its sins.
42   *spongy hydroptic*. One who suffers from dropsy so that the more he drinks (like a sponge soaking up liquid) the thirstier he gets.
44   *gallery*. An antechamber where suitors wait to have audience with the king.
46   *greatest King*. God.
52   *Nurse*. Donne may have been thinking of Juliet's nurse in *Romeo and Juliet*.

55 *Augur me better chance.* Cf. 'Sweetest love I do not go....' 11. 33-34
and 'A Valediction: Of Weeping' 11. 19-25. To augur is to predict or
prognosticate.
except. Unless.

HIS PICTURE

The poet hands a miniature portrait of himself to his mistress on
parting from her. Through a series of paradoxes he is able finally to
come to a proper understanding of the nature of his mistress's love
for himself.

His Picture

Here take my picture, though I bid farewell;
Thine, in my heart, where my soul dwells, shall dwell.
'Tis like me now, but I dead, 'twill be more
When we are shadows both, than 'twas before.
When weather-beaten I come back; my hand,
Perhaps with rude oars torn, or sun-beams tanned,
My face and breast of haircloth, and my head
With care's sudden hoariness o'erspread,
My body a sack of bones, broken within,
10   And powder's blue stain scattered on my skin;
If rival fools tax thee to have loved a man,
So foul, and coarse, as oh, I may seem then,
This shall say what I was: and thou shalt say,
Do his hurts reach me? doth my worth decay?
Or do they reach his judging mind, that he
Should now love less, what he did love to see?
That which in him was fair and delicate,
Was but the milk, which in love's childish state
Did nurse it: who now is grown strong enough
20   To feed on that, which to disused tastes seems tough.

NOTES

4   Portraits were sometimes called 'shadows'. Donne's meaning is that
        when he is a ghost ('shadow') the portrait ('shadow') will resemble
        him even more than it does now.

7   *haircloth.* Clothes made out of hair were worn by penitents.

8   i.e. my head covered ('o' erspread') with hair whose greyness ('hoar-
        iness') has been brought about suddenly by a rash of cares.

10   *powder's.* Gunpowder's. The poem may have been written when
        Donne was going off to Cadiz in 1596 on a military expedition.

13   *this.* i.e. my portrait.

14,15 *reach.* Afflict.

19   *it.* The mistress's love for him.

17-20 The poet hopes that his mistress will assert that his youthful beauty,
        as represented by the portrait, was the milk that nursed her immature
        love ('childish state', l. 18) for him. Now that her love is mature, it can
        feed on the 'meat' of his inner nature. The distinction between the
        child who needs milk and the mature man who feeds on meat is
        Biblical. See 1 Corinthians 3:1-2 and Hebrews 5:13-14. For another
        example of Donne's use of this metaphor see 'The Good-Morrow', ll.
        2-3 and note.

THE AUTUMNAL

The poem is supposed to have been addressed to Magdalen Herbert,
mother of the poets Sir Edward Herbert (later Lord Herbert of
Cherbury) and George Herbert. She was a rich and accomplished
lady whom Donne probably first met at Oxford around 1600, when
this poem was written, and with whom he later became good friends.
The poem consists of a series of witty paradoxes on the by then
conventional theme that age is preferable to youth in women. It
cannot be regarded either as an expression of the poet's beliefs or as
a seriously intended compliment to Mrs. Herbert. It is more in the
nature of a witty tribute that one poet may be expected to pay
another of the opposite sex. The fact that the sentiments are not
seriously intended is borne out by the title 'A Paradox of an Old
Woman' which some manuscripts give to the poem.

The Autumnal

No spring, nor summer beauty hath such grace,
    As I have seen in one autumnal face.
Young beauties force your love, and that's a rape,
    This doth but counsel, yet you cannot scape.
If 'twere a shame to love, here 'twere no shame,
    Affection here takes reverence's name.
Were her first years the Golden Age; that's true,
    But now she's gold oft tried, and ever new.
That was her torrid and inflaming time,
10   This is her tolerable tropic clime.
Fair eyes, who asks more heat than comes from hence,
    He in a fever wishes pestilence.
Call not these wrinkles, graves; if graves they were,
    They were Love's graves; for else he is no where.
Yet lies not Love dead here, but here doth sit
    Vowed to this trench, like an anachorit.
And here, till hers, which must be his death, come,
    He doth not dig a grave, but build a tomb.
Here dwells he; though he sojourn everywhere,
20   In Progress, yet his standing house is here.
Here, where still evening is; not noon, nor night;
    Where no voluptuousness, yet all delight.
In all her words, unto all hearers fit,
    You may at revels, you at council, sit.
This is Love's timber, youth his underwood;
    There he, as wine in June, enrages blood,
Which then comes seasonabliest, when our taste
    And appetite to other things is past.
Xerxes' strange Lydian love, the platan tree,
30   Was loved for age, none being so large as she,
Or else because, being young, nature did bless
    Her youth with age's glory, barrenness.
If we love things long sought, age is a thing
    Which we are fifty years in compassing.
If transitory things, which soon decay,
    Age must be loveliest at the latest day.
But name not winter-faces, whose skin's slack;
    Lank, as an unthrift's purse; but a soul's sack;

Whose eyes seek light within, for all here's shade;
40   Whose mouths are holes, rather worn out, than made;
Whose every tooth to a several place is gone,
       To vex their souls at Resurrection;
Name not these living death's-heads unto me,
       For these, not ancient, but antiques be.
I hate extremes; yet I had rather stay
       With tombs, than cradles, to wear out a day.
Since such love's natural lation is, may still
       My love descend, and journey down the hill,
Not panting after growing beauties, so,
50   I shall ebb out with them, who homeward go.

NOTES

1-2   Bacon in 'of Beauty' maintains that autumn is the most beautiful of
      all seasons. He may have got the idea from Plutarch.
4   *scape.* Escape.
6   i.e. love in this case ('here') turns into respect.
7   *Were her first years.* Inversion: her first years were...
      Golden Age. Associated with innocence. The next line suggests that
      now she has been tested by experience.
8   Just as gold is tested ('tried') for its purity, so she has been tried often;
      just as gold never becomes old so she is always new.
9-10 Her youthful years are compared to the hot climate of countries on
      the Equator ('torrid and inflaming'). Her present, though warm like
      the climate of the tropics, is not unbearable.
12   Pestilences were often ascribed to hot weather. The sense here is that
      to ask for more heat than she offers is to invite a pestilence.
16   *anachorit.* This would now be spelt 'anchorite' i.e a hermit who
      usually attached himself to a shrine out of a desire of penance.
19-20 i.e. this is his permanent home, though he may dwell in other places
      temporarily, like a king who has a palace but travels in state ('In
      Progress') through various parts of his realm.
23-4 Her words are full of delight as well as instruction so that she has
      something for every type of audience.
25   *timber...underwood.* Mature trees as opposed to undergrowth. Ben
      Jonson titled one collection of his poems *Underwoods,* while a
      collection of his critical prose is called *Timber, or Discoveries.*
26-8 i.e. in our youth love, like wine, overheats our blood. The best time
      for love and wine is when our taste for other things has been satiated.

29-31 Herodotus recounts how Xerxes found a plane tree which he decked
      with ornaments. Donne's meaning is that Xerxes' love for the tree
      arose either because it was old, its age being deduced from the fact
      of its size, or because though young it was barren and thus possessed
      the attributes of old age.

36   Because then it is on the point of disappearing altogether.

37   *winter-faces.* Old hags.

42   It was believed that when, on the Day of Resurrection, the dead rise
      from their graves they will possess exactly the same bodies that they
      had when alive. Since an old hag's fallen teeth are likely to have gone
      in several directions, there will be considerable vexation in getting
      them all together again in her mouth on the Last Day.

43   *death's-heads.* It was a common custom in the Middle Ages to keep
      a skull or a picture of a skull ('death's head') by one as a reminder of
      mortality.

44   *antiques.* With a pun on *antics* or grotesques. In *Richard II*, III. 2.
      162-3 death's heads are called antics.

47   *lation.* An obsolete astronomical term denoting movement. The idea
      in the last four lines is that love's natural movement is downward, and
      so Donne wants his love to 'ebb out' with the lives of those who are
      old and on their way to heaven ('homeward' in 1. 50 means 'heaven-
      ward'). He no longer wants to pant while running uphill in chase of
      'growing beauties'; 'down the hill' is the proper direction for him
      now.

SONGS AND SONNETS

Songs and Sonnets establishes Donne's preeminenece as a love
poet. Apart from the fact that the poems are consciously anti-
Petrarchan and therefore the poet is never abject before his mistress
and never thinks of himself as unworthy of her love, there is
probably no aspect of man-woman relationships that he has not
captured. He can be cynical, or mocking, or witty, or frankly carnal,
or desolate, or unfaithful; at other times he experiences a rapture in
love; often he seeks to explore and define the mystical union of souls
that love produces. Hie poems never describe the mistress, though
they often celebrate her. Their *forte* lies in the creation of specific
situations out of which they arise and with which they interact. The
shifts in a Donne poem both cause and mirror changes in the
situation with the result that by the end of the poem the situation is
never the same as it was at the beginning. Hand in hand with this

drama goes a great variety of metrical forms. His staples are the octosyllabic and decasyllabic lines, but he weaves everything into them from two-foot lines to alexandrines. There is equal variety in his stanza forms which range from quatrains through seven-line stanzas to complex stanzas of fourteen to twenty-four lines. Critics have commented upon Donne's colloquial rhythms, but the variations he rings on the inflections of the spoken voice always occur within rigid metrical patterns. It also needs to be remembered that quite a few of his poems are songs and were set to music.

Herbert J.C. Grierson, Donne's first twentieth-century editor, based his text on the 1635 edition of Donne except that he displaced 'The Flea', which opened *Songs and Sonnets*, from its pride of place. Recently Helen gardner has maintained that the 1633 edition provides better authority than that of 1635. Therefore her edition differs in several particulars from Grierson's. One important change is that whereas Grierson included fifty five poems under *Songs and Sonnets*, she admits only fifty four. Another lies in the order in which she prints the poems. She argues that poems in *Songs and Sonnets* can be divided into those whose style and metre are simple and those where they are complex and subtle. She associates this progression with Donne's reading of theology and Neoplatonic philosophy, and maintains that the first group was probably written before 1600, the second after 1602, most probably between 1607 and 1614. Therefore she prints *Songs and Sonnets* in two groups, the first consisting, from among those poems included in the present edition, of 'Song' ('Go and catch a falling star...'), 'Woman's Constancy', 'The Triple Fool' and 'The Flea', and the second of the rest.

While Gardner's arrangement has the merit of clarifying thematic links between the various poems and suggesting that Donne's genius was a developing, not static, one, it has not been accepted by later editors like John T. Shawcross, A.J. Smith and C.A. Patrides. The present edition follows Patrides, Donne's most recent editor, in restoring 'The Flea' to the head of the *Songs and Sonnets* sequence and thereafter adhering to the order in which the poems appeared in Grierson's text.

Of all the major twentieth-century editors, only Theodore Redpath prepared his edition specially for the use of students. He modernized spelling and simplified punctuation, retaining older forms only when there was a special reason for them. I have followed

Redpath's text of *Songs and Sonnets* for the most part. When I depart from him the reasons are explained in the notes.

THE FLEA

Helen Gardner points out that the use of the flea for erotic poems was popularized by the late medieval 'Carmen de Pulice' ascribed to Ovid. By Donne's time several poems on the flea existed. While other poets either wished to be a flea or envied the flea its death at the mistress's hands, Donne wittily makes the flea bring about the desired union by biting first him and then her. 'Donne may be reworking a French model which had...punned on "puce" (flea) and "pucelage" (maidenhead)' (Patrides). The drama of the poem lies in the way Donne is able to suggest the changing reactions of his mistress to successive stages in his argument and have a response to them ready, all the time keeping the upper hand. The ending where his ingenious wit enables him to turn the tables on his mistress has also been much admired.

The Flea

      Mark but this flea, and mark in this
      How little that which thou deny'st me is;
      Me it suck'd first, and now sucks thee,
      And in this flea our two bloods mingled be;
5   Confess it: this cannot be said
      A sin, or shame, or loss of maidenhead,
         Yet this enjoys before it woo,
         And pamper'd swells with one blood made of two,
         And this, alas, is more than we would do.

10   Oh stay, three lives in one flea spare,
      Where we almost, nay more than married are:
      This flea is you and I, and this
      Our marriage bed, and marriage temple is;
      Though parents grudge, and you, we're met
15   And cloister'd in these living walls of jet.
         Though use make you apt to kill me,

Let not to that, self-murder added be,
And sacrilege, three sins in killing three.

Cruel and sudden, hast thou since
20   Purpled thy nail in blood of innocence?
In what could this flea guilty be,
Except in that drop which it suck'd from thee?
Yet thou triumph'st, and say'st that thou
Find'st not thyself, nor me,the weaker now:
25   'Tis true; then learn how false, fears be;
Just so much honour, when thou yield'st to me,
Will waste, as this flea's death took life from thee.

NOTES

1   *Mark...mark.* The repetition of the word gives an objective, medita-
tive air to what is essentially a poem of seduction.
5   *Confess.* Admit.
9   *alas.* Because the mistress does not yield to the poet.
15   *cloister'd.* A cloister is a place of religious seclusion. Note the reli-
gious image in an erotic poem: this is characteristic of Donne.
Equally characteristic is the sense of the lovers' seclusion from the
rest of the world.
Jet. Black.
16   *use.* Habit.
18   *sacrilege.* Another religious term applied ironically here to the
'murder' of the flea. While the poet exaggerates the significance of
the killing of the flea, he regards her 'killing' of him to be a normal
occurrence.
20   *Purpled...innocence.* The beauty of the image is startling in the
context in which it occurs.

THE GOOD-MORROW

Very different from 'The Flea', this poem seeks the self-sufficiency
that Donne hopes to find in love. Gaining true love, he suggests, is
worth renouncing the whole world for; moreover, it is only through
such love that immortality can be attained. The poem possesses
qualities of seriousness and abstractness, yet is not devoid of collo-
quialisms and conceits.

The Good-Morrow

    I wonder, by my troth, what thou and I
    Did, till we lov'd? were we not wean'd till then?
    But suck'd on country pleasures, childishly?
    Or snorted we in the Seven Sleepers' den?
5   'Twas so; but this, all pleasures fancies be:
    If ever any beauty I did see,
    Which I desir'd, and got, 'twas but a dream of thee.

    And now good-morrow to our waking souls,
    Which watch not one another out of fear;
10   For love, all love of other sights controls,
    And makes one little room, an everywhere.
    Let sea-discoverers to new worlds have gone,
    Let maps to others, worlds on worlds have shown,
    Let us possess one world, each hath one, and is one.

15   My face in thine eye, thine in mine appears,
    And true plain hearts do in the faces rest;
    Where can we find two better hemispheres,
    Without sharp North, without declining West?
    Whatever dies, was not mix'd equally;
20   If our two loves be one, or, thou and I
    Love so alike, that none do slacken, none can die.

NOTES

1   *wonder.* The note of wonder is akin to that created by 'Mark...mark' in 'The Flea'.
    by my troth. An oath of assertion. Now obsolete.

2-3 *wean'd...childishly.* An infant suckles at its mother's breast; as it grows older it is weaned away from its mother's milk and introduced to solid food. Donne suggests that till they fell in love with each other his mistress and he were like infants or those unsophisticated people who enjoy only rustic ('country') pleasures, but their love has caused them to grow up. Now they are like those sophisticated people who can enjoy the pleasures of the city or court. Nowhere is it suggested that Donne and his mistress have not previously been in love; rather, their previous loves are belittled. The milk/meat contrast is Biblical. See 'His Picture' 11. 17-20 and note.

1-3   *I...childishly.* An ingenious but acceptable rhyme.

4   *snorted.* Snored. A colloquialism.

      Seven Sleepers' den. According to legend seven Christian youths sought shelter in a cave to escape the persecution of the Roman emperor Decius. The cave was walled up on the Roman emperor's orders so as to starve the youths to death, but they fell into a miraculous sleep and awoke after 187 years. The idea is again that before they fell in love the mistress and the poet could not be said to have been living, only sleeping.

5   *but this.* Except for our love.

      fancies. Imaginary, not real joy...

6-7   *beauty...thee. Beauty* here may be abstract, or used metonymically to refer to all beautiful women. Either way the meaning is that the poet's past experiences of love were like mere prefigurings ('dream') of his present love. Donne seems to be referring to the Platonic distinction between the Real and the world of appearances.

8   *good-morrow.* Good morning. An *aubade* is a love poem uttered at dawn, and 'The Good-Morrow' can be read as a spiritual *aubade* in which the poet's soul addresses that of his mistress at the moment of love's dawning.

10   Love takes away all desire to see other persons, places or things.

12-13 *worlds...worlds...worlds.* Continents. The Elizabethan age was remarkable for its voyages of discovery. Donne contrasts the ever-expanding sense of the universe with his 'little room' which the mistress's presence has turned into a self-sufficient world.

14   Commentators have argued about the number of worlds here: is there only one world made up of the lover and his mistress, or are there two worlds, those of the poet and the mistress, or four, each lover being one and also each possessing one? See also 11. 20-21, where again there is some ambiguity about whether the lovers together constitute one world or are each of them a separate world. A similar problem exists in 'A Valediction: Forbidding Mourning' 11. 21-26.

17   *hemispheres.* Here each lover's face is not the whole but just one hemisphere. Donne seems to have had in mind cordiforms or maps where hemispheres were shaped like hearts.

18   *sharp North...declining (West).* The reference is to cold north winds and the decline of the sun in the west. The world of lovers is superior to the physical world in that it is not afflicted by cold or subject to decline.

19   *equally.* Consistently, through and through.

21-2 The lines printed in this text are from the 1633 edition and favoured by most editors. However, Redpath, on whose text the present is based, rejects these lines, substituting them with the following emendation:

If our two loves be one, or, thou and I
Love just alike in all, none of these loves can die.

In rejecting the 1633 reading he argues that the last line is confusing.
If loving alike precludes the possibility of love dying, then no slack-
ening of love is possible. And if no slackening is possible, the mere
mention of this possibility in the 1633 text is absurd.

Redpath's emendation has the merit of adding greater conviction to
the hope for immortality that Donne expresses. But for precisely this
reason I feel uneasy with it. For the element of doubt and suspicion
which is introduced through contemplating the possibility that love
may one day slacken seems to me closer to Donne's own thinking on
love. He tries to find meaning and permanence in love, but even at
the moment of its highest affirmation is haunted by the fear that his
hopes may prove illusory. The 1633 reading captures his sceptical
temper, and hence I have followed it here.

SONG: GO AND CATCH A FALLING STAR

The jaunty melody of 'Song' suits the meaning. The poem first enu-
merates a number of bizarre or impossible actions and then con-
cludes with the idea that nothing is as impossible or bizarre as the
notion of a woman being both beautiful and faithful. This kind of
anti-feminism has a long history in the West and Donne's use of it
may have been merely witty and conventional. There is no need to
look for autobiographical facts behind the poem.

Song

Go and catch a falling star,
    Get with child a mandrake root,
Tell me where all past years are,
    Or who cleft the Devil's foot,
5   Teach me to hear mermaids singing,
      Or to keep off envy's stinging,
        And find
        What wind
Serves to advance an honest mind.

10   If thou be'st borne to strange sights,
      Things invisible to see,
Ride ten thousand days and nights,

Till age snow white hairs on thee,
Thou, when thou return'st, wilt tell me
15   All strange wonders that befell thee,
            And swear
            Nowhere
Lives a woman true, and fair.

If thou findst one, let me know,
20   Such a pilgrimage were sweet;–
Yet do not, I would not go,
      Though at next door we might meet;
Though she were true, when you met her,
      And last, till you write your letter,
25   Yet she
            Will be
False, ere I come, to two, or three.

NOTES

2   Make a mandrake root pregnant. The forked roots of *atropa man-
      dragora* resemble the human form. It was believed that the root
      uttered a human scream when pulled out of the ground. It was used
      as an aphrodisiac.
4   The Devil was popularly portrayed in the middle ages and the Renais-
      sance as having horns, a tail and cloven heels.
6   *to keep off envy's stinging*. To ward off jealousy.
8-9   *wind...mind.* How an honest man can gain promotion. Donne here
      mixes the concerns of the secular world with the mysteries, rareties
      and wonders described earlier.
24   *last*. Remain so.

WOMAN'S CONSTANCY

Another hectoring, 'anti-feminist' poem cast in the form of a dramatic
monologue. Unlike 'Song' it is addressed directly to the mistress; as
in 'The Flea' the poet's argumentative wit produces the dramatic turn
at the end. The title is ironic, the subject of the poem being woman's
inconstancy.

Woman's Constancy

Now thou hast lov'd me one whole day,
Tomorrow when thou leav'st, what wilt thou say?
Wilt thou then antedate some new-made vow?
    Or say that now
5   We are not just those persons which we were?
Or, that oaths made in reverential fear
Of Love, and his wrath, any may forswear?
Or, as true deaths true marriages untie,
So lovers'contracts, images of those,
10   Bind but till sleep, death's image, them unloose?
    Or, your own end to justify,
For having purpos'd change, and falsehood, you
Can have no way but falsehood to be true?
Vain lunatic, against these 'scapes I could
15   Dispute, and conquer, if I would;
    Which I abstain to do,
For by tomorrow, I may think so too.

NOTES

2   *when thou leavest.* 'when you stop loving me' (Redpath).
3   Will you claim that your vow of faithfulness, made recently, was in fact
    sworn a long time ago and is therefore not valid? Donne is anticipat-
    ing and countering the possible arguments the mistress may advance
    for her inconstancy.
6-7 Promises made under duress are not binding in law. The promise of
    fidelity was made in fear of the power of love. The idea contained in
    'reverential fear/Of Love' is a conventional one that goes back to
    courtly love in the middle ages.
7   *forswear.* Repudiate.
11-13 Can be paraphrased to mean: Will you argue, in order to justify the
    intention you have had all along to desert me, that your constancy
    lies in being unfaithful?
14   *Vain.* Ineffectual; but also containing a suggestion that the woman
    is proud and self-centred.
    lunatic. Under the moon's sway, therefore changeable and incon-
    stant.
    'scapes. Strategies of deception.
17   By tomorrow I may wish to leave you too.

THE UNDERTAKING OR PLATONIC LOVE

The poem has no title in most manuscripts and in the 1633 edition.
It is called 'Platonic Love' in some manuscripts and 'The Undertak-
ing' in the 1635 edition. Most editors have used the 1635 title;
following Redpath I retain both titles. The poem asserts the unique-
ness of the beloved and maintains after Plato that true beauty is
spiritual, that true love focuses only on the beauty of the soul, and
that sex is irrelevant to true lovers. Note the strict logic of the
argument: 'Just as... so also' (st. 2-3) and 'If...if...then' (st.5-7)

The Undertaking or Platonic Love

      I have done one braver thing
         Than all the Worthies did,
      And yet a braver thence doth spring,
         Which is, to keep that hid.

5   It were but madness now to impart
         The skill of specular stone,
      When he which can have learn'd the art,
         To cut it, can find none.

      So, if I now should utter this,
10   Others (because no more
      Such stuff to work upon there is)
         Would love but as before.

      But he who loveliness within
         Hath found, all outward loathes,
15   For he who colour loves, and skin,
         Loves but their oldest clothes.

      If, as I have, you also do
         Virtue attir'd in woman see,
      And dare love that, and say so too,
20   And forget the He and She;

      And if this love, though placed so,
         From profane men you hide,

Which will no faith on this bestow,
  Or, if they do, deride:

25 Then you have done a braver thing
      Than all the Worthies did;
    And a braver thence will spring,
      Which is, to keep that hid.

NOTES

1   *braver*. Greater.
2   *Worthies*. The nine Worthies consisted of three Gentiles, Hector, Alexander and Julius Caesar, three Christians, Arthur, Charlemagne and Godfrey of Buillon, and three Jews, Joshua, David and Judas Maccabaeus.
6   *specular stone*. Selenite. In ancient times it was cut into thin sheets and used for glazing. Donne believed that the stone no longer existed and there was therefore no point in teaching anyone to cut it.
11 *stuff*. Material, here meaning woman. In this stanza Donne suggests that there is no point in teaching anyone to love as he does, since another woman like Donne's mistress does not exist in the world.
15-16 Physical beauty is here compared to old clothes, both because like clothes it is external and because it ages and wears out.
17 *Virtue attir'd in woman*. A continuation of the clothes imagery. The woman's body is here seen Neoplatonically as the dress of virtue.
20 *He and She*. Sexual differences.
21 *though placed so*. Can be paraphrased: which is focused upon the mistress's spiritual beauty.
22 *profane men*. The phrase implies that Donne's love partakes of a religious mystery in which the average man is uninitiated.

THE SUN RISING

Another poem that expresses the self-sufficiency of lovers who are shut up in a room to the exclusion of the world outside. Opening with an exasperated expostulation it proceeds through a series of comparisons glorifying the mistress and ends on a note of restful calm. Such transitions of style, mood and feeling are common in the best poetry of this period.

The Sun Rising

Busy old fool, unruly Sun,
    Why dost thou thus,
Through windows, and through curtains, call on us?
Must to thy motions lovers' seasons run?
5   Saucy pedantic wretch, go chide
        Late schoolboys, and sour prentices,
    Go tell court-huntsmen that the King will ride,
    Call country ants to harvest offices;
Love, all alike, no season knows, nor clime,
10   Nor hours, days, months, which are the rags of time.

Thy beams, so reverend and strong
    Why shouldst thou think?
I could eclipse and cloud them with a wink,
But that I would not lose her sight so long:
15   If her eyes have not blinded thine,
        Look, and tomorrow late, tell me
    Whether both the Indias of spice and mine
    Be where thou leftst them, or lie here with me.
Ask for those Kings whom thou saw'st yesterday,
20   And thou shalt hear: 'All here in one bed lay.'

She is all States, and all Princes I,
    Nothing else is:
Princes do but play us; compar'd to this,
All honour's mimic, all wealth alchemy.
25   Thou, sun, art half as happy as we,
        In that the world's contracted thus;
    Thine age asks ease, and since thy duties be
    To warm the world, that's done in warming us.
Shine here to us, and thou art everywhere;
30   This bed thy centre is, these walls, thy sphere.

NOTES

4   Inverted syntax. The meaning is: Must lovers' seasons be dictated by
     the sun's movements?

5   *pedantic.* In the sense of one who lays excessive stress upon strict
     adherence to formal rules. But because the sun is asked to chide late
     schoolboys in the next line, the word also carries its primary meaning
     of a schoolmaster.

6   *prentices.* Apprentices; also more generally any disciple. Now obso-
     lete.

7   James I, who came to the throne in 1603, was fond of hunting. Com-
     mentators have seen the line as evidence that the poem must have
     been written after that date.

7-8 In these lines Donne rejects both the court and the country in favour
     of love.

10   *the rags of time.* 'The tattered clothing of time: or alternately, the
     shreds into which time is...subdivided' (Redpath).

11-12 Inversion: Why should you think your beams are...

17   *Indias of spice and mine.* The East Indies, associated with spices, and
     the West Indies, associated with gold.

21-2 Cf. 'The Anniversary' 1. 23.

24   *alchemy.* Counterfeit. Alchemy was a medieval pseudo-science that
     sought to turn base metals into gold.

30   *Sphere.* Orbit. The poem maintains the Ptolemaic view of the uni-
     verse according to which the sun moved in orbit round the earth.

THE CANONIZATION

To be canonized is to be elevated to sainthood in the Christian
church. In this poem the lovers are made into saints of love; just as
people pray to saints in the Roman Catholic church, so Donne
anticipates that other lovers will pray to his mistress and him after
they are dead. A colloquial, satirical and self-deprecatory opening
rapidly leads, in typical Donne fashion, to a celebration of love as a
mystery that shares the nature of a mystical religious experience.

The Canonization

For God's sake hold your tongue, and let me love,
   Or chide my palsy, or my gout,
My five gray hairs, or ruin'd fortune flout,
    With wealth your state, your mind with arts improve,
      Take you a course, get you a place,   5
      Observe his honour, or his grace,

Or the King's real, or his stamped face
   Contemplate; what you will, approve,
   So you will let me love.

Alas, alas, who's injured by my love?   10
   What merchant's ships have my sighs drown'd?
Who says my tears have overflow'd his ground?
   When did my colds a forward spring remove?
      When did the heats which my veins fill
      Add one man to the plaguy bill?   15
Soldiers find wars, and lawyers find out still
   Litigious men, which quarrels move,
   Though she and I do love.

Call us what you will, we are made such by love;
   Call her one, me another fly,   20
We are tapers too, and at our own cost die,
   And we in us find the Eagle and the Dove.
      The Phoenix riddle hath more wit
      By us; we two being one, are it.
So to one neutral thing both sexes fit,   25
   We die and rise the same, and prove
   Mysterious by this love.

We can die by it, if not live by love,
   And if unfit for tombs and hearse
Our legend be, it will be fit for verse;   30
   And if no piece of chronicle we prove,
      We'll build in sonnets pretty rooms;
      As well a well-wrought urn becomes
The greatest ashes, as half- acre tombs,
   And by these hymns, all shall approve   35
   Us *canoniz'd* for Love:

And thus invoke us: 'You, whom reverend love
   Made one another's hermitage;
You, to whom love was peace, that now is rage;
   Who did the whole world's soul contract, and drove   40
      Into the glasses of your eyes

(So made such mirrors, and such spies,
That they did all to you epitomize)
   Countries, towns, courts: beg from above
   A pattern of your love!'   45

NOTES

1   *love.* This word concludes the first and last lines of the poem.
2   *Or...or.* Either...or.
5   *place.* Job.
6   *observe.* Pay court to, attend to.
     honour...grace. Pay court to great men in the secular and religious spheres.
7-8 *Or...contemplate.* Become a courtier who finds his greatest satisfaction in gazing at the king's face. Or else go in for money making and think that your greatest good lies in looking at coins which have the king's image embossed ('stamped') on them. The references to the king indicate that the poem was written after 1603. See 'The Sun Rising' 1. 7 and note.
8   *approve.* Do, try. Now obsolete.
10-18 These examples of activities which the poet's love has *not* injured form a satirical list of some of the major concerns of the period: mercantile trade, agriculture, the weather, epidemics, wars and litigation. In exaggerating such symptoms of love as sighing, weeping and alternating between extremes of heat and cold Donne also satirizes the conventions of courtly love. The point he makes is that his love is free of these artificialities.
13   *forward spring remove.* Delay a Spring whch would otherwise have come early.
15   *plaguy bill.* A list of those killed by the plague. Printed bills began to be issued weekly in 1592. Plagues were endemic in Elizabethan England and were supposed to be caused by extreme warm weather. Redpath thinks that the word *bill*, by recalling 'playbill', carries the implication that, in case of a plague epidemic, playhouses would have been forced to close.
17   *which quarrels move.* Who start quarrels.
21   If we are flies, each of us is also a candle ('taper'). Each destroys the other as candles destroy flies, but we are also self-destructive ('at our own cost die') because in the mere act of burning we are diminishing ourselves as candles do. 'Die' was a common Elizabethan way of describing detumescence following the sex act. It also referred to the commonly held belief that the sex act shortened people's life span. This line refers to the destructive power of love. Later the poet will

talk of love's power to resurrect. Thus Christian notions underlie the consuming nature of sexual passion here.

22   *the Eagle and the Dove.* The birds stand respectively for the predatory and the gentle. But as chief of the birds the eagle in the middle ages also typified Christ. The Dove is traditionally a symbol of the Holy Ghost. Thus the naming of these birds introduces religious ideas into the poem.

23   *Phoenix riddle.* The phoenix was a mythical bird. Only one phoenix was supposed to exist at any time; a new phoenix, identical to the old, was supposed to rise from the ashes of the old when it died. The phoenix was a symbol of perfection because, being a creature of no sex, it could be said to contain both sexes in it. Because of its perfect nature and its power to resurrect itself it was also a symbol of Christ.

23-4 *hath more wit/...are it.* i.e. it makes more sense in light of our experience, for we too, by being joined in a perfect union, have transcended sexual differences ('are it').

26   *die and rise.* In the sense of detumescence after a sex act followed at a subsequent stage by fresh tumescence preparatory to another sex act. But dying and rising and the earlier references to the phoenix make it abundantly clear that the poet wants us to see similarities between his love and the mystery of Christ's death and resurrection.

31-2 *chronicle...sonnets.* If our lives and love are not worthy of history, they will be worthy of poetry.

35   *these.* Such as that in the last stanza.
       approve. prove.

40   *contract.* Helen Gardner prefers the reading *extract* as developing an alchemical metaphor.

41-4 *glasses of your eyes...courts.* Each lover saw ('spied') only the other lover; the eyes of each reflected ('mirrored') only the other. The person that each lover saw or reflected symbolized ('epitomized') to that lover the whole world ('countries, towns, courts'). Thus it could be said that the lovers had shrunk or distilled ('contract' or 'extract' 1. 40) and crammed ('drove' 1.40) the whole world into each other's eyes.

44   *beg from above. Beg* is in the imperative. The meaning is that just as Roman Catholics pray to saints to intercede with God on their behalf, so love's worshippers will ask the sainted lovers to beg God that they, the worshippers, might enjoy the same kind of love that the two lovers did when they were alive.

THE TRIPLE FOOL

The poem is noteworthy for the theory of love poetry that it propounds. The pain of love can be contained through the discipline of

versifying it: metre which serves as a restraint also proves an ano-
dyne. Such love poetry is best not published, for when it becomes
public property the pain it sought to allay is released once again.

The Triple Fool

    I am two fools, I know,
For loving, and for saying so
    In whining poetry;
But where's that wiseman, that would not be I,
    If she would not deny?   5
    Then, as the earth's inward narrow crooked lanes
Do purge sea-water's fretful salt away,
    I thought, if I could draw my pains
Through rhyme's vexation, I should them allay:
Grief brought to numbers cannot be so fierce;   10
For he tames it, that fetters it in verse.

    But when I have done so,
Some man, his art and voice to show,
    Doth set and sing my pain,
And, by delighting many, frees again
    Grief, which verse did restrain.
To love and grief tribute of verse belongs,
But not of such as pleases when'tis read;
    Both are increased by such songs:
For both their triumphs so are published,   20
And I, which was two fools, do so grow three;
Who are a little wise, the best fools be.

NOTES

Title. I am a fool because (a) I love, (b) because I write about love in po-
    etry, and (c) others set my verse to music and by publicizing it
    reawaken the pain of love.

3-5   Notice the poet's sense of simultaneous self-castigation and self-con-
    gratulation.

6-7   Many Ancients believed that the reason the seas were salt and rivers
    not was because sea water was desalinated in the course of its passage

through narrow subterranean channels before issuing forth in river
form.

6-11   The struggle to versify, till finally it is rewarded with success, is
       skilfully enacted in these lines. The struggle is suggested by the hard,
       clogged consonants and the dragging rhythm of lines 6-9, and the
       relief by the rhymed couplet with which the stanza closes.

10   *numbers*. Poetic metre.

14   *set*. Set to music.

17-19 The primary function of poetry is to offer tribute to love and grief, not
       to give pleasure to readers. When it starts doing the latter it fails in its
       primary function of being therapeutic.

22   See note to lines 3-5 above.

SONG: SWEETEST LOVE I DO NOT GO

This is one of Donne's several poems that deal with the subject of
parting and possesses a delicacy of phrasing and intensity of feeling.
It starts with an attempt to argue the mistress out of the fear that he
will not return, but gradually her foreboding affects his own mood.
Finally he overcomes fears with a calm assertion of the value of their
love.

Song

Sweetest love, I do not go for weariness of thee,
Nor in hope the world can show a fitter love for me;
            But since that I
      Must die at last,'tis best
      To use myself in jest,   5
            Thus by feign'd deaths to die;

Yesternight the Sun went hence, and yet is here today;
He hath no desire nor sense, nor half so short a way:
            Then fear not me,
      But believe that I shall make   10
      Speedier journeys, since I take
            More wings and spurs than he.

Oh how feeble is man's power; that if good fortune fall,
Cannot add another hour, nor a lost hour recall!

But come bad chance,   15
And we join to it our strength,
And we teach it art and length,
    Itself o'er us to advance.

When thou sigh'st, thou sigh'st not wind, but sigh'st my
                                            soul away,
When thou weep'st, unkindly kind, my life's blood doth decay. 20

    It cannot be
That thou lov'st me, as thou say'st,
If in thine my life thou waste;
    Thou art the best of me.

Let not thy divining heart forethink me any ill;   25
Destiny may take thy part, and may thy fears fulfil;
    But think that we
Are but turn'd aside to sleep;
They who one another keep
    Alive, ne'er parted be.   30

NOTES

5-6   By parting from you ('thus' in 1. 6) I should get used to the idea of
      dying eventually. The parting is a pretended ('feigned') death.
8   *nor half so short a way.* i.e. the sun has a much longer journey to
      perform than I do.
11-12 *since...be.* i.e. I have a greater reason to hurry back than the sun.
17   *length.* 'How to expand or stretch' its control over us (Redpath).
18   To get the upper hand of us.
20   *unkindly kind.* An oxymoron. The mistress cries out of the kindness
      of her heart, but since the poet's life is contained in her (11. 23-24)
      her crying also unintentionally destroys his life.
25   *divining.* Foreboding.
      forethink. The idea is that if she fears that evil will befall him and her
      fears come true, she will have *forethought* the evil, i.e. brought it
      about at a subsequent date by allowing the thought of it to enter her
      mind in the first place.

THE ANNIVERSARY

This poem (not to be confused with Donne's two long *Anniversaries* of 1611-1612) commemorates the beginning of the second year of his relationship with his mistress. The tone throughout is meditative, the rhythms slow and stately, and the use of abstractions gives it an exalted quality. The poem returns to such themes as time, death and immortality which we have encountered elsewhere but treats them differently.

The Anniversary

All Kings, and all their favourites,
   All glory of honours, beauties, wits,
The Sun itself, which makes times, as they pass,
Is elder by a year, now, than it was
When thou and I first one another saw: 5
All other things to their destruction draw,
   Only our love hath no decay;
This, no tomorrow hath, nor yesterday;
Running it never runs from us away,
But truly keeps his first, last, everlasting day.   10

   Two graves must hide thine and my corse;
   If one might, death were no divorce:
Alas, as well as other Princes, we
(Who Prince enough in one another be)
Must leave at last in death, these eyes, and ears,   15
Oft fed with true oaths, and with sweet salt tears;
   But souls where nothing dwells but love
(All other thoughts being inmates) then shall prove
This, or a love increased there above,
When bodies to their graves, souls from their graves remove.   20

   And then we shall be throughly blest,
   But we no more than all the rest;
Here upon earth, we are Kings, and none but we
Can be such Kings, nor of such subjects be:
Who is so safe as we, where none can do   25
Treason to us, except one of us two?

True and false fears let us refrain,
Let us love nobly, and live, and add again
Years and years unto years, till we attain
To write threescore; this is the second of our reign.   30

NOTES

3 The line has caused editors difficulties. The idea seems to be that the sun creates units of time like days, weeks, months, etc., referred to in this line as the plural *times*. By then causing these *times* to 'pass' (i.e. follow one another in chronological succession) it produces our sense of temporality. The sun can, therefore, be said to be the source or origin of time and should be free of time's ravages. But it is as much subject to ageing as anything else in nature.

6 Inverted syntax: All other things draw towards their destruction.

10 i.e. our love exists in the timeless present.

11 *Two graves*. Since their love is clandestine they cannot, unlike a married couple, hope to be buried in one grave.
corse. Corpse.

18 *inmates*. Temporary residents. Love is the only permanent dweller in our souls.

18-19 *then shall prove...above*. Donne says that after we are dead ('then') and go to heaven ('there above' in 1.19) we shall continue to experience ('prove') the same love ('This') as we do now, perhaps even greater.

20 When bodies go to their graves the souls leave their graves. Here the grave of souls is presumably the body. The idea that death liberates the soul from the body's bondage can be traced back to Neoplatonism and even earlier, but Donne does not usually think of the body as the grave of the soul.

21 *throughly*. Thoroughly.

21-2 'In heaven we shall be no more blessed than anyone else' (Redpath). According to Scholastic philosophy all are equally *content* in heaven. Donne here alters the notion of contentment to that of blessedness. Helen Gardner points out that the bliss the lovers enjoy here on earth is preferable to the bliss they will enjoy in heaven since here they are better off than the others while there they will enjoy only a common felicity.

23 Cf. 'The Sun Rising' 11.21-22. There the poet suggested that as prince he ruled over his mistress who represented his kingdom. Here the relationship is more equal since each is king of, and subject to, the other.

30   Today marks the beginning of the second year of the reign of our
      love. Let us live to celebrate its diamond jubilee. A score is twenty;
      threescore will be sixty years.

A VALEDICTION: OF WEEPING

This is another of Donne's poems of parting and can be grouped with
several of his other Valedictions. Individual lines in the poem present
difficulties in interpretation but the main idea is clear enough. The
poet exercises tight control over his imagery, though the detailed
and elaborate tear image and the uses to which it is put ally the poem
to such baroque works as Crashaw's 'The Weeper'. Indeed, it is the
tear image and the basic conceit associated with it—that the face
reflected in a tear is an emblem of death by drowning—that ties the
poem together. Interwoven with this image are others drawn from
geography, mintage, tides, storms and floods. Altogether the effect of
the poem is complex and satisfying.

A Valediction: of Weeping

        Let me pour forth
My tears before thy face, whilst I stay here,
For thy face coins them, and thy stamp they bear,
And by this mintage they are something worth,
        For thus they be   5
        Pregnant of thee;
Fruits of much grief they are, emblems of more,
When a tear falls, that thou falls which it bore,
So thou and I are nothing then, when on a diverse shore.

        On a round ball   10
A workman that hath copies by. can lay
An Europe, Africa, and an Asia,
And quickly make that, which was nothing, *All*;
        So doth each tear
        Which thee doth wear,   15
A globe, yea world, by that impression grow,
Till thy tears mixt with mine do overflow
This world, by waters sent from thee, my heaven dissolved so.

O more than Moon,
Draw not up seas to drown me in thy sphere,   20
Weep me not dead, in thine arms, but forbear
To teach the sea, what it may do too soon;
   Let not the wind
   Example find
To do me more harm than it purposeth;   25
Since thou and I sigh one another's breath,
Whoe'er sighs most, is cruellest, and hastes the other's death.

NOTES

3   My tears reflect your face. In this sense they are coins that your face
      mints. By stamping them with your image you give them value just as
      metal is given value by being stamped with an image in the process
      of being coined.

6   *pregnant*. Full.

7   My tears are the result of grief at the thought of parting from you and
      the signs ('emblems') of more to come.

8   Redpath explains the line to mean: When one of my tears falls, that
      particular Thou falls which the tear carried in it (i.e. the image of you
      in the tear falls).

9   *diverse shore*. Different countries. When we have separated I, like my
      fallen tear, will be nothing: likewise, you, the image in my fallen
      tear, will be nothing.

10   *round ball*. Globe.

11   *copies*. Maps.
       lay. Paste

14-15 So also each of my tears which reflects your image...

16   *impression*. Note that earlier in the poem his tears have been given
      value by her reflection in them (the coin minting image in 11.3-4)
      and have been impregnated by her reflection (1.6). Now her reflec-
      tion turns the poet's tears into a whole world.

18   *This world*. Refers both to the world into which the mistress's image
      has turned the poet's tears (1. 16 above) as also to the real physical
      world. When the phrase is interpreted in the latter sense the whole
      line can be taken to mean that once the mistress starts weeping, her
      copious tears joined to his will be enough to drown the whole world.
      my heaven. The mistress. By mixing her tears with his she blurs her
      image in his tears. Thus the poet's heaven is dissolved. Alternatively,
      if her tears cause a flooding of the physical world, she will perish in
      this flood; thus his heaven will be drowned ('dissolved').

19   *Moon*. Refers both to the mistress's beauty as also to her power to
     create a more powerful flood by her weeping than any tides that the
     moon controls.
20   *thy sphere*. According to the Ptolemaic system the moon's was the
     first sphere. The full meaning of the phrase is revealed when the next
     line is taken into account: the poet does not wish to be drowned
     when he is in the moon's own sphere (i.e. right in his mistress's arms).
     For that to happen would be a tragic irony, since in her arms is
     precisely where he wishes to be and since the danger of drowning
     comes precisely from the fact that he has to leave her arms and
     undertake a risky sea voyage.
21-25 She should cease weeping and sighing lest the waves and winds at sea
     learn a lesson from her and cause him to be shipwrecked on his
     journey.

THE APPARITION

In this dramatic monologue the poet threatens the unresponsive
mistress that if she kills him with her scorn his ghost will return to
haunt her. Both notions, that of the lover being killed by scorn and
of the lover's ghost's revenge, are conventional, but Donne puts
them to a vivid and different use. The situation of the mistress in bed
with another lover, in particular, is dramatically and comically
portrayed.

The Apparition

When by thy scorn, O murd'ress, I am dead,
   And that thou thinkst thee free
From all solicitation from me,
Then shall my ghost come to thy bed,
And thee, feign'd vestal, in worse arms shall see;   5
Then thy sick taper will begin to wink,
And he, whose thou art then, being tir'd before,
Will, if thou stir, or pinch to wake him, think
   Thou call'st for more,
And in false sleep will from thee shrink;   10
And then, poor aspen wretch, neglected thou
Bath'd in a cold quicksilver sweat wilt lie,

A verier ghost than I:
What I will say, I will not tell thee now,
Lest that preserve thee; and since my love is spent,   15
I had rather thou shouldst painfully repent,
Than by my threat'nings rest still innocent.

NOTES

5   *feign'd vestal.* Pretending to be a virgin.
6   The pale and weak candle by your bedside will begin to flicker. It was
     believed that the presence of ghosts made flames flicker.
7   *being tir'd before.* Being tired from an earlier bout of love making.
10   *false sleep.* The actions of both the woman and her new lover are
     characterized by falsehood.
11   *aspen.* Quivering or trembling like the leaves of an asp or willow tree.
12   *quicksilver sweat.* Alchemists combined mercury or quicksilver with
     ore to obtain gold or silver. The quicksilver was then removed,
     leaving only the precious metal. 'In a reversal the poet says that the
     woman will be left with a quicksilver sweat when her lover, who is like
     a precious metal, turns away' (Shawcross). Quicksilver sweat baths
     were also a treatment for syphilis.
14-18 The general sense of these lines is that if I told you now what my ghost
     will say, you would be so terrified that you would not take on another
     lover. But since I don't love you any more and want you to suffer, I
     shall keep silent now.

THE BROKEN HEART

A witty rather than a profound poem in which Donne plays with the
conventional notions of the transience of love, its destructive power,
and broken hearts. The first two stanzas lay out general propositions
which are then applied in the next two to his particular case. As with
so many of his other poems the ending is far removed from the
premises with which he began.

The Broken Heart

He is stark mad, who ever says
    That he hath been in love an hour;

Yet not that love so soon decays,
   But that it can ten in less space devour:
Who will believe me, if I swear   5
That I have had the plague a year?
   Who would not laugh at me, if I should say
   I saw a flask of powder burn a day?

Ah, what a trifle is a heart,
   If once into love's hands it come!   10
All other griefs allow a part
   To other griefs, and ask themselves but some;
They come to us, but us Love draws,
He swallows us, and never chaws:
   By him, as by chain'd shot, whole ranks do die;   15
   He is the tyrant pike, our hearts the fry.

If 'twere not so, what did become
   Of my heart, when I first saw thee?
I brought a heart into the room,
   But from the room I carried none with me: 20
If it had gone to thee, I know
Mine would have taught thine heart to show
   More pity unto me: but Love, alas,
   At one fierce blow did shiver it as glass.

Yet nothing can to nothing fall,   25
   Nor any place be empty quite,
Therefore I think my breast hath all
   Those pieces still, though they be not unite;
And now, as broken glasses show
A hundred lesser faces, so   30
   My rags of heart can like, wish, and adore,
   But after one such love, can love no more.

NOTES

8   *powder*. Gunpowder. A flask of gunpowder would burn in a flash
     rather than be consumed slowly, just as the plague would kill a man
     in much less time than a year (11. 5-6). Similarly love will destroy a
     man in less than an hour.

12   *but some.* Only some room, not all available space.
14   *chaws.* Chews.
15   *chain'd shot.* Chained cannonballs which could kill ranks of men.
16   *Fry* are small fish which the bigger *pike* eats.
25   Refers to the notion that matter is indestructible.
26   Refers to the notion that nature never allows a vacuum.
28   *unite.* Whole, united.
31-2 The sense is that just as fragments of a mirror may reflect parts of an
     object but cannot reflect the object in its entirety, so also the
     fragments of my heart can experience the constituent emotions of
     love but are incapable of experiencing love in its wholeness. The
     analogy is not apt since objects in their entirety can be reflected even
     in the broken pieces of a mirror.

A VALEDICTION: FORBIDDING MOURNING

In his *Life of Donne* Isaac Walton claimed that Donne addressed this
poem to his wife on the occasion of leaving her to accompany Sir
Robert Drury to France in 1611. This claim has been disputed by
Helen Gardner who says that in his poems Donne expresses the
viewpoint of the lover rather than of the husband or father, and that
the ideal nature of the lovers' union here is at odds with the
mundane details of Donne's married life. In this poem asking his
mistress not to mourn his absence becomes for the author an
occasion for exploring the nature of their love. The extended
compass image, though not original to Donne, has made the poem
a central text for the study of Metaphysical poetry, but its real
greatness lies in its achievement as a love lyric.

A Valediction: Forbidding Mourning

As virtuous men pass mildly away,
    And whisper to their souls, to go,
Whilst some of their sad friends do say:
    'The breath goes now', and some say: 'No':

So let us melt, and make no noise,   5
    No tear-floods, nor sigh-tempests move;
'Twere profanation of our joys
    To tell the laity our love.

Moving of the earth brings harms and fears;
    Men reckon what it did and meant: 10
But trepidation of the spheres,
    Though greater far, is innocent.

Dull sublunary lovers' love
    (Whose soul is sense) cannot admit
Absence, because it doth remove   15
    Those things which elemented it.

But we, by a love so much refin'd
    That our selves know not what it is,
Inter-assured of the mind,
    Care less, eyes, lips, and hands to miss.   20

Our two souls therefore, which are one,
    Though I must go, endure not yet
A breach, but an expansion,
    Like gold to airy thinness beat.

If they be two, they are two so   25
    As stiff twin compasses are two:
Thy soul, the fix'd foot, makes no show
    To move, but doth, if the other do;

And though it in the centre sit,
    Yet when the other far doth roam,   30
It leans, and hearkens after it,
    And grows erect, as that comes home.

Such wilt thou be to me, who must,
    Like the other foot, obliquely run:
Thy firmness makes my circle just,   35
    And makes me end where I begun.

NOTES

1   *pass mildly away*. Die a gentle death.
5   *melt*. Part, separate.
6   *move*. Raise.

7   *profanation.* 'The degradation or vulgarization of anything worthy of being held in reverence or respect' (O.E.D.). But the word also carries a religious overtone which continues in the word *laity* (1. 8) below. Donne wishes to suggest that his love is like a secret religious cult or practice which the uninitiated cannot understand.

8   *laity.* Lay persons as opposed to the clergy of a church or religion; therefore uninstructed, unlearned. See note to 1. 7 above.

9   *Moving of the earth.* Earthquakes.

10   *and meant.* Earthquakes were regarded as portents of important social or political changes.

11   *trepidation of the spheres.* 'A libration [oscillation] of the eighth or ninth spheres' (O.E.D.) It was believed that this astronomical phenomenon was more powerful than any earthquake but was not felt and caused no damage. Donne suggests that the most significant movements–such as the parting of the lovers–should remain unperceived to other men.

13   *sublunary.* Lit. 'below the moon'. Therefore earthly or ordinary and commonplace. The word also connotes people or phenomena that are subject to change and corruption.

14   *(Whose soul is sense).* i.e. whose lives are entirely sensual so that they cannot be said to have souls but only senses.
        admit. Tolerate.

16   *elemented it.* Formed the essential elements or ingredients of their love ('it').

21-4   Because we are not two souls but one, therefore when I part from you we shall not be separated ('endure not yet/A breach'). Rather, we shall simply be stretched out ('expansion'), just as when gold is beaten into thin leaf it does not break but merely expands. The poet's use of the gold image is a way of conferring worth upon his love, and 'airy thinness' may also suggest the transparency of bodies assumed by angels.

26   *stiff twin compasses* . A pair of compasses with two feet but joined at the head, used to draw circles. Donne compares his mistress to the fixed foot which remains at the centre of the circle while he is like the outer foot which draws the circumference. The stability of one ('firmness' in 1. 35 below) determines the successful completion of the task by the other.

31-2   When the circle is being drawn the fixed foot of the compass bends ('leans and hearkens') towards the moving foot. When the circle is completed and the compass is closed (Donne suggests this idea in the words 'comes home'), the fixed foot regains a vertical position ('grows erect'). Donne is saying that his mistress's sympathy will control his movement on the journey till such time as the journey is over and he can return to be beside her.

34   *obliquely*. Refers to the circle's curving shape.
35   *circle*. The circle is a symbol of perfection.
      just. perfect.
36   The circle ends at the point from where it began. The line poses a
      difficulty. The journey ends from where it began, i.e. from beside his
      mistress. But the circle (to which the journey is compared) does not
      begin from nor end at its centre, where the mistress is.

THE ECSTASY

This is a complex and richly wrought poem that draws upon horticul-
ture, medievel cosmology and psychology, alchemy, theology and
Platonism to argue that there is no dichotomy between body and
spirit. It has been read as a poem of seduction in which Donne uses
heavy philosophical concepts to make the girl friend acquiesce in the
act of love making. While the poem does not negate the importance
of sex in love, it would be a mistake to think that the philosophical
concepts are meant only to impress the woman. Through them
Donne is exploring and seeking to define the nature of an extraordi-
nary spiritual union.

The Ecstasy

Where, like a pillow on a bed,
   A pregnant bank swell'd up, to rest
The violet's reclining head,
   Sat we two, one another's best.

Our hands were firmly cemented   5
   With a fast balm, which thence did spring;
Our eye-beams twisted, and did thread
   Our eyes, upon one double string:

So to intergraft our hands, as yet
   Was all the means to make us one,   10
And pictures on our eyes to get
   Was all our propagation.

As,'twixt two equal armies, Fate
    Suspends uncertain victory,
Our souls (which to advance their state   15
    Were gone out) hung 'twixt her, and me.

And whilst our souls negotiate there,
    We like sepulchral statues lay;
All day, the same our postures were,
    And we said nothing, all the day.   20

If any, so by love refin'd
    That he soul's language understood,
And by good love were grown all mind,
    Within convenient distance stood,

He (though he knew not which soul spake,   25
    Because both meant, both spake the same)
Might thence a new concoction take,
    And part far purer than he came.

'This Ecstasy doth unperplex,'
    We said, 'and tell us what we love;   30
We see by this it was not sex;
    We see we saw not what did move:

'But as all several souls contain
    Mixture of things, they know not what,
Love these mix'd souls doth mix again,   35
    And makes both one, each this and that.

'A single violet transplant,—
    The strength, the colour, and the size,
All which before was poor, and scant,
    Redoubles still, and multiplies.   40

'When love, with one another so
    Interinanimates two souls,
That abler soul, which thence doth flow,
    Defects of loneliness controls.

'We then, who are this new soul, know   45
    Of what we are compos'd, and made,
For the atomies of which we grow,
    Are souls, whom no change can invade.

'But oh alas, so long, so far
    Our bodies why do we forbear?   50
They are ours, though they are not we, we are
    The intelligences, they the sphere.

'We owe them thanks, because they thus
    Did us, to us, at first convey,
Yielded their forces, sense, to us,   55
    Nor are dross to us, but allay.

'On man heaven's influence works not so,
    But that it first imprints the air;
So soul into the soul may flow,
    Though it to body first repair.   60

'As our blood labours to beget
    Spirits, as like souls as it can,
Because such fingers need to knit
  . That subtle knot, which makes us man:

'So must pure lovers' souls descend   65
    To affections, and to faculties,
Which sense may reach and apprehend,
    Else a great Prince in prison lies.

'To our bodies turn we then, that so
    Weak men on love reveal'd may look;   70
Love's mysteries in souls do grow,
    But yet the body is his book;

'And if some lover, such as we,
    Have heard this dialogue of one,
Let him still mark us, he shall see   75
    Small change, when we are to bodies gone.'

NOTES

Title.   The O.E.D gives several meanings for *ecstasy*, all them relevant
here:
(1) experience of an exalted state of feeling, or of rapture or intense
delight, (2) state of trance, and (3) a technical term used by mystical
writers to refer to a state of rapture in which the body becomes
incapable of sensation while the soul is engaged in a contempla-
tion of divine things. The fact that all manuscripts agree on the title
suggests that Donne himself may have given the poem its title.

2   *pregnant.* Rounded. The word, while used here to describe the
bank where the lovers are sitting, also serves to introduce right at
the outset the theme of sex and propagation which will be devel-
oped later.

6   *fast.* Fast-sticking.
balm. Lit. a sweet-smelling resin which exudes from trees. Here the
balm that cements the lovers' hands is the sweat of their palms. Cf.
Othello III. 4. 33-40, where a 'moist hand' argues 'fruitfulness and
a liberal heart'.

7-8   Since the lovers were looking intently into each other's eyes it
seemed that the light or rays from their eyes ('eyebeams') served as
a string which threaded the eyes together like beads. The string was
'double' presumably because one strand threaded the right eye of
one lover with the other lover's left eye, and the other threaded the
left eye of one lover with the other's right. The Renaissance was
uncertain whether sight resulted from beams from the eyes striking
objects or the other way round.

9   *so.* Thus, in this way.
intergraft. Join together. The image is from grafting plants or trees
upon one another.

11-12 Our only way thus far to have children ('propagation') was to cause
our eyes to reflect each other's image. Gardner points out that 'the
small image of oneself reflected in the pupils of another person was
called a "baby", from a pun on *pupilla*'.

13-16 In Homer's *Iliad*. xxii. 209 ff. Zeus suspends the scales holding the
fates of Hector and Achilles above the two warriors. In a similar way,
Donne says, our souls, having left our bodies, are hanging over us
to argue their case ('advance their state' in 1. 16 and 'negotiate' in
1. 17).

18   *sepulchral statues.* Statues erected on the sepulchres of those who
are buried there.

21, 27 *refin'd, concoction.* The process of refining metals involves their
separation from dross by heat; 'concoction' refers to a similar
process. The idea behind these lines is that only a man who had

been so refined that he could understand the soul's language would be able to overhear the conversation between our two souls. and the experience would refine him further.

23   *were grown*. Had turned into.

29   *unperplex*. End our confusion, explain.

31   *sex*. The O.E.D. records Donne as the first user of the word in this our modern sense.

32   We understand ('see') now that we did not previously understand what motivated our love ('did move').

36   *this and that*. Love so unifies the two souls, so makes them one, that it cannot be said that either soul is this or that soul. Alternatively, love so mixes together souls which already possess a mixture of various elements (such as the intellectual, sensuous, etc.) that each new soul now comes to possess an identical mixture of elements.

37   *transplant*. If you transplant.

37-40 Another horticultural image, related both to 'intergraft' in 1. 9 and 'interinanimates' in 1. 42 below. The image is beautiful but its application is unclear. Transplanting requires a movement from one place to another, the union of souls presumably a confluence of two souls into one.

41-2 Love gives new life to ('interinanimates') the two souls.

43   *abler soul*. The two souls join to form a new, more able soul.

44   Love is seen here as a way of overcoming the loneliness that each soul feels. The idea of the individual soul yearning for union with another is Neoplatonic.

47   *atomies*. Atoms.

50   *forbear*. Aviod, neglect.

52   According to the Ptolemaic theory of the universe as adapted to Christianity, each of the nine Spheres was ruled by a different order of angels. There are, obviously, two bodies in the poem, those of the lovers; describing them in this line with the singular *sphere* foreshadows the suggestion Donne will shortly make for physical union.

56   *dross, allay*.'Dross' is the waste produced in a refining process; 'allay' is alloy. By calling bodies alloy rather than dross Donne is saying that bodies are not worthless but possess some virtues ('forces, sense' in 1. 55) which the souls can profitably use.

57   *heaven's*. Of heavenly bodies.
      so. Directly.

57-8 It was believed that the superior intelligences that controlled heavenly bodies exercised their influence upon men's souls only mediately through the air. Donne is arguing that spiritual love requires the mediating agency of the body.

60   *repair*. Goes to.

61   *labours to beget.* The theme of sexual propagation resurfaces here
        in the words 'labour' and 'beget'.
61-4   'Spirits' were considered to be a thin vapour or refined liquid
        extracted from the blood or forming a part of it. They occupied an
        intermediate position between the body and soul; without them it
        was considered impossible for that knot between the body and soul
        to be tied which alone makes us into human beings. In Donne's
        words, these 'spirits' are the 'fingers' that 'knit/That subtle knot'.
65   Our gross blood tries to produce the more refined spirits (1. 61);
        conversely our refined souls need to descend to our grosser bodies.
66   *affections.* Passions.
        faculties. Power of action.
68   *Prince.* The soul. Paradoxically the soul is imprisoned till its entry
        into the body frees it and gives it capacity for action and passion.
70   'Weak men' are men whose faith is so weak that they need a sign or
        some other external manifestation of the mysteries of religion
        before they will believe. They will not believe in our spiritual and
        immaterial love (which constitutes a religion in itself) unless they
        see this love manifested in and through our bodies. The word
        'reveal'd' means made manifest, but it may also carry a suggestion
        of revealed religion; this would be in keeping with Donne's
        treatment of his love as a religious mystery which the lovers impart
        to the laity through their bodies. In 1. 72 below the bodies become
        a Bible in which others can read about the tenets of love's religion.
73   *some lover.* Such as that mentioned in 11. 21 ff.
74   *of one.* Of our two souls which speak as one.
76   i.e. the spiritual nature of our love will not change even after our
        souls assume their corporeal existence.

THE FUNERAL

The convention that dictated that lovers wear a wreath of their mis-
tress's hair becomes in this poem an occasion for using wit to find a
way that will ensure permanence in a decaying world. Even in the act
of meditating his death and the dissolution of his body Donne plans
stratagems that will help him to get even with his mistress.

The Funeral

Whoever comes to shroud me. do not harm
    Nor question much

That subtle wreath of hair, which crowns my arm;
The mystery, the sign, you must not touch,
    For 'tis my outward Soul,   5
Viceroy to that, which then to heaven being gone,
    Will leave this to control,
And keep these limbs, her provinces, from dissolution.

For if the sinewy thread my brain lets fall
    Through every part,   10
Can tie those parts, and make me one of all;
These hairs which upward grew, and strength and art
    Have from a better brain,
Can better do it; except she meant that I
    By this should know my pain,   15
As prisoners then are manacled, when they're condemn'd to die.

Whate'er she meant by it, bury it with me,
    For since I am
Love's martyr, it might breed idolatry,
If into others' hands these relics came;   20
    As 'twas humility
To afford to it all that a soul can do,
    So, 'tis some bravery,
That since you would save none of me, I bury some of you.

NOTES

3   *subtle*.Finely and delicately fashioned. Cf. 'The Relic', 1. 6.

5-8   As the soul of the poet mounts to heaven at the moment of his death,
it leaves behind the wreath of hair as its regent ('Viceroy' 1.6).
Because the wreath is worn on the arm it becomes the poet's
'outward Soul' (1. 5) as opposed to his inner soul. Just as the inner
soul kept the body alive and held it together, now it is the task of the
wreath to preserve the body from corruption in the grave.

9   *sinewy thread*. Thread-like nerves.

11   *One of all*. Coordinate all the various parts of my body.

12   *upward grew*. As opposed to the downward descent of the nerves
from his brain.

13   *better brain.* His mistress's.
14   *it.*   i.e. hold my body together after my death.
       except. Unless.
16   i.e. unless the wreath was devised as handcuffs to keep me chained
       at the moment of my death, just as condemned prisoners are man-
       acled.
19-20 Relics were the remains of Christian martyrs and saints. After their
       death their relics would be collected and venerated by other believ-
       ers. Donne sees himself as martyred for love and is therefore afraid
       that should the wreath fall into others' hands after his death it will
       become an object of veneration. The Protestant churches con-
       demned the Roman Catholics' use of relics and idols ('idolatry').
21-2 The idea is that the poet's praise of the wreath's power was born out
       of his humility.
21-4 Gardner says that just as the lady's gift of her hair may have been
       prompted by kindness or unkindness, so his act of burying it with
       him may show subservience or defiance.

THE RELIC

This poem further develops some of the ideas found in 'The Fu-
neral', but whereas the other ends with a show of bravado, this ends
on a note of hyperbolic praise for the mistress. The use of religious
imagery in a love poem which we find here is characteristic of
Donne.

The Relic

    When my grave is broke up again
    Some second guest to entertain
    (For graves have learn'd that woman-head,
      To be to more than one a bed),
        And he that digs it spies   5
A bracelet of bright hair about the bone,
        Will he not let us alone,
And think that there a loving couple lies,
Who thought that this device might be some way
To make their souls, at the last busy day,   10
Meet at this grave, and make a little stay?

If this fall in a time, or land,
Where mis-devotion doth command,
Then he that digs us up will bring
Us to the Bishop, and the King,   15
        To make us relics; then
Thou shalt be a Mary Magdalen, and I
        A something else thereby;
All women shall adore us, and some men;
And, since at such time miracles are sought,   20
I would have that age by this paper taught
What miracles we harmless lovers wrought

First, we lov'd well and faithfully,
Yet knew not what we lov'd, nor why;
Difference of sex we never knew,   25
No more than our guardian angels do;
        Coming and going, we
Perchance might kiss, but not between those meals;
        Our hands ne'er touch'd the seals
Which nature, injur'd by late law, sets free: 30
These miracles we did; but now, alas,
All measure, and all language, I should pass,
Should I tell what a miracle she was.

NOTES

1-2   The practice of using existing graves to accommodate new corpses
        began when graveyards became crowded and was commonplace in
        Donne's time.

3   *woman-head*. 'Womanly nature' (Redpath). The word is modelled
        on *maidenhead*.

6   A startling and vivid image. Cf.'The Funeral', 1.3.

10   *last busy day*. Day of the Resurrection, when Christians believe that
        the dead will rise from their graves and appear before Christ to be
        judged.

12   *this*. i.e. my body being dug up.

13   *mis-devotion*. False religion. Donne is here attacking Roman Catholi-
        cism. See 'The Funeral' 11. 19-20 and note.

15-16   While Roman Catholic bishops had the power to recognize relics,
        kings did not. Donne's reference to kings here is therefore puzzling.

17   *Mary Magdalen*. A former prostitute who became a follower of Jesus and ministered to His needs. She was present at the crucifixion and burial, and later saw the risen Christ. She is always portrayed as having long golden hair.

18   Redpath says that the poet is hinting obliquely that his bones will be mistaken to be Christ's. He adds that, according to Martin Luther, Christ and Mary Magdalen were lovers. However, Helen Gardner dismisses this interpretation and says that 'A something else' probably just means an unknown lover.

19   A hit at women's credulity and their interest in romances.

20   *miracles*. The Roman Catholic church maintained that miracles were performed in the presence of relics.

21   *paper*. i.e. poem.

27   *coming and going*. Kissing as a form of greeting at meeting and parting was sanctioned by the Bible.

29-30 We never had sexual intercourse which nature allows freely but which recent ('late') laws have limited.

32   *pass*. Exceed.

NEGATIVE LOVE

The poem attempts to define the perfect nature of the poet's love but realizes that it can only be done negatively. The theme is a Neoplatonic commonplace.

Negative Love

I never stoop'd so low, as they
Which on an eye, cheek, lip, can prey;
    Seldom to them, which soar no higher
    Than virtue or the mind to admire:
For sense, and understanding, may   5
    Know what gives fuel to their fire.
My love, though silly, is more brave,
For may I miss, whene'er I crave,
If I know yet, what I would have.

If that be simply perfectest   10
Which can by no way be express'd

But *negatives*, my love is so.
To All, which all love, I say no.
If any who deciphers best
   What we know not, our selves, can know,   15
Let him teach me that nothing; this
As yet my ease and comfort is:
Though I speed not, I cannot miss.

NOTES

1-2   i.e. purely physical lovers.
3   *seldom*. Note the contrast with 'never' in 1. 1.
3-4   i.e. lovers of a higher sort.
5-6   Through the exercise of sense and understanding one may figure out
        what attracts one to the beloved.
7   *brave*. Daring.
8   *miss*. Fail to attain. The poet's daring lies in his willingness to accept
        failure.
        crave. i.e. crave a woman's love.
9   i.e. if I know the nature of the thing I desire at the time I am desring
        it.
13   'I decline all the positive perfections, which are what everybody
        loves' (Redpath).
14-15   If there is any psychologist who can truly understand that which it is
        well-nigh impossible to know, *viz.* our own natures.
17   *As yet*. Meanwhile.
18   *speed*. Make progress.
        miss. Fail. The sense is that since the poet's love is *nothing* (i.e.
        capable of definition only by negatives), therefore even if he fails to
        attain it he will not have failed.

RELIGIOUS POEMS

In his *Life of Donne* Izaac Walton, Donne's first biographer, offered
a neat two-part division of the poet's career: the young Jack Donne
who was a great visitor of ladies, frequenter of plays, and author of
witty love poems, and the later Dr. John Donne, the respected Dean
of St. Paul's Cathedral, who wrote only religious poetry. Attractive
though this division is, it is not accurate. Donne grew up in a Roman
Catholic family at a time when religion was the most crucial aspect of

personal as well as social and political life and to be a Roman Catholic often invited persecution. Though in later life he became an Anglican, the religious influences he imbibed as a child never left him. One of his earliest poems, 'Satire III' 'is concerned with religion. His love poetry uses many religious ideas and metaphors. Therefore when he began to write religious poetry in his middle age while living in Mitcham and oppressed by poverty, family cares and ill health, he was not making a startling new beginning so much as allowing a life-long, if latent, concern to come to the fore.

His earliest religious poetry consisted of seven closely linked sonnets collectively called *La Corona* and probably sent to Mrs. Magdalen Herbert. Helen Gardner dates them around 1607. Twelve of his 'Holy Sonnets' were probably composed in the early part of 1609 and four more shortly thereafter. 'Good Friday, 1613. Riding Westward' dates itself. The sonnet beginning 'Since she whom I loved' was written some time after the death of his wife which occurred in 1617, and that beginning 'Show me dear Christ' around 1620. Walton says that 'A Hymn to God the Father' was written during his illness in 1623, and Donne had it set to music. This chronology suggests that, though it is true that Donne's last poems were religious not secular, it is by no means the case that they were written, as Walton suggests, after his ordination in 1615; indeed, many of the 'Holy Sonnets' were written at the same time as he was writing his best love poetry. (For the dating of his love poetry see headnote to *Songs and Sonnets* above).

The genre of religious poetry imposes some quite severe restrictions upon the practitioner. Samuel Johnson pointed out one when he said that such a poet is 'already in a higher state than poetry can confer.' T.S. Eliot pointed out another: a religious poet, he said, deals with a limited subject matter and has perforce to leave out much that others consider interesting. And Gardner adds a third: the religious poet has to work within the traditions and beliefs of his religion. He cannot afford to say that which has never been said before but only that which others of his faith have said or believed. For these reasons Gardner ranks Donne's achievement as a religious poet below that of his love poetry

She is right is maintaining that there is less of a sense of the variety of life's experiences in his religious than in his love poetry, and also that while Donne is as willing to argue with God as with his mistress, his confidence in his dialectical skills is constantly undercut by the acknowledgement in the religious poems: 'But who am I, that dare dispute with thee?' But to grant this is not to deny the greatness of his achievement as a religious poet. There is the same drama in his religious poems as in the love poems, the same total mastery of the form, so that the sonnet or hymn or whatever he chooses to write becomes the most natural medium for his ideas, and, as 'Good Friday, 1613' demonstrates, the same use of conceits and wit to explore, define and finally understand a situation. There is the same urgent importunity that comes out of the same strongly felt sense of the self. Many of his religious poems grow out of a sense of terror or despair at the thought that he is a sinner, and therefore his entreaties to Christ for salvation take on a powerful immediacy. Though there is in him none of that rapture which a soul in communion with God feels, nor the quiet, satisfying sense of a personal relationship with God that Herbert expresses, there is another equally moving quality: anguish at the sense of his own unworthiness and therefore a fear that accompanies the working out of his salvation face to face with his Maker, with no intercessors or intermediaries present. If some poems like 'A Hymn to God the Father' end on a note of acceptance or even of calm, that calm comes only as the conclusion to a storm of doubt, confusion or torment that the poems themselves embody. Nor does the humility or discursiveness of 'Good Friday 1613' conceal its passion and genuine penitential quality.

Louis L. Martz, in *The Poetry of Meditation*, has demonstrated the widespread use in the sixteenth century of spiritual exercises and meditation by Christians belonging both to the Roman Catholic and Reformed churches, and Helen Gardner uses the techniques of meditation laid down by Ignatius Loyola as a means of ordering as well as understanding Donne's 'Holy Sonnets'. She says that twelve out of nineteen are meditations on the Last Things--death, judgement, heaven and hell. Of these twelve the first six follow the form strictly and so constitute a coherent whole. The first, 'As due by many titles...', is a preparatory prayer, the second, 'O my black soul...vividly conjures up his deathbed, the third, 'This is my, play's last scene...'describes the moment of his death, the fourth, 'At the round earth's imagined corners...' summons a vision of Judgement Day, the fifth, 'If poisonous minerals...'meditates on damnation, and the sixth, 'Death be not proud...' on the death of Death which will come about with the salvation of the just. The next six are held together more loosely, but they too are meditations on love: the first three ('Spit in my face...', 'Why are we...' and 'what if the present were...') on God's love for man, and the last three ('Batter my heart...', Wilt

thou love God...' and Father, part of his...') on the love God deserves
from men. Gardner notes a histrionic and high-pitched tone in these
twelve sonnets, the result, she thinks, of the need in meditation to
stimulate emotion through the use of imagination.

Four other sonnets ('Thou hast made me...', 'I am a little world...',
'O might these sighs...' and 'If faithful souls...') Gardner calls peni-
tential: they deal, in different ways, with the theme of sin. Starting
with a prayer in the manner recommended by Ignatius, Donne
meditates on the way both his body and his soul have been afflicted
by sin. He then remembers the sin of having shed excessive tears in
front of his mistress. This leads to the final sonnet in which he leaves
it to God to decide on the value of his penitential tears.

The last three of the 'Holy Sonnets'. ('Since she whom I loved...',
'Show me dear Christ...' and 'Oh, to vex me...') are occasional poems
written at a much later date than the others and are found only in the
Westmoreland manuscript from which they were first printed in
1899.

In this present edition I give selections from all three groups of
Donne's 'Holy Sonnets). I also give two other religious poems by
him, 'Good Friday, 1613. Riding Westward' and 'A Hymn to God the
Father.' More extended discussions of these latter will be found in
headnotes to them.

The order in which these poems appear here is that of Gardner's
text except that in the interest of chronology I put 'Good Friday,
1613' between the first two groups of the 'Holy Sonnets' and the last.
The text is the modernized version of A.J. Smith.

DEATH BE NOT PROUD

In this sonnet Donne affirms the Christian belief that the death of
Christ on the cross has freed mankind from the fear of death. The
idea that after death our souls will sleep till they awake on the Day
of Judgement helps to date the poem and the other 'Holy Sonnets'
to which it is linked. Gardner says that it was not till Donne started
writing the prose work *Pseudo-Martyr* in August 1609 that he
thought clearly about the problem of what happens to the soul at
death, and the conclusion he came to was that the souls of the
righteous are admitted to God's presence at the moment of death
rather than having to wait till the Day of Judgement. The idea
contained in this poem, that death is followed by a short sleep,
means that it must have been written before August 1609.

Death be not proud

Death be not proud, though some have called thee
Mighty and dreadful, for, thou art not so,
For, those, whom thou think'st, thou dost overthrow,
Die not, poor death, nor yet canst thou kill me;
From rest and sleep, which but thy pictures be,
Much pleasure, then from thee, much more must flow,
And soonest our best men with thee do go,
Rest of their bones, and soul's delivery;.
Thou art slave to fate, chance, kings, and desperate men,
10   And dost with poison, war, and sickness dwell,
And poppy, or charms can make us sleep as well,
And better than thy stroke; why swell'st thou then?
One short sleep past, we wake eternally,
And death shall be no more, Death thou shalt die.

NOTES

5-6   Rest and sleep are 'pictures' or images of death. If we derive pleasure
       from rest, we must derive even greater pleasure from death which is
       the real thing.
7   Either that the best men die young, or that the best men are most
       willing to part with their lives. Compare the second interpretation
       with 'A Valediction: Forbidding Mourning' 11. 1-4.
9   *slave to*. i.e. you are used or exploited by.
11   *poppy, or charms*. Poppy or opium is a soporific. Charms may refer
       to other sleep-inducing drugs.
12   *swell'st*. i.e. why do you puff up with pride?
13   See headnote to the poem. The eternal awakening refers to the Day
       of Judgement.
14   Cf. 1 Corinthians 15: 26, 54: 'The last enemy that shall be destroyed
       is death....Death is swallowed up in victory.'

BATTER MY HEART, THREE-PERSONED GOD

This is a powerful and dramatic sonnet whose vigour arises from its
direct colloquialisms, force of expression, and the startling use of
sexual imagery. The poet demands extreme measures from God as
being the only way his soul can be won over.

Batter my heart, three-personed God

> Batter my heart, three-personed God; for, you
> As yet but knock, breathe, shine, and seek to mend;
> That I may rise, and stand, o'erthrow me, and bend
> Your force, to break, blow, burn, and make me new.
> I, like an usurped town, to another due,
> Labour to admit you, but oh, to no end,
> Reason your viceroy in me, me should defend,
> But is captived, and proves weak or untrue,
> Yet dearly I love you, and would be loved fain,
> 10   But am betrothed unto your enemy,
> Divorce me, untie, or break that knot again,
> Take me to you, imprison me, for I
> Except you enthral me, never shall be free,
> Nor ever chaste, except you ravish me.

NOTES

1   *heart*. The poet here images his heart as a door that needs to be forcefully battered down whereas God is at present only knocking at it (1. 2).
     three-personed God. The Christian God is conceived of as being triune or three in one. The Trinity consists of the Father, Son and Holy Ghost.

7   *Reason your viceroy in me*. Compare the role of reason in the individual to that of nature in the world in 'Good Friday 1613', 1. 19. The notion that Reason is God's representative in man is traditional.

8   The meaning of the the line is that Reason should preserve Donne's soul for God, but it has either been imprisoned by the usurping enemy Satan in the some way that a town's governor may be imprisoned by an invader, or that it has proved too weak in its post as God's viceroy, or else that, like a traitor, it has allied itself to the enemy.

9   *fain*. Gladly.

10   The image changes now from Donne's reason as having been captured by an invader to that of Donne as a girl having been forcibly betrothed to God's rival.

GOOD FRIDAY, 1613. RIDING WESTWARD

The poem was written on Good Friday, 2 April 1613, when the poet was on his way to Sir Edward Herbert in Wales. The poem opens in typical 'Metaphysical' fashion, an extended and learned conceit of the movement of the spheres being used to understand the contradiction that Donne is riding west on a day when he should be contemplating Christ in the east. The attempt to understand is carried on through puns and paradoxes. These devices are abruptly abandoned as understanding dawns. Christ is no longer a mere object of contemplation but enters the poem as a real person and the poet now addresses him in the second person. The beauty and drama of the poem lie in this turn which enables the poet to understand the meaning both of his actions and of Christ's, who has permitted his actions. The ending is one of penitence and humility.

Good Friday, 1613. Riding Westward

Let man's soul be a sphere, and then, in this,
The intelligence that moves, devotion is,
And as the other spheres, by being grown
Subject to foreign motions, lose their own,
And being by others hurried every day,
Scarce in a year their natural form obey;
Pleasure or business, so, our souls admit
For their first mover, and are whirled by it.
Hence is't, that I am carried towards the west
10   This day, when my soul's form bends toward the east,
There I should see a sun, by rising set,
And by that setting endless day beget;
But that Christ on this Cross, did rise and fall,
Sin had eternally benighted all.
Yet dare I almost be glad, I do not see
That spectacle of too much weight for me.
Who sees God's face, that is self life, must die;
What a death were it then to see God die?
It made his own lieutenant Nature shrink,
20   It made his footstool crack, and the sun wink.
Could I behold those hands which span the poles,

And turn all spheres at once, pierced with those holes?
Could I behold that endless height which is
Zenith to us, and to'our antipodes,
Humbled below us? or that blood which is
The seat of all our souls, if not of his,
Made dirt of dust, or that flesh which was worn,
By God, for his apparel, ragged, and torn?
If on these things I durst not look, durst I
30 Upon his miserable mother cast mine eye,
Who was God's partner here, and furnished thus
Half of that sacrifice, which ransomed us?
Though these things, as I ride, be from mine eye,
They are present yet unto my memory,
For that looks towards them; and thou look'st towards me,
O Saviour, as thou hang'st upon the tree;
I turn my back to thee, but to receive
Corrections, till thy mercies bid thee leave.
O think me worth thine anger, punish me,
40 Burn off my rusts, and my deformity,
Restore thine image, so much, by thy grace,
That thou mayst know me, and I'll turn my face.

NOTES

1-2   For the image of spheres and intelligences see 'The Ecstasy' 1. 52. In
      'Good Friday, 1613' devotion becomes the 'intelligence' that causes
      our bodies ('spheres') to move.
3-6   In the Ptolemaic theory of the universe each sphere was supposed to
      move from west to east, but the Primum Mobile or First Mover caused
      them to move in the opposite direction, from east to west. In this
      aberrant movement of the spheres Donne sees a parallel to his own
      journey which is taking him westward when his natural inclination
      would be to travel east. He ascribes this aberration to the influence
      of 'foreign motions' of 'pleasure or business' (1. 8), thinking that
      these emotions are the 'first mover' of the soul. But at the end of the
      poem he realizes that the aberration is no aberration at all but part
      of God's design, and God wants him to travel westward for a purpose.
      The Primum Mobile or First Mover was often used as a term for the
      Christian God.
8   *For.* As.

11   *sun*.The pun on *sun-son* was very common in Donne's time. *Son* is, of course, Jesus Christ, the Son of God.

11   There are a number of witty paradoxes here. Christ's crucifixion is like the setting of the sun, but while the sun sets in the west, Christ was crucified at Calvary which is to the east (of England). The *rising* of the Son on the cross caused the sun to *set*. The reference is to the eclipse that occurred at the time of the crucifixion (Matthew 27:45). Or, by being raised ('rising') on the cross, Christ died; thus his sun set.

12   *endless day beget*. The hope of salvation became possible with Christ's death on the cross for mankind's sins.

13   *But that*. Had it not happened that.

17   *that is self life*. i.e. that is life itself.

17   In Exodus 23:20 God told Moses: 'Thou canst not see my face: for there shall no man see me, and live.'

19   *lieutenant Nature*. Nature is seen as God's deputy or viceregent on earth.

20   The line refers to the earthquake and eclipse that occurred at the crucifixion. See note to l. 11, and also Matthew 27:51. The earth is called God's footstool in Isaiah 66:1.

22   *turn*.Some editors like Gardner prefer *tune*. This reading would give the sense that Christ is the composer of the music that the spheres were supposed to produce as they moved. *Turn* suggests Christ in the role of Prime Mover. Smith mentions a fourteenth-century fresco in Pisa which shows Christ controlling the spheres.

24   *antipodes*. The other side of the globe. The sense is that Christ represents the highest point imaginable ('Zenith') to all people irrespective of where they live.

26   Donne does not literally mean that our souls are contained in our blood. However, he does want to convey the sense that Christ's blood is the seat of our souls since they find new life through it.

27   *dirt of dust*. Smith explains: '(a) mingled with dust, and so made muddy dirt; (b) made still less than the dust of its human incarnation [i.e. the dust of the human body], lower than the low.'

29   *durst*. Dare.

30   *miserable*. Made miserable.

31-2   The 'sacrifice' which 'ransomed us' (l. 32) is Christ's laying down of His life for the sake of mankind. In ascribing half of mankind's salvation to Christ's mother, Mary, Donne is expressing a Mariolatry that Anglicans would not accept.

33   *be from*. i.e. be away from.

35   *and thou*. From here on Christ is addressed in the second person.

36   *the tree*. The cross.

41   *thine image*. According to Genesis 1:27, God made man in His own image. Donne says that he has so disfigured this image in him that

God would not be able to recognize him. Therefore Donne has
turned his face away from God. He wants God to lash the back that
confronts Him. When the poet's sins have been beaten away he will
regain his likeness to God and then he will turn his face.

SINCE SHE WHOM I LOVED

From the note of resignation in the poem Gardner concludes that it
was written some time after the death of Donne's wife on 15 August
1617. She offers May 1619 as a conjectural date of composition. In
this Sonnet Donne expresses his love for his wife and emphasizes
how all his thoughts are now turned heavenwards.

Since she whom I loved

Since she whom I loved hath paid her last debt
To nature, and to hers, and my good is dead,
And her soul early into heaven ravished,
Wholly in heavenly things my mind is set.
Here the admiring her my mind did whet
To seek thee God; so streams do show the head,
But though I have found thee, and thou my thirst hast fed,
A holy thirsty dropsy melts me yet.
But why should I beg more love, when as thou
10 Dost woo my soul for hers; offering all thine:
And dost not only fear lest I allow
My love to saints and angels, things divine,
But in thy tender jealousy dost doubt
Lest the world, flesh, yea Devil put thee out.

NOTES

1-2 To pay one's last debt to nature is to die.
2   *and to hers...dead.* The line is ambiguous: (1) she has paid her debt
     to nature, and to her human or mortal nature; she, who was my good,
     is dead. (2) she has paid her debt to nature and is dead, for her good
     and for mine, since by dying she has gone to heaven and set my
     thoughts in that direction also. Neither sense is satisfactory.

5   *Here.* While she was alive.

5-6   My admiration for her sharpened ('did whet') my quest for God.

6   *streams...bead.* She was the stream whose source is God. By follow-
       ing a stream up its course we can reach the source.

8   Dropsy causes an unquenchable thirst. For the use of this image in a
       love poem see 'On his mistress' 1. 42.

9-10   There is no need for me to ask for more of your love since you already
       love me. Indeed, you are wooing my soul in order to unite it with my
       wife's in heaven, just as a father may woo an eligible young man to
       marry his daughter here on earth. And just as the father may offer the
       young man a dowry, so also you have offered me a dowry of all that
       you possess: your only Son ('all thine' in 1. 10). Cf. John 3:16: 'For
       God so loved the world that he gave his only begotten Son, that
       whoever believes in him shall not perish but have eternal life.'

11-14 The idea is that man need not doubt God's love, though God may,
       with good reason, doubt man's love for Him. The lines may be
       paraphrased: You are afraid not only that I might give my love to
       divine beings like saints and angels instead of to you, but also that I
       might allow the world, the flesh and the devil to usurp the affection
       that should rightly belong only to you. Therefore you have taken
       away my wife, the best of saints and angels. You have also sent me
       worldly disappointments as a way of guarding me against the tempta-
       tions of this life.

SHOW ME DEAR CHRIST

Critics like Grierson have read this sonnet, found only in the Westmore-
land manuscript and not printed till 1899, as of a piece with 'Satire
III'. In that poem, written at the outset of his career, Donne wonders
where the true Church is to be found. Grierson saw this sonnet as
continuing that sceptical questioning and therefore argued that its
non-inclusion in the other manuscripts resulted from the embarrass-
ing fact that, even after being ordained an Anglican priest, Donne
continued to doubt the truth of his Church.

However, Helen Gardner maintains that the theme of the sonnet
is: What is the mark of the true Church? Having mocked the other
answers Donne offers his own, which is 'unity and godly love'.
Gardner says that Donne is not contrasting the three Churches of
Rome, Geneva (or Germany) and Canterbury in this poem but is
instead wondering if either of the two figures he describes—the
proud harlot and the ravished virgin—can be said to be the true

Bride of Christ. In opposition to them he contrasts the third, as yet hidden figure of the Church Universal, whom he describes as the bride who will be hospitable to all comers. Gardner's conclusion is that though Donne sees the limitations of both Roman Catholicism and Puritanism, he does not reject them as totally false. Rather, he is critical of those who would confine the truth to either of them. And he hopes for the day when these divisions will be overcome and the Church United revealed. Gardner sees this view as being perfectly compatible with the Anglican faith which, while it prided itself on harking back to the traditions of the primitive church and the apostolic succession, did not deny that the other churches were also Christian. Seen thus, the poem becomes an Anglican lament at the rifts which have historically characterized Christianity rather than an anguished utterance of a man who continues to have doubts about the church he has chosen to serve.

Gardner dates the poem at around 1620 or later. See explanatory notes below for a fuller discussion.

Show me dear Christ

> Show me dear Christ, thy spouse, so bright and clear.
> What, is it she, which on the other shore
> Goes richly painted? or which robbed and tore
> Laments and mourns in Germany and here?
> Sleeps she a thousand, then peeps up one year?
> Is she self truth and errs? now new, now outwore?
> Doth she, and did she, and shall she evermore
> On one, on seven, or on no hill appear?
> Dwells she with us, or like adventuring knights
> 10 First travail we to seek and then make love?
> Betray kind husband thy spouse to our sights,
> And let mine amorous soul court thy mild dove,
> Who is most true, and pleasing to thee, then
> When she is embraced and open to most men.

NOTES

1   *thy spouse.* The Church is the Bride of Christ. Cf. Revelation 19:7: 'The marriage of the Lamb is come, and his wife hath made herself ready.'

2   *on the other shore.* In Rome.

3   *richly painted.* The Roman Catholic church was often identified with
      the Whore of Babylon. The 'richly painted' woman is very unlike the
      true Bride described in 1. 1.

3-4   *robbed and tore...here.* According to Gardner these lines do not
      apply to Calvin's church, and the raped and robbed virgin described
      here is not the 'plain, simple, sullen...contemptuous yet unhand-
      some' woman who stands for Puritanism in 'Satire III'. Instead, they
      refer to the loss of Protestant hopes in Germany with the defeat of the
      Elector of Hanover in October 1620. The hopes of the Anglicans were
      tied up with those of the German Protestants, and so when the
      Elector lost, the mourning was heard not only among German Prot-
      estants but also in England ('here', 1. 4.). Donne compares the loss
      of hope in Germany to the desolation of Jerusalem. In *Lamentations*
      the captive Jerusalem is mourned as though it were a raped and
      robbed daughter, and this imagery may explain why Donne uses the
      image of a ravaged woman in talking of Protestant Germany's defeat
      in 1. 4.

      Gardner's interpretation would place the composition of the
      sonnet after 24 November 1620, when news of the Elector's defeat
      reached England.

5   The Calvinists claimed that the truths of the primitive Church
      remained forgotten till the time of the Reformation. In this line
      Donne is making fun of this assertion by asking whether the true
      Church slept for a thousand years.

6   *Is she...errs?* Donne mocks the Roman Catholic claim to infallibility
      by asking why, if that Church is the true one, it has been guilty of so
      many errors.

8   One hill refers to Mount Moriah where Solomon built his temple.
      The seven hills are those of Rome, and 'no hill' is the Calvinist Church
      in Geneva.

9-10 Donne wonders whether the true Church can be found at home or
      only abroad. 'Adventuring Knights' refers to the medieval knights of
      chivalric romance who travelled in quest of adventure and love.
      There are so few references to the world of medieval chivalry in
      Donne that the present one has to be suspected of sarcasm. The
      implication would be that it is not necessary to quest abroad for the
      true Church.

10   *travail.* (1) Labour, (2) travel.

11   *Betray.* Reveal. There is also the suggestion here of Christ acting as
      a pandar or pimp. Donne says that the more open the church is to the
      embraces of all men, the purer she will be, meaning that only the true
      Church will unite all Christians. The sexual image is startling and
      strong but it has Biblical sanction. See 1. 12 and note below.

12   *amorous soul...mild dove.* Cf. Song of Solomon 5:2: 'Open to me, my
      sister, my love, my dove, my undefiled.' The eroticism of the *Song of
      Solomon* is explained as the address of Christ to the Church.

A HYMN TO GOD THE FATHER

For the date of the poem, see note 'Religious Poetry' above. Written
in the expectation that he was going to die, Donne is full of a sense
of urgency as he asks God to forgive his sins and importunes Him for
salvation. The urgency is only enhanced by the witty pun that runs
through the poem on Donne's name.

A Hymn to God the Father

I

Wilt thou forgive that sin where I begun,
  Which was my sin, though it were done before?
Wilt thou forgive that sin, through which I run,
  And do run still: though still I do deplore?
    When thou hast done, thou hast not done,
      For, I have more.

II

Wilt thou forgive that sin which I have won
  Others to sin? and, made my sin their door?
Wilt thou forgive that sin which I did shun
10   A year, or two: but wallowed in, a score?
    When thou hast done, thou hast not done,
      For I have more.

III

I have a sin of fear, that when I have spun
  My last thread, I shall perish on the shore;
But swear by thy self, that at my death thy son
  Shall shine as he shines now, and heretofore;
    And, having done that, thou hast done,
      I fear no more.

NOTES

1-2   *Where I...before.* The original sin, the consequence of Adam's fall,
      which afflicts us all though we did not commit it.
3   *that sin.* i.e. my daily round of sins.
5   *done.* Pun on the poet's name.
7,8,9 *sin, sin, sin.* Refers most probably to his licentious elegies and *Songs
      and Sonnets.* Donne here laments that his secular poems may have
      led his readers to sin (1. 8).
14   *perish on the shore.* Left behind on the earth instead of being
      transported to heaven.
15   *Swear by thy self.* In Genesis 22:6, the angel reports to Abraham: 'By
      myself have I sworn, saith the Lord.'
      son. Pun on *son-sun.* See 'Good Friday 1613' 1. 11 and note.

GEORGE HERBERT

George Herbert (1593-1633) belonged to an old and aristocratic family. His father died when he was three years old, and he was brought up by his mother Magdalene, a woman of culture, high intelligence, uprightness, and a friend of poets like Donne who, besides 'The Autumnal', also consecrated a sermon to her. Herbert was educated at Westminster School and at Trinity College, Cambridge. Shortly after he entered university he decided that he would write poetry only on religious subjects, as the two sonnets sent to his mother in 1610 state. His choice of a career proved more problematic. Upon graduation he was appointed to a succession of university posts. In 1616 he was elected to a major fellowship at Trinity and in 1620 became University Orator. This latter position had proved to be a stepping stone to important secular offices for a number of previous incumbents. Herbert's earliest biographer Izaac Walton maintained that Herbert entertained hopes of a career in a similar direction, but they were dashed in 1625 with the death of his patrons including James I, whereupon he turned to a career in the Church. This view is controverted by his most recent biographer Amy M. Charles, who thinks that Herbert had always intended to take holy orders. But if this was so it is difficult to explain why he was not ordained by or before 1623 as the terms of his major fellowship at Trinity required, but instead allowed himself to be nominated to Parliament in that year and served as M.P. till the following year. He was ordained deacon sometime between leaving his seat in Parliament and 1626. In 1629 he married Jane Danvers, and the following year was ordained a priest and appointed to the parish of Bemerton, where he undertook the repairs of the church at his own expense, wrote his prose *A Priest to the Temple, or, The Country Parson* as also a majority of his English poems, discharged his parish duties conscientiously and earned a reputation for his saintly living. He also became intimate with a group of Anglican theologians led by Nicholas Ferrar who had set up a retreat at the nearby Little Gidding. Never in the best of health, he died at the age of 40.

Apart from a few Latin verses Herbert published no poetry in his lifetime. From his deathbed he sent his manuscript of poems to Nicholas Ferrar who undertook their publication at the end of 1633. The printer Thomas Buck was extraordinarily capable and painstaking, with the result that this first edition, entitled *The Temple: Sacred Poems and Private Ejaculations* offers a close approximation to what Herbert actually wrote. It was used as the basis for the current standard edition of Herbert's works edited by F.E. Hutchinson who also included six poems from the Williams Manuscript not included in the first edition of *The Temple*. The text given in the present edition is Hutchinson's.

Apart from a few pieces like the two sonnets Herbert sent his mother on New Years' Day, 1610, and some others, the poems are impossible to date though we know that some must have been written as early as his undergraduate days. An early twentieth-century editor, George Herbert Palmer, tried to arrange them chronologically, dividing them into three sections entitled, respectively, the 'Cambridge Poems', 'The Crisis', and 'Bemerton Poems'. The division is flawed for two reasons. First, it presupposes that Walton was right in claiming that the poet experienced a crisis after graduation when he was in two minds about following a secular or a religious calling—a point of view which later biographers have questioned. Second, it assumes that once Herbert settled in Bemerton he overcame his spiritual crisis, when the fact seems to be that he was always a man characterized by mood changes, as a priest no less than at any other time. It is impossible to detect a chronology in the moods the poems express.

However, in so far as Palmer's arrangement reveals a desire to find an organizational principle which may confer a sense of unity upon the 164 poems that constitute *The Temple*, his efforts have been seconded by other scholars. Helen White thinks that Herbert was engaged in rearranging the poems into some sort of a unified order when he died and was not able to complete the task. Louis Martz suggests that the rearrangement was substantially completed and that the poems fall into a threefold division of Christian life, the active, the contemplative, and the newly active. An order can certainly be discerned in various clusters of poems, if not the whole, of *The Temple*, and making the reader perceive this order is part of the meaning that these poems convey. Thus the tripartite ordering of the poems recalls ecclesiastical architecture: 'The Church-Porch' preaches various do's and dont's of the Christian life, after which the reader is allowed to enter 'The Church' itself, but not without first passing through a 'Superliminare' or threshold over which is inscribed a verse warning the profane not to enter. The first poem in 'The Church' is 'The Altar' because the altar is not only the most important part of the church but also what the person entering the church first sees. The altar puts the poet in mind of Christ's sacrifice on the Cross, and so 'The Altar' is followed by 'The Sacrifice', a monologue spoken by Christ on the cross in which He meditates upon His sacrifice and offers a series of mocking paradoxes underlining the irony of the fact that He is dying for the sins of man. Christ's sacrifice leads the poet to offer Him thanks in the next poem which is entitled, appropriately enough, 'The Thanksgiving'. Another group of poems which is united by imagery drawn from articles of daily and common use in the church as also thematically (a meditation on man's sin, hard-heartedness and death) consists of 'The Church-Floor', 'Church-Lock and Key', 'Church Monuments', and 'The Windows'. Christian observances and rituals form another group: to this may be assigned poems such as 'Good Friday', 'Sepulchre', 'Easter', and 'Easter-wings'. Sometimes poem answers poem. Thus 'Longing' expresses the poet's despair that God does not hear his prayers. The next poem, 'The Bag', shows how ill-founded the poet's despair is. For the wounds of Christ are the bag into which all men may put their petitions to God with the certainty that they will be presented to Him and be accepted. When a dialectic is thus set up between two poems Herbert does more than just link them thematically. The interval between the end of one poem and the beginning of the next becomes the interval in which God accepts the poet's prayer and grants him the grace that was requested. Through this device Herbert suggests that grace is a living thing, available to those who seek it; and by showing its operation in the second poem he makes God an equal participant in the drama that is being depicted. A reciprocal relation-ship exists between God and man: man prays and God grants; indeed, God has granted man's wishes even before the prayer has been made, so that prayer sometimes becomes man's means not of asking God for something but of learning to recognize His gifts.

I have thought it necessary to comment at some length on the unifying features of the poems in *The Temple* because, in any selection from that work such as the present, a sense of this unity can be easily lost. The selection opens with Herbert's two 1610 sonnets to his mother; thereafter the poems follow the order in which Hutchinson prints them.

SONNETS FROM WALTON'S *LIVES*

First printed in Walton's biography of Herbert (1670), they were written when the poet was just over sixteen years old. In a letter to his mother with which they were enclosed Herbert wrote: 'For my own part, my meaning...is in these Sonnets, to declare my resolution to be, that my poor Abilities in *Poetry*, shall be all, and ever consecrated to God's glory'. The rejection of love in favour of something higher was a common pose for young Elizabethan gentlemen (cf. *Love's Labour's Lost*), but in Herbert's case it proved to be genuine. See also 'Jordan-I' below.

Sonnet 1

My God, where is that ancient heat towards thee
    Wherewith whole showls of *Martyrs* once did burn
    Besides their other flames? Doth Poetry
Wear *Venus* Livery? only serve her turn?
5   Why are not *Sonnets* made of thee? and layes
    Upon thine Altar burnt? Cannot thy love
    Heighten a spirit to sound out thy praise
As well as any she? Cannot thy *Dove*
    Out-strip their *Cupid* easily in flight?
10   Or, since thy wayes are deep, and still the same,
    Will not a verse run smooth that bears thy name?
Why doth that fire, which by thy power and might
    Each breast does feel, no braver fuel choose
    Than that, which one day Worms may chance refuse.

NOTES

2   *showls.* Shoals.
    Martyrs were the early Christians who were persecuted for their faith and often burnt at the stake. Herbert implies that two kinds of fire consumed them, that in which they were burnt and that passion (*heat* in 1. 1) which they felt for Christ.
4-9   Herbert satirizes the conventions of courtly love poetry. To 'wear *Venus* livery' is to declare oneself a servant of the goddess of love; building altars to the lady love, addressing sonnets to her and then burning them on these altars as a sacrifice to her were as much

conventions of sixteenth-century love poetry as were invocations to
Cupid, the winged god of love and the son of Venus.
5   *layes.* Songs or poems.
8   *Dove.* Symbol of the Holy Spirit. But the term is also applied in *Song of Songs* to the mistress. Herbert's use of this word enables him to combine the amorous with the religious.
14 *one day...refuse.* Though the lover may think his lady beautiful, the reality underneath the skin is so ugly that when she dies the worms in the grave may refuse to feed on her. Images of worms feeding on corpses are commonplace in Elizabethan and Jacobean poetry.

Sonnet 2

>Sure, Lord, there is enough in thee to dry
>   Oceans of *Ink;* for, as the Deluge did
>   Cover the Earth, so doth thy Majesty:
>Each Cloud distills thy praise, and doth forbid
>5   *Poets* to turn it to another use.
>   *Roses* and *Lillies* speak thee; and to make
>   A pair of Cheeks of them, is thy abuse.
>Why should I *Womens eyes* for for Chrystal take?
>Such poor invention burns in their low mind
>10   Whose fire is wild, and doth not upward go
>   To praise, and on thee, Lord, some *Ink* bestow.
>Open the bones, and you shall nothing find
>   In the best *face* but *filth,* when, Lord, in thee
>   The *beauty* lies in the *discovery.*

NOTES

1   *dry.* Use up.
2   *Deluge.* Noah's Flood.
4-5   i.e., each object in Nature, by praising God, forbids that poets put it to such sacrilegious uses as comparing it to the mistress's beauty.
6   *Roses and Lillies* were common comparisons in Elizabethan love poetry for the mistress's complexion.
      speak. Express.
8   *Chrystal.* Precious glass.
12-13 *Open....filth.* Go beneath the beautiful woman's skin to the bone, and it will be seen to be ugly.
14   *discovery.* Used in the sense of to explore, to reveal, or to uncover.

THE AGONIE

The range of references and terseness of expression (as in line 2) recall Donne, as does the complex image in stanza 2. The slow movement of the verse in stanza 1 and the poet's intense concentration on the Crucifixion are in the meditative tradition which is used here to better understand the mystery of Christ's suffering and His love for man. In this respect the poem illuminates the point made in the second of the sonnets above: 'Lord, in thee/The beauty lies in the *discovery*'. At the same time, the imagery and paradoxes of the poem, though they may appear recondite to the modern reader, would have come naturally to a man steeped in the Bible and Christian doctrine. There is, too, a Christian 'wit' in the way Herbert makes the bleeding Christ emblematic of two such seemingly diverse concepts as sin and love: man's causing Him to bleed is the greatest sin imaginable, and His bleeding for man the greatest act of love.

The Agonie.

Philosophers have measur'd mountains,
Fathom'd the depths of seas, of states, and kings,
Walk'd with a staffe to heav'n, and traced fountains:
But there are two vast, spacious things,
The which to measure it doth more behove: 5
Yet few there are that sound them; Sinne and Love.

Who would know Sinne, let him repair
Unto Mount Olivet; there shall he see
A man so wrung with pains, that all his hair,
His skinne, his garments bloudie be.   10
Sinne is that presse and vice, which forceth pain
To hunt his cruell food through ev'ry vein.

Who knows not Love, let him assay
And taste that juice, which on the crosse a pike
Did set again abroach; then let him say   15
If ever he did taste the like.
Love is that liquour sweet and most divine,
Which my God feels as bloud; but I, as wine.

NOTES

2   i.e. natural philosophers or scientists have measured the depth of seas; political philosophers have taken the measure of the deep policies of kings and kingdoms.

3   *staffe*. Measuring rod with which the height of the sky has been calculated.

       traced fountains. Discovered the source of rivers.

8   *Mount Olivet*. On the night that Jesus was betrayed by Judas he retreated to the Mount of Olives to pray. 'And being in an agony he prayed more earnestly; and his sweat was as it were great drops of blood falling down to the ground'. (Luke 22: 44).

11-12 Hutchinson points out that the principal image is suggested by Isaiah 63: 1-3: 'Who is this that cometh from Edom, with dyed garments from Bozrah?....I that speak in righteousness, mighty to save....I have trodden the winepress alone'. *Vice* is a pun, meaning both evil and a screw-press; in the latter sense the *OED* lists Herbert's as the first usage. The metaphor in these lines is from wine making: just as the screw- press squeezes and crushes the grapes, so sin and evil force pain to be pumped up through every vein in the body. Herbert suggests that pain feeds upon the blood and in coursing through veins is, in fact, in pursuit of its food. He also wishes to suggest a comparison between the purple-stained clothes of the wine presser and the bloodied garments of Christ.

14   *juice* Liquid; here, Christ's blood. See 'The Bag' 1. 26.

       pike. Spear. The reference is to the wound in Christ's side made by a spear at the time of His crucifixion.

15   *abroach*. To broach is to stab or pierce; the *OED* also points out that another meaning is to tap a cask of wine in order to set it flowing.

17-18 These lines reverse the symbolism of the Eucharist. In the communion service the wine stands for the blood of Christ. However, Herbert says that he experiences the blood as wine: presumably being washed in the blood of Christ (or symbolically partaking of it in the communion) gives him the heady feeling of well-being that comes from drinking wine. If God expresses His love for man by shedding blood on his behalf, man experiences God's love by partaking of His sacrifice as though it were a health-giving liquid.

REDEMPTION

The 'story' in this sonnet is told allegorically, and the legal metaphors are as essential to its meaning as the naive character of the narrator.

The metaphors have their roots in the idea of the old Covenant of Works and the new Covenant of Grace. In the poem the narrator, not profiting under the old lease (the Covenant of Works which requires that man lead a just and virtuous life on pain of death), goes to negotiate a new lease with God. But he finds that God has already granted his request by offering him the Covenant of Grace through which all sinners can be saved. The drama of the poem derives from the sudden illumination dawning upon the ignorant narrator that what he wants to ask for is already his, that he has been living under the new lease when all along he had thought that he was living under the old. There are other reversals. God, who remains unseen and inaccessible until the penultimate line, suddenly emerges as the hero of the poem, and the narrator, who has hitherto had a wrong notion of God, suddenly has his understanding cleared. Two visions, that of failure and ignorance and that of salvation and enlightenment, are simultaneously contained in the poem, but at the beginning the second is concealed by the first. As the poem progresses there is a displacement of the first by the second.

Redemption.

Having been tenant long to a rich Lord,
    Not thriving, I resolved to be bold,
    And make a suit unto him, to afford
A new small-rented lease, and cancell th' old.
In heaven at his manour I him sought: 5
    They told me there, that he was lately gone
    About some land, which he had dearly bought
Long since on earth, to take possession.
I straight return'd, and knowing his great birth,
    Sought him accordingly in great resorts;   10
    In cities, theatres, gardens, parks, and courts:
At length I heard a ragged noise and mirth
    Of theeves and murderers: there I him espied,
    Who straight, *Your suit is granted,* said, & died.

NOTES

2   *I.* The first person singular here, as so often in Herbert, is both the individual speaker and every Christian man and woman, and his quest is both personal and that of Everyman.

3   · *afford.* Grant.

6   *lately.* Recently.

7   *land.* i.e. mankind.

      dearly. A pun: (1) dear, and (2) at great price

12-13 *ragged...murderers.* Refers to the criminals who were crucified along with Christ. Note how the narrator finally gains a better understanding of the nature of Christ.

14   God grants the suit even before the narrator has a chance to express it, and His death voids the old Covenant and seals the new.

EASTER-WINGS

When seen sideways, the shape of the printed poem on the page resembles two wings. Herbert used the technique of making the physical appearance of the poem suggest the poem's subject in 'The Altar' also. In 'Easter-Wings' the effect is created by the use of gradually shorter lines followed by gradually longer ones; these contracting and expanding lines enact the meaning they express of the growing poverty and thinness of the poet followed by an increasing sense of victory and hope.

Easter-Wings.

Lord, who createdst man in wealth and store,
    Though foolishly he lost the same,
        Decaying more and more,
            Till he became
                Most poore: 5
                With thee
             O let me rise
        As larks, harmoniously,
    And sing this day thy victories:
Then shall the fall further the flight in me.   10

My tender age in sorrow did beginne:
   And still with sicknesses and shame
     Thou didst so punish sinne,
       That I became
         Most thinne.   15
        With thee
      Let me combine
   And feel this day thy victorie:
For, if I imp my wing on thine,
Affliction shall advance the flight in me.   20

NOTES

1   *store.* i.e. with a wealth of (spiritual) goods.
8   The mention of larks is appropriate, since their falling and rising
       notes recreate a sense of the poem's contracting and expanding lines
       and hence of its falling and rising rhythm.
10   The notion that Adam's fall occasioned Christ's sacrifice and man's
       redemption was commonplace in Herbert's time.
11-15 'Sickness' and 'sorrow' refer not just generally to the Christian's
       sense of original sin and unworthiness but may also have a more
       specific reference to Herbert's own frequent ill health.
19-20 In falconry to imp is 'to engraft feathers in a damaged wing, so as to
       restore or improve the powers of flight' (*OED*). Herbert implies that
       by imping his broken and afflicted wing on Christ he will reach
       salvation more easily.

AFFLICTION (1)

This is the first of Herbert's five 'Affliction' poems. Intensely power-
ful and autobiographical with an enigmatic ending, it is reminiscent
of Job's cries of despair at being forsaken by God and shares, too, the
Psalmist's willingness to complain bitterly against God's dealings.
The God portrayed here is, far from being benevolent and loving, a
fickle, perverse and arbitrary betrayer, but though Herbert recog-
nizes God's nature, his aspiration remains a full commitment to Him.
At the same time the poem begins, as Helen Vendler has noted, with
a favourable self - characterization of the poet which is, however,
gradually stripped of all illusions by the inexorable realities of life,
and the rage the poet feels at having his personality come unstuck is
also part of the total effect. For a possible dating see 1. 32 n.

Affliction (1).

When first thou didst entice to thee my heart,
        I thought the service brave:
So many joyes I writ down for my part,
        Besides what I might have
Out of my stock of naturall delights,   5
Augmented with thy gracious benefits.

I looked on thy furniture so fine,
        And made it fine to me:
Thy glorious houshold-stuffe did me entwine,
        And 'tice me unto thee.   10
Such starres I counted mine: both heav'n and earth
Payd me my wages in a world of mirth.

What pleasures could I want, whose King I served,
        Where joyes my fellows were?
Thus argu'd into hopes, my thoughts reserved   15
        No place for grief or fear.
Therefore my sudden soul caught at the place,
And made her youth and fiercenesse seek thy face.

At first thou gav'st me milk and sweetnesses;
        I had my wish and way: 20
My dayes were straw'd with flow'rs and happinesse;
        There was no moneth but May.
But with my yeares sorrow did twist and grow,
And made a partie unawares for wo.

My flesh began unto my soul in pain,   25
        Sicknesses cleave my bones;
Consuming agues dwell in ev'ry vein,
        And tune my breath to grones.
Sorrow was all my soul; I scarce beleeved,
Till grief did tell me roundly, that I lived.   30

When I got health, thou took'st away my life,
        And more; for my friends die:
My mirth and edge was lost; a blunted knife
        Was of more use then I.

Thus thinne and lean without a fence or friend,   35
I Was blown through with ev'ry storm and winde.

Whereas my birth and spirit rather took
                    The way that takes the town;
Thou didst betray me to a lingring book,
                    And wrap me in a gown.   40
I was entangled in the world of strife,
Before I had the power to change my life.

Yet, for I threatned oft the siege to raise,
                    Not simpring all mine age,
Thou often didst with Academick praise   45
                    Melt and dissolve my rage.
I took thy sweetned pill, till I came where
I could not go away, nor persevere.

Yet lest perchance I should too happie be
                    In my unhappinesse,   50
Turning my purge to food, thou throwest me
                    Into more sicknesses.
Thus doth thy power crosse-bias me, not making
Thine own gift good, yet me from my wayes taking.

Now I am here, what thou wilt do with me   55
                    None of my books will show.
I reade, and sigh, and wish I were a tree;
                    For sure then I should grow
To fruit or shade: at least some bird would trust
Her houshold to me, and I should be just.

                                                                   60
Yet, though thou troublest me, I must be meek;
                    In weaknesse must be stout.
Well, I will change the service, and go seek
                    Some other master out.
Ah my deare God! though I am clean forgot,   65
Let me not love thee, if I love thee not.

NOTES

1   *entice.* Vendler says that the word suggests seduction; a sense of
        duplicity is also present.

2   *brave.* Splendid, fine.

7-10   In 1. 12 the poet will address God as the king, thus casting himself in
        the role of a courtier. In these lines he suggests that in the initial
        period of his service he began to think of all of God's possessions as
        being his own, and this 'tice [d]' (1.10), i.e. enticed him further.

17   My soul, acting in an unpremeditated way and without forethought
        ('sudden') snatched the opportunity presented to hold a place as
        your courtier.

22   *moneth.* Month.

25   *began.* Began to complain.

26   *cleave.* Clung to.

32   Hutchinson points out that Herbert's friend the Duke of Lennox and
        Richmond died in 1624, Lord Hamilton and King James the following
        year, Bacon and Lancelot Andrewes in 1626, and Herbert's mother in
        1627. It is conjectured that the poem must have been written shortly
        after that last date.

35   *fence.* Means of defence.

37-40   'The way that takes the town' may refer to Herbert's ambitions for
        secular advancement, in which case he is saying that he abandoned
        these ambitions in favour of an academic life. But the scholar's life
        proved to be a betrayal like everything else mentioned in the poem,
        and the scholar's gown little better than a shroud.

51   *Turning....food.* Drawing sustenance from Your chastisements.

53-4   Hutchinson points out that the metaphor in the phrase 'cross-bias' is
        from the game of bowls and means, in Grierson's words to 'give me
        an inclination other than my own'. Herbert wants to say that God is
        constantly thwarting him in his purposes ('Me from my wayes tak-
        ing'). This does not mean that He has other purposes for him ('not
        making/Thine own gift good'). His only intention seems to be to
        prevent the poet from realizing any purpose at all.

64   Vendler suggests that, given the traditional opposition between God
        and the Devil, the 'other master' could only refer to the Devil. The
        thought is abandoned as soon as it is expressed, not only because it
        is blasphemous but also because, as the poet has earlier hinted, he
        feels a loss of all volition or coherence and is unlikely to be able to
        make a new beginning.

65-6   The lines are condensed and a little obscure. The only thing the poet
        has left at this point is his love for God, and he wants no half measures
        here. It has got to be total love or nothing at all, and he tells God that
        rather than loving Him conditionally or imperfectly ('if I love thee
        not') he would prefer not to love at all.

PRAYER (1)

The sonnet may be read as a string of epithets used to evoke and
understand the nature of prayer, but it also possesses dynamism and
drama. As Vendler points out, it opens frigidly as though the poet
were sitting down to understand the nature of prayer out of a sense
of duty and could think of little more than a series of doctrinal com-
monplaces. But when he turns to his own feelings his definition of
prayer takes on an angry and violent edge. It is now seen as a defence
against God's thunderbolts; indeed, it becomes man's way of assault-
ing God.The violent anger is replaced by a sense of softness and
peace in the sestet, and the sonnet closes on a note of understand-
ing: prayer is a complex made up of all the preceding emotions. This
understanding makes all metaphors redundant, and they are there-
fore abandoned at the end.

Prayer (1)

Prayer the Churches banquet, Angels age,
   Gods breath in man returning to his birth,
   The soul in paraphrase, heart in pilgrimage,
The Christian plummet sounding heav'n and earth;
Engine against th' Almightie, sinners towre,   5
   Reversed thunder, Christ-side-piercing spear,
   The six-daies world transposing in an houre,
A kinde of tune, which all things heare and fear;
Softnesse, and peace, and joy, and love, and blisse,
   Exalted Manna, gladnesse of the best,   10
   Heaven in ordinarie, man well drest,
The milkie way, the bird of Paradise,
   Church-bels beyond the starres heard, the souls bloud,
   The land of spices; something understood.

NOTES

1   *Angels age.* According to Vendler, angels' age may be told by how
    long they have been praying.
3   *The soul in paraphrase* . Prayer paraphrases and thus opens out and
    explains the soul to itself.

4   *plummet.* A device for measuring ('sounding') depths (and here heights).
5   *Engine.* Weapon.
     towre. Tower, a defensive position.
6   *Reversed thunder.* The metre requires *reversed* to be pronounced with three syllables. Prayer enables man to seize the thunderbolts that God shoots at him and hurl them back. Since it is the classical Jove rather than the Christian God who is normally portrayed with thunderbolts, and since Jove's enemies had no way of retaliation, Herbert seems to be saying that the superiority of Christian over pagan prayer lies in the ability of the former to enter into a more equal relationship with God.
7   'An hour of prayer may affect a universe which took six days to set in order'. (Hutchinson).
10   *Manna.* A heavenly food with which Israelites were fed in the desert on their way from Egypt to the Chosen Land. See Exodus 16:35.
12   *bird of Paradise.* A bird with bright plumage. Hutchinson says that the image may also have been chosen because birds of paradise were believed to reside constantly in the air. Birds of paradise were also mistakenly believed in medieval times to be phoenixes and peacocks. The former is a symbol of the risen Christ, the latter was associated with the Nativity.

THE TEMPER (1)

This autobiographical poem reveals the poet's recognition of the extreme swings of mood to which he was subject. Ascribing these swings to God's desire to torture him, he first begs God to grant him stability but soon realizes that God wishes not to rack but tune the poet as though he were a musical instrument. The poem ends with the belief that whatever God may do to the author, he is never bereft of God even in his darkest moments.

The Temper (1)

How should I praise thee, Lord! how should my rymes
   Gladly engrave thy love in steel,
  If what my soul doth feel sometimes,
    My soul might ever feel!

Although there were some fourtie heav'ns, or more,   5
    Sometimes I peere above them all;
    Sometimes I hardly reach a score,
      Sometimes to hell I fall.

O rack me not to such a vast extent;
    Those distances belong to thee: 10
    The world's too little for thy tent,
      A grave too big for me.

Wilt thou meet arms with man, that thou dost stretch
    A crumme of dust from heav'n to hell?
    Will great God measure with a wretch?   15
      Shall he thy stature spell?

O let me, when thy roof my soul hath hid,
    O let me roost and nestle there:
    Then of a sinner thou art rid,
      And I of hope and fear.   20

Yet take thy way; for sure thy way is best:
    Stretch or contract me, thy poore debter:
    This is but tuning of my breast,
      To make the musick better,

Whether I flie with angels, fall with dust,   25
    Thy hands made both, and I am there:
    Thy power and love, my love and trust
      Make one place ev'ry where.

NOTES

5   *Fourtie heav'ns.* Jewish apocalypses speak of seven heavens. Herbert
      says that sometimes he is so elated that he could reach beyond forty,
      assuming there were so many.

9   'To rack' was to torture a prisoner by tying him to an instrument like
      a wheel which would stretch and break his limbs. See Vaughan, 'The
      Charnel-house', line 20

11   *Tent.* Habitation.

13 *Meet arms with.* The metaphor is taken from fencing, where the duellists measured their opponents' weapons against their own before the duel began. See *measure* in 1.15 below.

23-4 The image is that of a musician who tunes his musical instrument by tightening its strings. Whereas at the beginning of the poem Herbert said that his poetry would become an abiding expression of his love for God if God did not subject him to violent changes of mood, in these lines he sees himself not as the artist but as the Divine Artist's instrument and implies that his mood changes are a way to make him produce better music.

25-8 Herbert here abandons the concepts of height and depth because they do not exist for God. He comes to understand that wherever he is, in Heaven or Hell, he is with God and therefore everywhere. The notion of being everywhere does not terrify him as it did at the beginning of the poem.

JORDAN (1)

In this poem Herbert satirizes the artificialities of pastoral love poetry and rejects that genre in favour of simple and direct religious poetry. But he does so in a manner that, far from being simple and direct, is sophisticated and witty: even his proud flaunting of a loss of rhyme at the end is carried on in impeccable rhymed verse. See also 'Jordan (II)' below.

Jordan (1)

Who sayes that fictions onely and false hair
Become a verse? Is there in truth no beautie?
Is all good structure in a winding stair?
May no lines passe, except they do their dutie
    Not to a true, but painted chair?   5

Is it no verse, except enchanted groves
And sudden arbours shadow course-spunne lines?
Must purling streams refresh a lovers loves?
Must all be vail'd, while he that reades, divines,
    Catching the sense at two removes?   10

Shepherds are honest people; let them sing:
Riddle who list, for me, and pull for Prime:
I envie no mans nightingale or spring;
Nor let them punish me with losse of rime,
    Who plainly say, *My God, My King.*   15

NOTES

Title. Interpretation of the title has generated much controversy. The
classical poets claimed poetic inspiration in the waters of the Heli-
con. Christ was baptized in the river Jordan, and its waters have
become associated for the Christian with divine grace. By calling his
poem 'Jordan' Herbert may therefore be signalling a rejection of
classical or pagan in favour of Christian poetry.

1   *fictions...and false hair.* Fictions may be a reference to allegorical
    fictions, and by false hair Herbert is satirizing love poets who address
    verses to their mistresses' hair, sometimes not even realizing that the
    hair is false.

3   Is a complex structure like that of a spiralling staircase the only
    criterion for judging a poem's construction? Herbert implies that his
    own poems' structure is simple and straightforward.

5   *chair.* Used here to represent all objects. Herbert's question is:
    should poetry deal only with the outward manifestations or surface
    beauty of things?

7   *sudden arbours.* Arbours that spring suddenly to view, as is so often
    the case in pastoral romances.
    course-spunne lines. Herbert's point is that even if the lines of verse
    are poor ('coarse') they are admired if they describe ('shadow')
    strange and incredible incidents.

8   This line is a satire on the conventional language and sentiments of
    much contemporary love poetry.

9-10 A satire against the allegorist's habit of concealing his true subject
    and expressing his meaning obliquely.

11 *Shepherds.* Refers to pastoral poets who pretend they are shepherds.
    Herbert does not deny them the right to write as they choose; he
    grants that they are 'honest people'. Rather, his objection is against
    the tendency to see their kind of poetry as being the only legitimate
    kind.

12 *pull for Prime.* 'To draw a card or cards which will make the player
    prime. (OED) Herbert refuses to compete with those who 'riddle' (al-
    legorical poets) or those who write about the nightingale and spring
    (love poets).

15 These words are the Psalmist's, and in quoting them Herbert implies
    a repudiation of classical inspiration in favour of the Bible.

DENIALL

Like 'Affliction (I)' this poem grows out of a sense of being aban-
doned by God. The abandonment not only shatters the poet's unity
of being into fragments (stanza 2) but also leads to a physical
disorganization so that his heart leaves his breast and lodges in his
knees. It is also represented by the breaking of a bow, of a flower, and
of the rhyme scheme of the verse so that the poet is not able to find
the appropriate rhymes at the end of stanzas. But with a request to
God to 'tune' him a sense of unity returns. The musical metaphor
(reminiscent of 'The Temper - I') reestablishes harmony between
God and the poet and enables the broken music of his verse to be
mended.

Deniall.

    When my devotions could not pierce
            Thy silent eares;
Then was my heart broken, as was my verse:
    My breast was full of fears
            And disorder: 5

    My bent thoughts, like a brittle bow,
            Did flie asunder:
Each took his way; some would to pleasures go,
    Some to the warres and thunder
            Of alarms.   10

    As good go any where, they say,
            As to benumme
Both knees and heart, in crying night and day,
    Come,come, my God, o come,
            But no hearing.   15

    O that thou shouldst give dust a tongue
            To crie to thee,
And then not heare it crying! all day long
    My heart was in my knee,
            But no hearing.   20

Therefore my soul lay out of sight,
                    Untun'd, unstrung.
My feeble spirit, unable to look right,
            Like a nipt blossome, hung
                            Discontented.   25

O cheer and tune my heartlesse breast,
                    Deferre no time;
That so thy favours granting my request,
            They and my minde may chime,
                            And mend my ryme.   30

NOTES

5-6   My thoughts were bent (by tension of suffering?) instead of being
       straight. A brittle bow, when bent, will crack, and my thoughts
       sundered likewise and flew off in several directions. The image
       changes in mid-line: from being compared to a bow that snaps under
       pressure the poet's thoughts become like bent arrows that go
       everywhere except to the target.
19   i.e. I was praying on my knees and my heart was praying with me. But
       the image of the poet's heart in his knees also suggests that his heart
       was heavy and drooping instead of experiencing a heavenwards
       motion.

VANITIE (I)

This poem describes the uselessness ('vanity') of the activities of the
astronomer, the pearl diver and the alchemist, who, the poet main-
tains, are motivated only by pride ('vanity'). As against their labours
we are urged to follow God's commandments, for whereas obedi-
ence to God gives life, vanities are productive of death. Part of the
poem's subtlety lies in the way Herbert is able to weave images
suggestive of perversity, destruction or death in his description of
the three human activities. Herbert's attitude may seem to be anti-
intellectual, but what he is arguing against is not man's endeavours
as such but the danger of these endeavours becoming an end in
themselves instead of a means of perceiving the glory of God's
creation.

Vanitie (I)

The fleet Astronomer can bore,
And thred the spheres with his quick-piercing minde:
He views their stations, walks from doore to doore,
    Surveys, as if he had design'd
To make a purchase there: he sees their dances,   5
        And knoweth long before
Both their full-ey'd aspects, and secret glances.

The nimble Diver with his side
Cuts through the working waves, that he may fetch
His dearely-earned pearl, which God did hide   10
    On purpose from the ventrous wretch;
That he might save his life, and also hers,
        Who with excessive pride
Her own destruction and his danger wears.

The subtil Chymick can devest   15
And strip the creature naked, till he finde
The callow principles within their nest:
    There he imparts to them his minde,
Admitted to their bed-chamber, before
        They appeare trim and drest   20
To ordinarie suitours at the doore.

What hath not man sought out and found,
But his deare God? who yet his glorious law
Embosomes in us, mellowing the ground
    With showres and frosts, with love & aw,   25
So that we need not say, Where's this command?
        Poore man, thou searchest round
To finde out *death*, but missest *life* at hand.

NOTES

2   *thred the spheres.* Mary Ellen Rickey says that the familiar image of
      threading the spheres probably originated in 'diagrams of the universe
      in which the lines tracing planetary orbits look much like strings
      transfixing the heavenly bodies'. She also suggests that the words
      bore and *piercing* convey an impression of damage or destruction.

3-7   Herbert uses a number of technical terms in this stanza. *Stations* is
      the position of the planets, *purchase* the application of mechanical
      force, and *aspects* 'the relative positions of the heavenly bodies as
      they appear to an observer on the earth's surface at a given time'.
      (C.T.Onions, qtd. in Hutchinson). But the stanza is also, as Rickey
      suggests, shot through with sexual innuendoes. For *purchase* also
      meant concubinage in Elizabethan English, and the poet suggests
      that there is something perverse in the astronomer's interest in his
      subject matter. He studies the stars almost as if he were inspecting
      women in a brothel.Seen thus, technical terms like *dances, full-ey'd
      aspects* and *secret glances* take on another significance.
9   *working.* Constantly moving.
11   The diver's quest for pearls is no different from the quest of the
      astronomer or the alchemist: all are engaged in finding the hidden.
      But Herbert seems to treat the diver with greater harshness and
      suggests that while the astronomer and the alchemist are simply
      looking for that which is hidden, the diver is in search of something
      that God wanted to remain hidden.
12-14 Herbert means that the diver's mistress is so vain that for her not to
      have the pearl would be tantamount to death. By fulfilling her wishes
      the diver thinks that he is saving her from this fate, even though in
      doing so he has risked his life. What he --and she--do not realize is that
      her vanity condemns her to spiritual death.
15   *Chymick.* The alchemist here is also an anatomist.
      devest. Unclothe.
17   *callow.* Featherless. Herbert means that the anatomist strips and
      dissects his subject till he is able to find its innermost principles
      nestling inside.
18-21 'He can give his mind to their study with better opportunity than
      those can who only see them emerge from the door fully drest'.
      (Hutchinson). It needs to be pointed out that there is something
      perverse in the alchemist's experiments as there is in the efforts of the
      astronomer and the diver. The alchemist is admitted to the very
      'bedchamber' of his experimental subject where he proceeds with
      his dissection as lovingly as if he were undressing his mistress.
24-6 The image is of God as a gardener who has not only planted ('Em-
      bosomes') his 'glorious law' in our hearts but also fertilized the
      ground with 'showres and frosts, with love & aw' so that the plant may
      thrive and we may have no difficulty in perceiving it.

VERTUE

Though not in the *carpe diem* tradition the poem is reminiscent of
it. Inaugurated by Ovid, this poetic tradition urges the mistress to

seize the day since time is fleeting. In his poem Herbert fastens upon
virtue as a counter to time's transience. The delicacy, refined tact and
assured understatement of the poem have made it much admired: in
the eighteenth century John Wesley adapted it as a hymn and in the
nineteenth Coleridge singled it out for praise. On the surface 'Vertue'
seems simple enough. The first three stanzas, which begin identi-
cally, address the day, the rose and Spring respectively—all sweet but
transient natural phenomena—while the final stanza affirms the con-
trasting permanence of a virtuous soul. But the poem is full of com-
plexities and puzzles. Recently they have been well analysed by
Helen Vendler, who reads the poem as 'a miniature autobiography'
in which Herbert is concerned with the Wordsworthian problem of
the values to live by once the enthusiasms of youth have faded and
concludes that in it Herbert defines the need for a certain strength
or moral staunchness to accompany beauty.

Vertue.

Sweet day, so cool, so calm, so bright,
The bridall of the earth and skie:
The dew shall weep thy fall to night;
       For thou must die.

Sweet rose, whose hue angrie and brave   5
Bids the rash gazer wipe his eye:
Thy root is ever in its grave,
       And thou must die.

Sweet spring, full of sweet dayes and roses,
A box where sweets compacted lie;   10
My musick shows ye have your closes,
       And all must die.

Onely a sweet and vertuous soul,
Like season'd timber, never gives;
But though the whole world turn to coal,   15
       Then chiefly lives.

NOTES

2   *bridall.* The clear beauty of the day seems to join earth and sky
      together.
5   *angrie.* 'Having the colour of an angry face, red'. (*OED*)

6   Vendler suggests that the beauty of the rose is like a thorn that pricks
       the rash gazer. She also finds the description of the rose one of the
       puzzles of the poem: how can its 'angry and brave' nature be
       reconciled with its sweetness?

11   *closes.* A technical term in music, meaning cadences. This line is the
       only place in the poem where the poet makes a direct reference to
       himself.

16   *chiefly lives.* The soul is alive at present, but after the end of the world
       it will become more so.

THE PEARL. MATTH. 13.45.

The poem is based on the parable of the merchant in Matthew 13: 45-
46: 'Again, the kingdom of heaven is like unto a merchant man
seeking goodly pearls: who, when he hath found one pearl of great
price, went and sold all that he had, and bought it'. Herbert here
expresses his repudiation of the pleasures of the world in favour of
God's kingdom. But even as he does so, worldly pleasures are
described in great and loving detail, showing that they had a strong
appeal for him and giving them up could not have come easily. They
are not condemned, except perhaps when Herbert associates Honour
with liquor in stanza 2, since he recognizes that they, too, are the
work of God, but they are clearly seen as inferior to God's service.
Joseph Summers points out that in this poem Herbert speaks as a
courtier and the pleasures he repudiates--of learning, honour and
pleasure--form 'the courtly trinity'.

The Pearl. Matth. 13.45.

I know the wayes of Learning; both the head
And pipes that feed the presse, and make it runne,
What reason hath from nature borrowed,
Or of it self, like a good huswife, spunne
In laws and policie; what the starres conspire,   5
What willing nature speaks, what forc'd by fire;
Both th'old discoveries, and the new-found seas,
The stock and surplus, cause and historie:
All these stand open, or I have the keyes:
                Yet I love thee.   10

I know the wayes of Honour, what maintains
The quick returns of courtesie and wit:
In vies of favours whether partie gains,
When glorie swells the heart, and moldeth it
To all expressions both of hand and eye,   15
Which on the world a true-love-knot may tie,
And bear the bundle, wheresoe're it goes:
How many drammes of spirit there must be
To sell my life unto my friends or foes:
          Yet I love thee.   20

I know the wayes of Pleasure, the sweet strains,
The lullings and the relishes of it;
The propositions of hot bloud and brains;
What mirth and musick mean; what love and wit
Have done these twentie hundred yeares, and more: 25
I know the projects of unbridled store:
My stuffe is flesh, not brasse; my senses live,
And grumble oft, that they have more in me
Then he that curbs them, being but one to five:
          Yet I love thee.   30

I know all these, and have them in my hand:
Therefore not sealed, but with open eyes
I flie to thee, and fully understand
Both the main sale, and the commodities;
And at what rate and price I have thy love;   35
With all the circumstances that may move:
Yet through these labyrinths, not my groveling wit,
But thy silk twist let down from heav'n to me,
Did both conduct and teach me, how by it
          To climbe to thee.   40

NOTES

1-2   *bead...presse.* Hutchinson sees here a probable allusion to Zechar-
iah 4: 12: 'two olive branches, which through the two golden pipes
empty the golden oil out of themselves', and adds that perhaps the
bead is the fountain of knowledge, the two universities, and the *pipes*
are those who mediate that knowledge to the world. Following H.C.
Beeching, Mary Ellen Rickey says that the *presse* is the printing press,

the *head* the intellect and the *pipes* the two organs of sight and sound.

3-4   I know what Reason has learned from an observation of Nature and what it has produced (*spunne*) out of its own understanding.

5   *what the starres conspire.* What influence the heavenly bodies have upon the earth and its inhabitants.

6   *what forc'd by fire.* The reference is to the alchemical practice of heating substances in order to change their nature and create new ones.

8   *Stock and surplus.* Hutchinson quotes Beeching: 'The learning we inherit, and that which we add to it'.

12   *returns.* Repartees.

13-17 'I know how to gauge by the rules of courtesy who wins in a contest of doing favours; when each party is urged by ambition to do all he can by look or deed to win the world and bind it on his back'. (Beeching, qtd. in Hutchinson).

18-19 I know how much liquor one must consume before one is ready either to sacrifice one's life for one's friends or undertake a fight with one's enemies which may cost one's life. Herbert is here referring contemptuously to 'Dutch courage' which grows out of excessive drinking but passes as honour in the world of the court.

21-3 In these lines *strains, lulling, relish* and *propositions* are all technical terms from music. Herbert, a skilled musician, associates pleasure primarily with music in this stanza. He must have found a repudiation of the pleasures of secular music particularly difficult.

26   I know the activities (*projects*) which are capable of yielding limitless amounts (*unbridled store*) of pleasure.

27-9 *my senses...five.* My senses grumble that though they are five in number they have to yield to the authority of one man.

29   *then.* Than.

34   I understand the conditions of sale and the nature of the goods I am selling (*commodities*). The metaphor of sale is, of course, from the parable as recounted in Matthew.

37-40 'Thy silk twist' is the silken cord of God's love for man. Its having been lowered down from heaven so that man may climb up with its help is a reference to Christ coming down as a man so that His sacrifice may prove to be mankind's salvation. Herbert says that if he is willing to leave the *labyrinths* or tortuous paths of learning, honour and pleasure, he was led to this decision not through the exercise of his own intelligence, which is low (*groveling*) but by God, thus echoing the Anglican belief that it is not through his own volition but only by God's grace that man can be saved. The mention of the silk twist and labyrinths is reminiscent of Ariadne helping Theseus to find his way back after slaying the Minotaur.

MAN

This is generally seen as a poem expressing common seventeenth-century beliefs that man is a microcosm, the highest of God's creations, and that in the symmetry and order that is revealed in him, as well as in the intricate relationships that exist between him and all of nature, may be studied the 'neatness' and 'wit' of God the artist. Recently Diana Benet has argued that if the poem glorifies man, it also undercuts his pride and selfishness, and it is only when Herbert's ambiguous attitude is understood that his prayer at the end of the poem to allow man to be God's servant gains full significance.

Man

     My God, I heard this day,
That none doth build a stately habitation,
     But he that means to dwell therein.
     What house more stately hath there been,
Or can be, then is Man? to whose creation   5
     All things are in decay.

     For Man is ev'ry thing,
And more: He is a tree, yet bears more fruit;
     A beast, yet is, or should be more:
     Reason and speech we onely bring.   10
Parrats may thank us, if they are not mute,
     They go upon the score.

     Man is all symmetrie,
Full of proportions, one limbe to another,
     And all to all the world besides: 15
     Each part may call the furthest, brother:
For head with foot hath private amitie,
     And both with moons and tides.

     Nothing hath got so farre,
But Man hath caught and kept it, as his prey.   20
     His eyes dismount the highest starre:
     He is in little all the sphere.
Herbs gladly cure our flesh; because that they
     Finde their acquaintance there.

                For us the windes do blow,   25
The earth doth rest, heav'n move, and fountains flow.
                Nothing we see, but means our good,
                As our delight, or as our treasure:
The whole is, either our cupboard of food,
                Or cabinet of pleasure.   30

                The starres have us to bed;
Night draws the curtain, which the sunne withdraws;
                Musick and light attend our head.
                All things unto our flesh are kinde
In their descent and being; to our minde   35
                In their ascent and cause.

                Each thing is full of dutie:
Waters united are our navigation;
                Distinguished, our habitation;
                Below our drink; above, our meat;   40
Both are our cleanlinesse. Hath one such beautie?
                Then how are all things neat?

                More servants wait on Man,
Then he'l take notice of: in ev'ry path
                He treads down that which doth befriend him,   45
                When sicknesse makes him pale and wan,
Oh mightie love! Man is one world, and hath
                Another to attend him.

                Since then, my God, thou hast
So brave a Palace built; O dwell in it,   50
                That it may dwell with thee at last!
                Till then, afford us so much wit;
That, as the world serves us, we may serve thee,
                And both thy servants be.

NOTES

1   *I heard this day.* Perhaps in a sermon. Such colloquial and casual
        openings are not uncommon in Herbert.
2-5   The image of man as a building is Biblical. cf. Paul's words to the
        Corinthians: 'Ye are God's building'(1 Corinthians 3:2).

2, 4 *stately.* Benet points out that the word means not only dignified but also arrogant. Already the undercutting of man's nobility has started.

8 *More fruit.* Hutchinson says that his reading is an emendation of the Bodleian manuscript and the 1633 edition, both of which read 'no fruit'. Benet accepts 'no fruit' as lending greater support to her interpretation.

11 *parrats.* Parrots.

12 i.e. 'they are in man's debt' (Hutchinson);

15 i.e. every part of the human body is related to all aspects; of the universe. The point is explained further in line 18 where we are told that the moon and tides can affect the well-being of man's head and limbs.

21 *dismount.* Bring down to the level of his field of vision.

24 *acquaintance.* Natural affinities with the body's chemical properties.

34-6 All things are kind to our bodies in their downward motions and to our minds in their upward motions. The downward and upward motions signify the hierarchical relationship between the body (which was considered lower) and the mind (which was considered higher).

39 *Distinguished.* Parted or separated, and thus revealing land.

40 *Above, our meat.* The rain that falls from above causes our food (*'meat'*) to grow.

41-2 If one element possesses such a diversity of beautiful uses, how wonderful must the total structure of the world created by an integration of all elements be. The *OED* defines *neat* as cleverly contrived and executed and characterized by elegance of form or arrangement, with freedom from all unnecessary additions; and Herbert's use of the word here to characterize the world is meant to reveal God's skill in contriving it.

44-6 The indifference of man to his servants further reveals the ambiguity of his nature and lends support to Benet's reading of the poem.

49-54 In the last stanza Herbert expresses two wishes. He hopes that God will dwell in man, but before that can happen he hopes that man will learn to serve God as all natural objects serve man. The contrast is between Nature's fidelity and man's dereliction of duty prompted by grandiose notions of the self.

LIFE

The posy or garland that the poet makes is emblematic of the sweetness that he hopes his life will have, and when the flowers wither he learns a lesson about the nature of death. The poem ends with the hope that the poet's own death will enhance the value of his

life as has happened in the case of the flowers. Thus 'Life' moves from
an aesthetic contemplation of flowers to the realization of a moral
meaning in the aesthetic act. The tone is courtly throughout, and the
same delicacy with which the speaker addresses the dead flowers is
found in death's courteous treatment of them. Vendler points out
that though the poem expresses a light acquiescence in death, the
tone is sad throughout. 'The day runs by; the flowers steal away and
wither; the poet takes an admonition...Even Herbert's stanza itself is
made up of two dying falls, reinforcing the many lamenting cadences
found in the diction and syntax...'

Life

I made a posie, while the day ran by:
Here will I smell my remnant out, and tie
        My life within this band.
But Time did becken to the flowers, and they
By noon most cunningly did steal away,   5
        And wither'd in my hand.

My hand was next to them, and then my heart;
I took, without more thinking, in good part
        Times gentle admonition
Who did so sweetly deaths sad taste convey,   10
Making my minde to smell my fatall day;
        Yet sugring the suspicion.

Farewell deare flowers, sweetly your time ye spent,
Fit, while ye liv'd, for smell or ornament,
        And after death for cures;   15
I follow straight without complaints or grief,
Since if my sent be good, I care not if
        It be as short as yours.

NOTES

1-3   No editor has, to my knowledge, satisfactorily glossed these lines,
      whose general meaning is clear but which pose problems of precise
      interpretation. Does Herbert mean that his act of making the posy
      marked a withdrawal of some sort from life, that while the day ran by

he decided that he would spend the remainder of his days in smelling
the flowers? In what sense could his life be *tied* within the posy?

12   *sugring the suspicion.* Sweetening the hint of my approaching death.·
15   *cures.* Withered flowers were used for medicinal purposes. Hutchin-
son quotes Donne, *The First Anniversary,* 11. 403-4:
Since herbes, and roots, by dying lose not all,
But they, yea Ashes too, are medicinall.
17   *Sent.* Scent. Herbert says that he will not mind an early death if his life
can have the same beauty as the flowers did, and if his death can prove
valuable to others, as is the case with the dead flowers.

MORTIFICATION

Like 'Life' the subject of 'Mortification' is death, but whereas in 'Life'
Herbert talks of death from a personal point of view, in 'Mortifica-
tion' it is treated more impersonally as a universal phenomenon. The
perception that death is present at each new beginning of life,
whether we realize it or not, is more characteristic of some of
Donne's sermons than of Herbert; and Herbert's use of it here shows
him working within a homiletic tradition, driving home to his audi-
tors the ever-present reality of death with an insistence bordering on
the morbid in order that the prayer with which the poem closes may
carry more conviction. Throughout the poem Herbert maintains full
control over his subject, as can be seen partly in the way in which the
different stages of life are enumerated sequentially and logically, and
partly in the verse structure: the third line of each stanza ends with
breath and the last line with the rhyming *death.*

Mortification

How soon doth man decay!
When clothes are taken from a chest of sweets
To swaddle infants, whose young breath
Scarce knows the way;
Those clouts are little winding sheets,   5
Which do consigne and send them unto death.

When boyes go first to bed,
They step into their voluntarie graves,

Sleep bindes them fast; onely their breath
        Makes them not dead: 10
Successive nights, like rolling waves,
Convey them quickly, who are bound for death.

        When youth is frank and free,
And calls for musick, while his veins do swell,
        All day exchanging mirth and breath   15
                In companie;
        That musick summons to the knell,
Which shall befriend him at the houre of death.

        When man grows staid and wise,
Getting a house and home, where he may move   20
        Within the circle of his breath,
                Schooling his eyes;
        That dumbe inclosure maketh love
Unto the coffin, that attends his death.

        When age grows low and weak,   25
Marking his grave, and thawing ev'ry yeare,
        Till all do melt, and drown his breath
                When he would speak;
        A chair or litter shows the biere,
Which shall convey him to the house of death.   30

        Man, ere he is aware.
Hath put together a solemnitie,
        And drest his herse, while he has breath
                As yet to spare:
        Yet Lord, instruct us so to die,   35
That all these dyings may be life in death.

NOTES

2   *chest of sweets.* Sweet-smelling closet. The word *sweet* is often used
     by Herbert to mean sweet odours or fragrances.
5   *clouts.* Swaddling clothes; clothes in which an infant is dressed.
8   i.e. they step voluntarily into their beds which are a prefiguration of
     their graves.

11-12 The metaphor is of a ship carrying its passengers to their destination.

17-18 Hutchinson mentions the seventeenth-century custom of tolling the knell when a man was dying rather than after he was dead, the idea being that people who heard the knell would pause to pray for the soul of the dying man. In these lines the music that the young man calls for becomes the knell which, by exhorting others to pray for him, will prove to be his true friend.

21 *circle of his breath.* The suggestion is of growing limitations: the man's activities are now confined to an area only large enough to allow him to send his breath to its farthest boundaries.

22 *schooling his eyes.* Teaching his eyes to see objects close to him now that he has become short-sighted.

23-4 The middle aged man's silent house (*dumbe enclosure*) resembles the coffin that awaits him.

26-8 *thawing...speak.* As the old man weakens, his vital functions melt or dissolve ('thaw') till finally his speech is drowned by the rheum in his throat. The image of thawing goes together with that of drowning.

36 i.e. may our death lead us to immortal life on the other side of the grave.

JORDAN (II)

Like the first 'Jordan' this poem expresses a preference for a simple, direct and unaffected style of poetry over a sophisticated and ingenious manner. But the technique of expressing the idea varies in the two poems. While the first is wholly in the poet's voice, the second falls into two parts. In the first part, he describes his subtle and ingenious methods of writing; in the second, the voice of his 'friend' (God) advises him, in direct language, to abandon complexity in favour of simplicity. The presence of the two voices makes this poem more dialectical than 'Jordan (1).'

Jordan (II).

When first my lines of heav'nly joyes made mention,
Such was their lustre, they did so excell,
That I sought out quaint words, and trim invention;
My thoughts began to burnish, sprout, and swell,
Curling with metaphors a plain intention,   5
Decking the sense, as if it were to sell.

Thousands of notions in my brain did runne,
Off'ring their service, if I were not sped:
I often blotted what I had begunne;
This was not quick enough, and that was dead.   10
Nothing could seem too rich to clothe the sunne,
Much lesse those joyes which trample on his head.

As flames do work and winde, when they ascend,
So did I weave my self into the sense.
But while I bustled, I might heare a friend   15
Whisper, *How wide is all this long pretence!*
There is in love a sweetnesse readie penn'd:
Copie out onely that, and save expense.

NOTES

1-6   For one trained in the tradition of classical rhetoric 'quaint words',
      'trim invention', and an inclination to 'deck' or decorate the mean-
      ing with 'curling...metaphors' would have come naturally; and Her-
      bert's Latin orations made when he was at Cambridge are character-
      ized by these stylistic devices. His development as a poet may be seen
      partly as a conscious effort to move away from an Euphuistic or Meta-
      physical style.

8   *if I were not sped.* If my work as a poet did not make good progress.

10   *quick.* Lively

11   *sunne.* Whenever the word is encountered in sixteenth and seven-
      teenth century poetry we must suspect a pun on *sun/son.* In 'The
      Sonne' Herbert expresses a preference for English over all other
      languages because it alone enables this pun.

12   *trample.* In what sense can joys be said to *trample* on the head of
      either the sun or Christ? The meaning is obscure, perhaps intention-
      ally, as an example of the kind of poetry Herbert eventually rejects in
      this poem, though the obscurity does not interfere with the general
      sense. His commentators have left the line unglossed.

14   The image of weaving suggests both the intense labour involved in
      writing poetry as well as its complex patterns in order to achieve
      which the poet has had to follow tortuous and intricate paths.

17   *readie.* Already. The reference is to the Scriptures which the poet is
      being exhorted to copy. It may be added that for the poet to follow
      this advice would result in abdicating his role as a creator for that of
      a mere copier or secretary—a role that Herbert never performed. But
      the main point of God's advice is to commend not this latter role but
      rather a Scriptural directness.

18   Hutchinson quotes from the first sonnet in Philip Sidney's *Astropbel
      and Stella* for comparison: 'Foole said my *Muse* to mee, look in thy
      heart and write'. But as Stanley Fish points out, Sidney's poet 'is asked
      to call on his own resources; Herbert is reminded that his resources
      are not his own'.

DIALOGUE

What is remarkable about Herbert's dialogue with God here is not
that God speaks—He does so in several other poems including
'Jordan (2)'—but that He speaks on terms of equality with Herbert.
If the poet, more concerned about the standards that God should
uphold than God himself seems to be, speaks courteously but shows
at times a capability for logic-chopping, stubbornness, self-abase-
ment, and truculence, God too, while being forbearing, can speak
ironically, punningly and in warning tones while preserving His
essential mystery. The poem suggests that God so loves man that He
will use any stratagem to win him, but He will not force man to love
Him. Man has to give Him his love freely, for God is no tyrant and
respects man's right to his free will. The poem will make better sense
if the speaker's opening speech is seen as a response to an earlier
speech of God regarding the possession of man's soul.

Dialogue

Sweetest Saviour, if my soul
Were but worth the having,
Quickly should I then controll
  Any thought of waving.
But when all my care and pains   5
Cannot give the name of gains
To thy wretch so full of stains,
What delight or hope remains?

What Child, is the ballance thine,
  Thine the poise and measure?   10
If I say, Thou shalt be mine;
  Finger not my treasure.
What the gains in having thee

Do amount to, onely be,
Who for man was sold, can see;   15
That transferr'd th' accounts to me.

But as I can see no merit,
  Leading to this favour:
So the way to fit me for it
  Is beyond my savour.   20
As the reason then is thine;
So the way is none of mine:
I disclaim the whole designe:
Sinne disclaims and I resigne.

That is all, if that I could   25
  Get without repining;
And my clay, my creature, would
  Follow my resigning:
That as I did freely part
With my glorie and desert,   30
Left all joyes to feel all smart—
Ah! no more: thou break'st my heart.

NOTES

4   *waving.* Hutchinson points out the pun in this word: to wave is to
        waver and to waive or decline an offer. In the former sense the
        passage means: were I but convinced that my soul was worth God's
        having, I would immediately stop wavering about the question. In
        the second sense the meaning is: I would immediately abandon any
        thought of waiving or declining god's right to my soul. The poem
        abounds with legal terms like *waiver.*
6   *give the name of gains.* Make me worthy of or useful to you.
8   This ambiguous line is meant by the poet to apply both to himself and
        to God. In so far as God is concerned, He is asked what delight He can
        hope to get by possessing the stained soul of the poet. In so far as the
        line applies to the poet, it means that since man is incapable of
        making himself worthy of God, his case is sad and hopeless. The point
        that God is making is, however, that He wants the poet's soul as it is:
        for Him it is a 'treasure' (1.12). A situation that should give joy is seen
        by the poet, because of his holier-than-God attitude, as one of
        dejection.

Stanzas 2 and 4. God's speeches are printed in italics.

9-10 God asks ironically whether man is the judge or He. A balance or pair of scales was traditionally associated with the figure of Justice who *poised* and *measured* evidence.

12   *Finger.* Trifle or play with; or perhaps accuse. For *treasure* see note to line 8 above.

14-15 Herbert's God can be a meticulous and legalistic bookkeeper, as here.

20   *savour.* Perception, understanding.

22-3 'I deny all responsibility for the bargain; it was none of my making' (Hutchinson).

25   *That is all.* That settles it. Note that God has deliberately misunder-stood the poet's word *resign* to come to this conclusion. What the poet meant by that word in line 24 was that he refused to have any further part in the discussion. But God understands him to mean 'I yield' or 'I surrender'--in much the same way that Christ yielded or surrendered His glory in heaven when He came down to earth as a man (lines 28-31).

26   *repining.* For a gloss on this word, see Herbert's 'The Pulley'.

LONGING

Like 'Deniall' this poem expresses a sense of abandonment by God, but whereas in the former, harmony is reestablished at the end between the speaker and God, in 'Longing' God does not respond to the poet's prayer. The poet's alienation from God leads to a fragmen-tation, even disintegration of his self: instead of remaining a whole man he becomes a collection of eyes, knees, bones, throat, heart and dust. God, too, is seen as the bowels of pity, ear, head and feet. The sense of fragmentation is further enhanced by the short, choppy lines of verse. Herbert's tone ranges from the abject to the bitter. He begs, grovels, implores, hectors and accuses God and expresses in-credulous bafflement that after dying for man God should have left him to his own devices. The early parts of the poem express the vast distance that separates man from God. Though by the end this distance has been bridged somewhat--man is now seen to be at the feet of Christ—the hoped-for reconciliation has to wait till the next poem, 'The Bag'. For further comments on 'Longing' and 'The Bag' see the general introduction to Herbert above.

Longing.

With sick and famisht eyes,
With doubling knees and weary bones
   To thee my cries,
   To thee my grones,
To thee my sighs, my tears ascend: 5
    No end?

My throat, my soul is hoarse;
My heart is wither'd like a ground
   Which thou dost curse.
   My thoughts turn round,   10
And make me giddie; Lord, I fall,
    Yet call.

From thee all pitie flows.
Mothers are kinde, because thou art,
   And dost dispose   15
   To them a part:
Their infants, them; and they suck thee
    More free.

Bowels of pitie, heare!
Lord of my soul, love of my minde,   20
   Bow down thine eare!
   Let not the winde
Scatter my words, and in the same
    Thy name!

Look on my sorrows round!   25
Mark well my furnace! O what flames,
   What heats abound!
   What griefs,what shames!
Consider, Lord; Lord, bow thine eare,
    And heare!   30

Lord Jesu, thou didst bow
Thy dying head upon the tree:
   O be not now
   More dead to me!

Lord heare! *Shall he that made the eare,*   35
          Not heare?

          Behold, thy dust doth stirre,
It moves, it creeps, it aims at thee:
               Wilt thou deferre
                  To succour me,   40
Thy pile of dust, wherein each crumme
               Sayes, Come?

          To thee help appertains.
Hast thou left all things to their course,
               And laid the reins   45
               Upon the horse?
Is all lockt? hath a sinners plea
               No key?

          Indeed the world's thy book,
Where all things have their leafe assign'd: 50
               Yet a meek look
               Hath interlin'd.
  Thy board is full, yet humble guests
               Finde nests.

          Thou tarriest, while I die,   55
And fall to nothing: thou dost reigne,
               And rule on high,
               While I remain
In bitter grief: yet am I stil'd
               Thy childe.   60

          Lord, didst thou leave thy throne,
Not to relieve? how can it be,
               That thou art grown
               Thus hard to me?
Were sinne alive, good cause there were   65
               To bear.

          But now both sinne is dead,
And all thy promises live and bide.
          That wants his head;

These speak and chide,   70
And in thy bosome poure my tears,
         As theirs.

Lord JESU, heare my heart,
Which hath been broken now so long,
      That ev'ry part   75
         Hath got a tongue!
Thy beggars grow; rid them away
         To day.

My love, my sweetnesse, heare!
By these thy feet, at which my heart
      Lies all the yeare,   80
         Pluck out thy dart,
And heal my troubled breast which cryes,
         Which dyes.

NOTES

10   *turn round.* Spin round.
16-17 The line is condensed. The infants suck their mothers, and the
      mothers draw sustenance from Thee, more freely because they
      possess a share of Thy love.
26   *furnace.* Cf. Isaiah 48: 10: 'I have refined thee, but not with silver: I
      have chosen thee in the furnace of affliction'. Also Ezekiel 22: 20: 'As
      they gather silver, and brass, and iron, and lead and tin into the midst
      of the furnace, to blow and fire upon it, to melt it; so will I gather you
      in mine anger and in my fury, and I will leave you there, and melt you'.
29   Cf. Psalm 31:2: 'Bow down thy ear to me...'
35-6 An almost verbatim quotation from Psalm 94:9: 'He that planted the
      ear, shall he not hear?'
51-2 A meek look underlines the pages of Your book.
61   Refers to the Incarnation or God coming to earth as a man.
67-70 Christ's sacrifice put an end to sin and promised salvation to man.
      Therefore sin is now 'headless' and the promises reproach Christ
      because they are not being kept.

THE BAG

Vendler quotes Robert Graves' sexual interpretation of the poem:
Christ is a female figure who comes down from heaven undressing all

the way, is pierced, and then displays his open wound as a bag into which anyone can thrust a petition. Though this interpretation has not been generally accepted, 'The Bag' remains a curious poem. After expressing joy in the first stanza that God has not become deaf to man's entreaties, as 'Longing' feared, the poem goes on to narrate the story of Christ almost as though the poet were preaching a homily to a rustic congregation who needed to have the story simplified. But it is a strange narration. Christ's birth is told almost as a fairy tale and there is neither any grief in the depiction of the crucifixion nor any mention of the Resurrection. The focus is on the wounded figure of Christ. Though the image of the wound as a bag is baroque if not grotesque, a permanently wounded Christ is in keeping with the image in 'Longing' of a permanently wounded man.

The Bag.

Away despair! my gracious Lord doth heare.
    Though windes and waves assault my keel,
    He doth preserve it: he doth steer,
    Ev'n when the boat seems most to reel.
    Storms are the triumph of his art: 5
Well may he close his eyes, but not his heart.

Hast thou not heard, that my Lord JESUS di'd?
    Then let me tell thee a strange storie.
    The God of power, as he did ride
    In his majestick robes of glorie,   10
    Resolv'd to light; and so one day
He did descend, undressing all the way.

The starres his tire of light and rings obtain'd,
    The cloud his bow, the fire his spear,
    The sky his azure mantle gain'd.   15
    And when they ask'd, what he would wear;
    He smil'd and said as he did go,
He had new clothes a making here below.

When he was come, as travellers are wont,
    He did repair unto an inne.   20
    Both then, and after, many a brunt

He did endure to cancell sinne:
  And having giv'n the rest before,
Here he gave up his life to pay our score.

But as he was returning, there came one   25
  That ran upon him with a spear.
  He, who came hither all alone,
  Bringing nor man, nor arms, nor fear,
  Receiv'd the blow upon his side,
And straight he turn'd, and to his brethren cry'd,   30

If ye have any thing to send or write,
  I have no bag, but here is room:
  Unto my Fathers hands and sight,
  Beleeve me, it shall safely come.
  That I shall minde, what you impart,   35
Look, you may put it very neare my heart.

Or if hereafter any of my friends
  Will use me in this kinde, the doore
  Shall still be open; what he sends
  I will present, and somewhat more,   40
  Not to his hurt. Sighs will convey
Any thing to me. Harke, Despair away.

NOTES

2-4   The image is of Christ as the helmsman of the poet's ship, steering it
      through storms with closed eyes (as he seemed to have in 'Longing').
11   *light.* Alight on earth.
13   *tire.* Attire. The whole stanza describes in a fanciful or myth-making
      way why the stars are bright or how the rainbow and thunder were
      formed or why the sky came to be blue: these are the articles of
      clothing Christ shed on His way to earth where He was going to
      clothe Himself in the human body (line 18 below).
23   *rest.* i.e. the rest of his belongings.
25   *returning.* Returning to heaven after being crucified.
26   See 'The Agonie', line 14 and note.
30   *brethren.* Christians see Christ as God's Son but also as the perfect
      Man. In addressing other men here as His brothers He reveals His
      human attributes.

42   The last words of the poem recall the first, and together they provide
      an answer to man's entreaties in 'Longing'.

THE COLLAR

In the best poems of Donne the act of writing becomes a strenuous
wrestling bout with a given problem at which we feel we are present.
In Herbert's 'The Collar' the problem of rebellion against God has
been resolved before the writing of the poem; yet so vividly is the
struggle recreated that it gains the immediacy of unfolding before
our eyes. An original use of rhyme and metre helps to achieve this
immediacy. In what must be one of the earliest examples in English
of free verse, unequal lines and irregular rhyming recreate the wild
raving of the rebellious poet till calm is established at the end with
the help of a regular four-lined stanza.

  'The Collar' recalls three Biblical texts: Luke 15: 13-21 (the
parable of the Prodigal Son): 'And not many days after the younger
son gathered all together, and took his journey into a far country,
and there wasted his substance with riotous living', Matthew 11: 29-
30: 'My yoke is easy, and my burden is light', and John 20:16: 'Jesus
saith unto her, Mary. She turned herself, and saith unto him,
Rabboni; which is to say, Master'. There are a number of other
Biblical references and puns (identified in the notes) in the 'raving'
speech of the poet which suggest that though he thinks he wants
freedom from God's service, in reality it is God he is searching for,
and when at the end of the poem he recognizes God, we are meant
to realize the 'correct' or Christian meaning underlying words that
had initially seemed expressive of revolt. In this sense the poem may
be said to superimpose one reading on top of another and requires
to be read at both levels for its full meaning.

The Collar.

I struck the board, and cry'd, No more.
                    I will abroad.
  What? shall I ever sigh and pine?
My lines and life are free; free as the rode,
  Loose as the winde, as large as store.   5
                  Shall I be still in suit?

Have I no harvest but a thorn
To let me bloud, and not restore
What I have lost with cordiall fruit?
        Sure there was wine   10
Before my sighs did drie it: there was corn
      Before my tears did drown it.
Is the yeare onely lost to me?
      Have I no bayes to crown it?
No flowers, no garlands gay? all blasted?   15
      All wasted?
Not so, my heart: but there is fruit,
      And thou hast hands.
Recover all thy sigh-blown age
On double pleasures: leave thy cold dispute   20
Of what is fit, and not. Forsake thy cage,
      Thy rope of sands,
Which pettie thoughts have made, and made to thee
    Good cable, to enforce and draw,
        And be thy law,   25
  While thou didst wink and wouldst not see.
      Away; take heed:
      I will abroad.
Call in thy deaths head there: tie up thy fears.
      He that forbears   30
    To suit and serve his need,
    Deserves his load.
But as I rav'd and grew more fierce and wilde
    At every word,
Me thoughts I heard one calling, *Child!*   35
    And I reply'd, *My Lord.*

NOTES

Title. The collar was a common seventeenth-century term for discipline; but there is a pun here, with the secondary meaning of *choler* (anger) also present.

1   *board.* May refer to the communion table (Herbert was a priest), or the dining table (recalling the Prodigal Son), or the table in the hall of a noble lord. In this last case the word would recall a master-servant relationship, which is found again later in the word *suit* in line 6.

6   *still in suit.* The word *still* is used in the Elizabethan sense of 'always'.
        The phrase means: Must I be a perpetual suitor? But *suit* being the
        livery of a noble lord worn by his servants, the phrase may also mean:
        Must I continue to be a servant for ever? Either way the suggestion is
        that God is the other partner in this unequal and unsatisfactory rela-
        tionship.

7-8   *Have I...bloud.* Have I been able to produce no harvest but rather
        only thorns that have caused me to bleed? Though the rebellious
        persona is probably not aware, Herbert wants us to recall here
        Christ's bleeding brow crowned with a wreath of thorns.

9   *cordiall fruit.* Cordial means health-giving or restorative. But it also
        connotes something that comes from the heart (Latin *cor* = heart);
        as such, Herbert is using a pun to suggest that the rebellious persona,
        in asking for a restorative drink, thinks he is asking for wine when in
        reality what he is asking for is the true restorative, Christ's blood

10-12   The *corn* and *wine* that the speaker desires represent food and drink,
        but they are also the elements of the Eucharist, bread and wine.

10-18   Vendler says that the speaker's rage is directed not merely against
        God but also against himself for having lived an ascetic life so long
        that now he can no longer enjoy the pleasures of the world. The des-
        peration with which he wants to reclaim them expresses his sense of
        anger with himself at knowing that they will not really please.

21-6   The speaker imagines that all this while he has been living in a prison
        ('cage', line 21) made out of his 'pettie thoughts' (line 23). The same
        thoughts also deceived him ;into thinking that the prison was made
        of strong rods ('good cable', line 24), when in fact it was made of
        easily destructible material ('rope of sands', line 22). The whole
        scheme was engineered by God while the speaker was not paying
        attention (line 26) in order to impose His will and service on the
        speaker. The point of this elaborate image is, first, that God's service
        is an enforced obligation, and second, that man was deceived into
        accepting it.

29   *Death's head* was the skull traditionally placed at a prominent place
        during feasts to remind diners of mortality. The speaker asks for this
        skull to be taken away.

35-6   *Child...Lord.* So immediate is the speaker's recognition of, and re-
        sponse to, God's voice that the nature of his rebellion is shown to
        have been unreal. Note that man addresses God as his master, but
        God sees man as His child.

THE PULLEY

If God is perfect, how could He create man who so obviously is not?
This is the question the poem answers. Herbert suggests that the very

imperfections of man show the perfect plan of God, for by making man restless and incapable of happiness God has ensured that he will always turn to Him. This answer is provided through an imaginative re-telling of the story of Creation. The sources for this poem are both Genesis and the story of Pandora, but Herbert alters them. Genesis describes the physical creation of man; Herbert the psychological. Pandora's story allows man to keep only Hope; Herbert makes God give man everything but rest.

The Pulley.

When God at first made man,
Having a glasse of blessings standing by;
Let us (said he) poure on him all we can:
Let the worlds riches, which dispersed lie,
  Contract into a span.   5

So strength first made a way;
Then beautie flow'd, then wisdome, honour, pleasure;
When almost all was out, God made a stay,
Perceiving that alone of all his treasure
  Rest in the bottome lay.   10

For if I should (said he)
Bestow this jewell also on my creature,
He would adore my gifts in stead of me,
And rest in Nature, not the God of Nature:
  So both should losers be.   15

Yet let him keep the rest,
But keep them with repining restlesnesse:
Let him be rich and wearie, that at least,
If goodnesse leade him not, yet wearinesse
  May tosse him to my breast.   20

NOTES

Title. A pulley is a mechanical contrivance for raising or lifting weights. In the poem man's restlessness serves as the pulley which enables him to be pulled up to heaven.

13-14 If man became all-sufficient he would not need God; at most, he would thank Nature for his existence.

15   *both*. Both man and God. The way man would be a loser is clear. But God would be a loser too, since He loves man and wants man to reciprocate this love freely.

16-17 God's pun on *rest...restlesnesse* has been much admired. However, it is not clear from where *repining* comes into the poem. Restlessness does not necessarily involve repining, and God has said nothing earlier about endowing man with this quality also.

19-20 Herbert's God so loves man that He will use any stratagem to win him over.

THE FLOWER

'The Flower' returns to Herbert's common theme of alienation from God, but with a difference. Using the image of the flower it creates meanings only to repudiate them in favour of other meanings. The presence of a number of meanings, none satisfactory, is itself part of the total meaning of the poem. The first stanza suggests that when harmony is reestablished between man and God, man's memories of the earlier alienation are annihilated. That this view does not satisfy is clear from stanzas 2 and 3; but whereas in the second stanza the alienation is seen as a cyclical natural phenomenon which will end as inevitably as it has occurred, in the third stanza it is seen as intensely painful, the result of the will of a powerful God. In the fourth and fifth stanzas Herbert's depiction of God undergoes a change: instead of blaming Him for averting His face from man the poet acknowledges that God's action is a suitable punishment for man's presumptuousness. In the final stanza Herbert accepts the inadequacy of the foregoing explanations by coming to the realization that both burgeoning and shrivelling are part of human existence decreed not by an arbitrary but by a loving God. The whole poem becomes, thus, an exemplification of the view put forward in stanza 3 that any attempt on man's part to define the human condition is bound to be limited; at the same time, the writing of the poem is evidence that man cannot but make the attempt constantly.

The Flower.

How fresh, O Lord, how sweet and clean
Are thy returns! ev'n as the flowers in spring;

To which, besides their own demean,
The late-past frosts tributes of pleasure bring.
                    Grief melts away   5
                    Like snow in May,
As if there were no such cold thing.

            Who would have thought my shrivel'd heart
Could have recover'd greennesse? It was gone
            Quite under ground; as flowers depart   10
To see their mother-root, when they have blown;
                    Where they together
                    All the hard weather,
Dead to the world, keep house unknown.

            These are thy wonders, Lord of power,   15
Killing and quickning, bringing down to hell
            And up to heaven in an houre;
Making a chiming of a passing-bell.
                    We say amisse,
                    This or that is: 20
Thy word is all, if we could spell.

            O that I once past changing were,
Fast in thy Paradise, where no flower can wither!
            Many a spring I shoot up fair,
Offring at heav'n, growing and groning thither: 25
                    Nor doth my flower
                    Want a spring-showre,
My sinnes and I joining together.

            But while I grow in a straight line,
Still upwards bent, as if heav'n were mine own,   30
            Thy anger comes, and I decline:
What frost to that? what pole is not the zone,
                    Where all things burn,
                    When thou dost turn,
And the least frown of thine is shown?   35

            And now in age I bud again,
After so many deaths I live and write;
            I once more smell the dew and rain,

And relish versing: O my onely light,
         It cannot be   40
         That I am he
On whom thy tempests fell all night.

These are thy wonders, Lord of love,
To make us see we are but flowers that glide:
    Which when we once can finde and prove,   45
Thou hast a garden for us, where to bide.
         Who would be more,
         Swelling through store,
Forfeit their Paradise by their pride.

NOTES

2   *thy returns.* The return of God's grace to man.

3   *demean.* Demeanour or bearing; also, *demesne* or estate. The
        passage means that the beauty of the newly-blossoming Spring flower
        is made up partly of itself and partly of the memory of the past winter.
        But lines 5-8 argue against this meaning, for they suggest that when
        the Spring comes it obliterates all memories of the winter. The
        constant pitting of one meaning against another is characteristic of
        the dialectic of 'The Flower'.

11   *blown.* Finished blooming. The suggestion is that the period when
        Herbert was alienated from God was like winter when the bloom
        fades and the sap of the plant retreats to the root; but the poet's use
        of the image in the stanza suggests a cosy warmth which assorts ill
        with his heart being shrivelled. This is another example of the restless
        jostling of meanings that marks this poem, thus dramatizing the truth
        of the remark in lines 19-20 that any human utterance is of necessity
        going to be less than the whole truth.

16   *down to bell.* Here the grief experienced at being bereft of God's
        grace is neither capable of being forgotten (as in stanza 1) nor seen
        as something possessing its own peculiar comfort (stanza 2) but as the
        painful experience defined in 'Affliction (1)' and 'Deniall'.

18   *chiming....bell.* Converting a death knell into a musical peal of bells.

25   *Offring.* Aiming towards.

27   *want.* Need, lack.

32   *zone.* Torrid zone or the hot equatorial climate.

40-2   The poet finds such a gulf between his present state of grace and his
        previous experience of a lack of it that he cannot believe that he is the
        same person.

43 *Lord of love.* Contrast this with 'Lord of power' in line 15 above.

44 *flowers that glide.* The phrase may refer to the blooming and
    shrivelling of flowers; it may imply, too, that after death human
    beings will be transplanted (glide = move from one place to another)
    into God's never-fading garden (lines 45-46). But flowers that *glide*
    are, properly speaking, not flowers at all, since flowers are incapable
    of moving from place to place. Thus Herbert here also repudiates the
    flower metaphor which he has used throughout the poem.

AARON

Aaron, Moses's brother, is the type of the perfect priest in the Bible
(see Exodus 28 and Hebrews 5: 4). The question that Herbert poses
in this poem is: given man's sinful nature, how can anyone become
a true priest? The answer is that the descent of God's grace into man's
heart leads to a spiritual conversion: the old sinner dies and a new
man is born worthy to preach God's word. The new man is not just
God's mouthpiece but represents rather a full flowering of his own
personality which is, at the same time, in consonance with Christian
doctrine. Each stanza in the poem uses the same five words to end
the lines: head, breast, dead, rest and drest, thereby suggesting that
these are five key words in the composition of the poem. Part of the
success of 'Aaron' lies in the skill with which these words, antici-
pated when they come, also fit so perfectly into the changed context
of each stanza.

Aaron.

      Holinesse on the head,
        Light and perfections on the breast,
Harmonious bells below, raising the dead
      To leade them unto life and rest:
        Thus are true Aarons drest.   5

      Profanenesse in my head,
        Defects and darknesse in my breast,
A noise of passions ringing me for dead
      Unto a place where is no rest:
        Poore priest thus am I drest.   10

>   Onely another head
>   I have, another heart and breast,
>   Another musick, making live not dead,
>   Without whom I could have no rest:
>   In him I am well drest.   15

>   Christ is my onely head,
>   My alone onely heart and breast,
>   My onely musick, striking me ev'n dead;
>   That to the old man I may rest,
>   And be in him new drest.   20

>   So, holy in my head,
>   Perfect and light in my deare breast,
>   My doctrine tun'd by Christ,(who is not dead,
>   But lives in me while I do rest)
>   Come people; Aaron's drest.   25

NOTES

1-5   The description of Aaron derives from that given in Exodus 28.

8-9   Herbert, in contrasting his unworthiness as a priest with Aaron, is particularly conscious of his jangling passions which have the power to convey him to hell.

11-20 The third and fourth stanzas describe sinful man's spiritual transformation. The process does not occur at once, so that for a while Herbert seems to have two heads, two hearts, two breasts (lines 11-12). Once divine grace has taken full possession of him Paul's words become applicable: 'I live, yet not I, but Christ liveth in me' (Galatians, 2:20). The old Adam dies in him and the new man is born. In the excitement of the new birth Herbert maintains that there has been a total extinction of his personality and he has no music but that which God gives him.

21-3 In this stanza Herbert goes beyond the vision of St.Paul by denying what he said in the fourth and suggesting that his spiritual rebirth has not resulted in an extinction of his personality after all. Note the reiteration of *my* in lines 21 and 22 and the view in line 23 that the poet has his own music, though it is tuned by Christ.

25   The poet- priest has become a type of Aaron and invites the congregation to join him in worship.

THE FORERUNNERS

Noticing grey hair on his head, Herbert wonders whether old age will rob him of his poetic powers. Though he is willing to let them go so long as he has the ability left to acknowledge God in the simplest of language, his loving description of his creative ability shows the regret he must have felt at the thought that one day he might lose the power of writing poetry.

The Forerunners.

The harbingers are come. See, see their mark:
White is their colour, and behold my head.
But must they have my brain? must they dispark
Those sparkling notions, which therein were bred?
      Must dulnesse turn me to a clod?
Yet have they left me, *Thou art still my God.*

Good men ye be, to leave me my best room,
Ev'n all my heart, and what is lodged there:
I passe not, I, what of the rest become,
So *Thou art still my God,* be out of fear.   10
      He will be pleased with that dittie;
And if I please him, I write fine and wittie.

Farewell sweet phrases, lovely metaphors.
But will ye leave me thus? when ye before
Of stews and brothels onely knew the doores,   15
Then did I wash you with my tears, and more,
      Brought you to Church well drest and clad
My God must have my best, ev'n all I had.

Lovely enchanting language, sugar-cane,
Hony of roses, whither wilt thou flie?   20
Hath some fond lover tic'd thee to thy bane?
And wilt thou leave the Church, and love a stie?
      Fie, thou wilt soil thy broider'd coat,
And hurt thy self, and him that sings the note.

Let foolish lovers, if they will love dung,   25
With canvas, not with arras, clothe their shame:
Let follie speak in her own native tongue.
True beautie dwells on high: ours is a flame
    But borrow'd thence to light us thither.
Beautie and beauteous words should go together.   30

Yet if you go, I passe not; take your way:
For, *Thou art still my God* is all that ye
Perhaps with more embellishment can say.
Go birds of spring: let winter have his fee;
    Let a bleak palenesse chalk the doore,   35
So all within be livelier then before.

NOTES

1   *barbingers.* 'Harbingers were sent in advance of a royal progress to purvey lodgings by chalking the doors' (Hutchinson). Death's harbingers or forerunners have begun to mark Herbert's hair with white.

3-4 *dispark...notions.* Hutchinson points out that *dispark* means *disimpark* or turn out of a park; however, as Rickey says, the word also puns on *sparkling* in line 4.

6   *Thou art still my God.* An almost verbatim quotation from Psalms, 31: 14.

7   *ye.* i.e. the harbingers.

9   *I passe not.* I don't care.

10   So long as I have the ability to acknowledge God, I am not afraid.

14   Whereas in the first stanza Herbert claimed that his poetic faculties were being forcibly evicted from his brain, here he says that they are forsaking him willingly. The line is a quotation from Thomas Wyatt.

15-18 Herbert claims that he was the first to use language for religious poetry; previously it had been used only for love poetry.

19-30 There is great poignancy in Herbert's apostrophe to the language of poetry as he contemplates the possibility that in old age he might lose his mastery of it. He addresses it as if it were a beloved mistress who is being enticed away by another man with whom her future is sure to be one of degradation.

33   *embellishment.* Is there any bitterness in Herbert's dismissal of poetic language as mere embellishment?

34-5 Winter being associated with old age, its mention here is appropriate. *Bleak palenesse* in line 35 goes with winter, but the metaphor of *chalking* the door (as with snow) takes us back to the first line of the poem. See note on line 1 above.

DISCIPLINE

The poem asks God to replace His wrath by love since the latter is a more potent weapon. At the same time the poet says that he wants of his own free will to subjugate his will completely to God (lines 7-8). Vendler sees the speaker's tone as light and bantering, that of a favoured child addressing an indulgent parent; but it may also be regarded as arising from a total stripping away of all embellishments in favour of the most direct form of utterance, the result of a strenuous self-imposed discipline.

Discipline.

Throw away thy rod,
Throw away thy wrath:
     O my God,
Take the gentle path.

For my hearts desire   5
Unto thine is bent:
     I aspire
To a full consent.

Not a word or look
I affect to own,   10
     But by book.
And thy book alone.

Though I fail, I weep:
Though I halt in pace,
     Yet I creep   15
To the throne of grace.

Then let wrath remove;
Love will do the deed:
      For with love
Stonie hearts will bleed.   20

Love is swift of foot;
Love's a man of warre,
      And can shoot,
And can hit from farre.

Who can scape his bow?   25
That which wrought on thee,
      Brought thee low,
Needs must work on me.

Throw away thy rod;
Though man frailties hath,   30
      Thou art God:
Throw away thy wrath.

NOTES

22   *man of warre*. A battleship. The reference is to Exodus 15: 3, where
       Moses uses this term to describe God. Herbert suggests that ironically
       love may be a more powerful weapon than God's wrath.
25   In classical mythology Cupid, the god of love, is armed with a bow.
       Christ has here been turned into a divine Cupid.
27-28 Love proved too powerful even for God, for it caused Him to
       incarnate Himself as man. *Brought thee low* suggests that God was
       humbled, but Herbert is also referring to Christ's descent to earth
       and subsequent death on the cross.
30-31 Vendler explains these lines: '*Man* has frailties but *thou* art God, and
       need not succumb to a frailty, even a godlike one like anger—
       therefore throw away thy wrath'.

DEATH

This poem should be compared with Donne's 'Death be not proud'.
Herbert makes a distinction between death as it was before Christ
and as it is now. Then it was hideous and ugly, but after Christ's

redemption of man it has become a desirable and cheerful prospect, no different from sleep.

Death.

Death, thou wast once an uncouth hideous thing,
        Nothing but bones,
    The sad effect of sadder grones:
Thy mouth was open, but thou couldst not sing.
For we consider'd thee as at some six   5
        Or ten yeares hence,
    After the losse of life and sense,
Flesh being turn'd to dust, and bones to sticks.
We lookt on this side of thee, shooting short;
        Where we did finde   10
    The shells of fledge souls left behinde,
Dry dust, which sheds no tears, but may extort.
But since our Saviours death did put some bloud
        Into thy face;
    Thou art grown fair and full of grace,   15
Much in request, much sought for as a good.
For we do now behold thee gay and glad,
        As at dooms-day;
    When souls shall wear their new aray,
And all thy bones with beautie shall be clad.   20
Therefore we can go die as sleep, and trust
        Half that we have
    Unto an honest faithfull grave;
Making our pillows either down, or dust.

NOTES

5-8   i.e. we thought of you in terms of the corpse that has been rotting in the grave for some half dozen or ten years.

9   i.e. our view of you fell short of the mark.

11   The image is that of the chrysalis after the buttterfly has emerged. We thought of death as the empty shell left behind by the soul which has fled.

19-20 The poet thinks that on the Day of Judgement not only will the dead
       souls rise again new-clothed in their bodies but death also will be
       beautified and joy in the event.
24   Death being no different now from sleep, it does not matter whether
       we lay our heads down on dust (that is, die) or on downy pillows.

LOVE (III)

This poem, which ends *The Temple,* has been much commented on.
It describes the reception of the redeemed soul in heaven, and
recalls the communicant partaking of the Eucharist, Christ washing
the feet of his disciples and serving them at the Last Supper (John 13:
12-16), and , as Martz reminds us, the admission of the redeemed to
the 'marriage supper' (Revelation 19:9). Vendler points to another
source, Luke 12:37: 'Blessed are those servants, whom the lord when
he cometh shall find watching: verily I say unto you, that he shall gird
himself, and make them to sit down to meat, and will come forth and
serve them'. She adds that the poem can be seen as a contest in
courtesy between man and God such as was common in medieval
poetry. A study of the sources barely accounts for the power of a
poem which shows Christ in a benign, smiling aspect. Herbert's God,
we have seen, can be baffling and wrathful, but He is also full of wit,
good humour and solicitousness. As the poem progresses the speaker,
from being gauche and uncomfortable, begins to feel more at home
till all distance between him and God is annihilated.

Love (III)

Love bade me welcome: yet my soul drew back
       Guiltie of dust and sinne.
But quick-ey'd Love, observing me grow slack
       From my first entrance in,
Drew nearer to me, sweetly questioning,   5
       If I lack'd any thing.

A guest, I answer'd, worthy to be here:
       Love said, You shall be he .
I the unkinde, ungratefull? Ah my deare,
       I cannot look on thee.   10

Love took my hand, and smiling did reply,
  Who made the eyes but I?

Truth Lord, but I have marr'd them: let my shame
  Go where it doth deserve.
And know you not, sayes Love, who bore the blame?   15
  My deare, then I will serve.
You must sit down, sayes Love, and taste my meat:
  So I did sit and eat.

NOTES

10   Cf. Exodus 33: 20: 'Thou canst not see my [God's] face: for there shall
      no man see me, and live'.
17   *meat*. Food.

RICHARD CRASHAW

Richard Crashaw (1612?- 1649) was the son of a Puritan preacher. His mother having died when he was a young boy, and his stepmother (for his father remarried) when he was eight, he was brought up by his father. Crashaw was educated at the Charterhouse and entered Pembroke College, Cambridge in 1631. 1634, when he took his B.A., also saw the appearance of his *Epigrammata Sacra,* a collection of Greek and Latin epigrams including some written while he was still at school. By this date he seems to have switched from the Puritan faith of his father to High Anglicanism. The following year he was elected to a Fellowship at Peterhouse, the most High Church of all Cambridge colleges. He was ordained shortly thereafter and appointed Curate of Little St. Mary's Church, next door to Peterhouse. He also became a frequent visitor to the community at Little Gidding. His happy years at Cambridge came to an end in 1643 when, fearing that the Puritans would eject him from his position owing to his High Church views, he fled to Holland. He returned to Oxford the following year and entered service with Queen Henrietta Maria who, with her husband Charles I, had set up court there. But she went to the Continent shortly thereafter and Crashaw followed suit. There he spent some time in Paris, where Abraham Cowley befriended him, converted to Roman Catholicism, became a friend of the Countess of Denbigh, and eventually obtained an introduction to the Pope from Henrietta Maria. But when Crashaw went to Rome he found the Vatican to be indifferent to him. Finally in 1647 he obtained a post under Cardinal Palotto, and in 1649 the Cardinal appointed him to a vacancy in Loretto, where he died shortly after his arrival.

While at Cambridge Crashaw published several poems in magazines besides *Epigrammata Sacra.* When fleeing England he entrusted a manuscript of poems to an unknown friend in Lincolnshire who arranged its publication. This work, consisting of religious and secular poems, was divided into two corresponding parts and published as *Steps to the Temple. Sacred Poems, with other Delights of the Muses* in 1646. In 1648, for the second edition, Crashaw revised a number of poems and added some more. In 1652 *Carmen Deo Nostro* appeared posthumously in Paris. It drew on the work published in the 1646 and 1648 editions but quite a few of the old poems appeared here in considerably revised and expanded form. It also included new poems being published for the first time. All the above volumes, together with a number of manuscripts, were used by L.C. Martin in preparing his monumental edition of *The Poems of Richard Crashaw* (2nd. ed. 1957). The present text is taken from Martin's edition. I have not modernized the spelling, but it should pose few problems once it is realized that *v* was written as *u* except when beginning words, and *j* as *i*.

Crashaw was a constant reviser of his work, with the result that in the case of some poems more than one version exists. Thus the 1646 and 1652 versions of 'The Weeper' are so different as almost to be two poems. In recognition of this fact Martin prints both versions. Of course all poets revise their work, but in Crashaw's case the constant revisions and additions cause the poems to keep evolving, changing their form and never quite stabilizing. This fluidity of form is a characteristic of much baroque poetry. But it poses a dilemma to the anthologizer who has to decide which of the versions of a given poem he should include in his anthology. My own choice has been to include the version found in the *Carmen Deo Nostro* (1652) as representing the poet's final revisions, though the text presents some corruptions owing to its having been printed in a foreign country after the poet's death.

A word needs to be said about the religious content of Crashaw's work. Though Donne and Herbert require some knowledge of the Bible to be understood, their works speak so directly to our religious sensibilities that they can be enjoyed by people with little grounding in Christian theology. Crashaw requires more knowledge of Christianity on the reader's part. But that should not make it impossible for non-Christian readers to respond to him. Indeed, with the help of the annotations provided here Indian readers may be better able to appreciate Crashaw than many others. Baroque embellishments and the emblematic quality of his images will not appear foreign to audiences familiar with the icons of Indian religions. His emphasis on celebratory ritual will be immediately accessible to those brought up on the tradition of communal worship. His use of humour in religious worship is not alien to many branches of Hinduism. The Muslim, the Sikh, the Hindu–all will have an instinctive understanding of Crashaw's mystical insights. Their religious traditions also provide many similarities to the meditative techniques that he exploits in his poetry.

THE WEEPER

Crashaw has at least a dozen poems in which Mary Magdalen figures, of which the present is the best known. On Crashaw's fascination with Mary Magdalen, see the general introduction to this book. Much adverse criticism has been directed against some of the hyperbolical images in this poem which may have come from the example of Marino, and against its seeming lack of structure. However, the poem is not formless. Marc Bertonasco sees it as modelled on the structure of meditation recommended by St. Francis de Sales. The whole can be read as an attempt to understand, by means of a variety of images, the epigram with which it opens. The paradoxes of the poem celebrate three theologically interrelated ideas: those of the penitent sinner, of God's love which turns this penitence into a beautiful thing, and the Catholic belief that the forgiveness of a sinner has beneficial consequences for the whole of humanity.

Sainte
Mary
Magdalene
or
The Weeper.

Loe where a WOVNDED HEART with Bleeding EYES conspire.
Is she a FLAMING Fountain, or a Weeping fire!

THE
WEEPER

I.

Hail, sister springs!
Parents of syluer-footed rills!
    Euer bubling things!

Thawing crystall! snowy hills,
Still spending, neuer spent! I mean
Thy fair eyes, sweet MAGDALENE!

II.

Heauens thy fair eyes be;
Heauens of euer-falling starres.
'Tis seed-time still with thee
And starres thou sow'st, whose haruest dares   10
Promise the earth to counter shine
Whateuer makes heaun's forhead fine.

III.

But we'are deceiued all.
Starres indeed they are too true;
For they but seem to fall,
As Heaun's other spangles doe.
It is not for our earth & vs
To shine in Things so pretious.

IV.

Vpwards thou dost weep.
Heaun's bosome drinks the gentle stream.   20
Where th'milky riuers creep,
Thine floates aboue; & is the cream.
Waters aboue th'Heauns, what they be
We'are taught best by thy TEARES & thee.

V.

Euery morn from hence
A brisk Cherub somthing sippes
Whose sacred influence
Addes sweetnes to his sweetest Lippes.
Then to his musick. And his song
Tasts of this Breakfast all day long.   30

VI.

Not in the euening's eyes
When they Red with weeping are
For the Sun that dyes,
Sitts sorrow with a face so fair,
No where but here did euer meet
Sweetnesse so sad, sadnesse so sweet.

VII.

When sorrow would be seen
In her brightest majesty
(For she is a Queen)
Then is she drest by none but thee.   40
Then, & only then, she weares
Her proudest pearles; I mean, thy TEARES.

VIII.

The deaw no more will weep
The primrose's pale cheek to deck,
The deaw no more will sleep
Nuzzel'd in the lilly's neck;
Much reather would it be thy TEAR,
And leaue them Both to tremble here.

IX.

There's no need at all
That the balsom-sweating bough   50
So coyly should let fall
His med'cinable teares; for now
Nature hath learn't to'extract a deaw
More soueraign & sweet from you.

X.

Yet let the poore drops weep
(Weeping is the ease of woe)

Softly let them creep,
Sad that they are vanquish't so.
They, though to others no releife,
Balsom maybe, for their own greife.   60

XI.

Such the maiden gemme
By the purpling vine put on,
Peeps from her parent stemme
And blushes at the bridegroome sun.
This watry Blossom of thy eyn,
Ripe, will make the richer wine.

XII.

When some new bright Guest
Takes vp among the starres a room,
And heaun will make a feast,
Angels with crystall violls come   70
And draw from these full eyes of thine
Their master's Water· their own Wine.

XIII.

Golden though he be,
Golden Tagus murmures tho;
Were his way by thee,
Content & quiet he would goe.
So much more rich would he esteem
Thy syluer, then his golden stream.

XIV.

Well does the May that lyes
Smiling in thy cheeks, confesse   80
The April in thine eyes.
Mutuall sweetness they expresse.
No April ere lent kinder showres,
Nor May return'd more faithfull flowres.

XV.

O cheeks! Bedds of chast loues
By your own showres seasonably dash't
Eyes! nests of milky doues
In your own wells decently washt,
O wit of loue! that thus could place
Fountain & Garden in one face.   90

XVI.

O sweet Contest; of woes
With loues, of teares with smiles disputing!
O fair, & Freindly Foes,
Each other kissing & confuting!
While rain & sunshine, Cheekes & Eyes
Close in kind contrarietyes.

XVII.

But can these fair Flouds be
Freinds with the bosom fires that fill thee
Can so great flames agree
Aeternall Teares should thus distill thee!   100
O flouds, o fires! o suns o showres!
Mixt & made freinds by loue's sweet powres.

XVIII.

Twas his well-pointed dart
That digg'd these wells,& drest this Vine;
And taught the wounded HEART
The way into these weeping Eyn.
Vain loues auant! bold hands forbear!
The lamb hath dipp't his white foot here.

XIX.

And now where're he strayes,
Among the Galilean mountaines,   110

Or more vnwellcome wayes,
He's follow'd by two faithfull fountaines;
Two walking baths; two weeping motions;
Portable, & compendious oceans.

XX.

O Thou, thy lord's fair store!
In thy so rich & rare expenses,
Euen when he show'd most poor,
He might prouoke the wealth of Princes.
What Prince's wanton'st pride e're could
Wash with Syluer, wipe with Gold.   120

XXI.

Who is that King, but he
Who calls't his Crown to be call'd thine,
That thus can boast to be
Waited on by a wandring mine,
A voluntary mint, that strowes
Warm syluer shoures where're he goes!

XXII.

O pretious Prodigall!
Fair spend-thrift of thy self! thy measure
(Mercilesse loue!) is all.
Euen to the last Pearle in thy treasure.   130
All places, Times,& obiects be
Thy teare's sweet opportunity.

XXIII.

Does the day-starre rise?
Still thy starres doe fall & fall
Does day close his eyes?
Still the FOVNTAIN weeps for all.
Let night or day doe what they will,
Thou hast thy task; thou weepest still.

XXIV.

Does thy song lull the air?
Thy falling teares keep faith full time.   140
Does thy sweet-breath'd praire
Vp in clouds of incense climb?
Still at each sigh, that is, each stop,
A bead, that is, A TEAR, does drop.

XXV.

At these thy weeping gates,
(Watching their watry motion)
Each winged moment waits,
Takes his TEAR, & gets him gone.
By thine Ey's tinct enobled thus
Time layes him vp; he's pretious.   150

XXVI.

Not, so long she liued,
Shall thy tomb report of thee;
But, so long she greiued,
Thus must we date thy memory.
Others by moments, months,& yeares
Measure their ages; thou, by TEARES.

XXVII.

So doe perfumes expire.
So sigh tormented sweets, opprest
With proud vnpittying fire.   160
Such Teares the suffring Rose that's vext
With vngentle flames does shed,
Sweating in a too warm bed.

XXVIII.

Say, ye bright brothers,
The fugitiue sons of those fair Eyes

Your fruitfull mothers!
What make you here? What hopes can tice
You to be born? what cause can borrow
You from Those nests of noble sorrow?

XXIX.

Whither away so fast?
For sure the sordid earth   170
Your Sweetnes cannot tast
Nor does the dust deserue your birth.
Sweet, whither hast you then? o say
Why you trip so fast away?

XXX.

We goe not to seek,
The darlings of Auroras bed,
The rose's modest Cheek
Nor the violet's humble head.
Though the Feild's eyes too WEEPERS be
Because they want such TEARES as we.   180

XXXI.

Much lesse mean we to trace
The Fortune of inferior gemmes,
Preferr'd to some proud face
Or pertch't vpon fear'd Diadems.
Crown'd Heads are toyes.We goe to meet
A worthy object, our lord's FEET.

NOTES

1,3   *springs/bubling.* Cf. Psalm 119:136: 'Rivers of water run down mine
       eyes, because they keep not thy law'.
4   The comparison of the weeping eyes to crystal (a hard, solid sub-
       stance) and frozen hills suggests the warmth of Magdalen's passion
       which causes these substances to melt.
12   *counter shine.* Outline.

13-18	i.e. the tears do not actually fall to the ground (for the reason explained in the following stanza). For them to do so would be tantamount to the earth coming in possession of things as precious as those possessed by heaven.
21	*milky riuers*. The Milky Way, regarded as a pathway to heaven.
23	*Waters aboue th' Heauns*. Cf. Genesis 1:7: 'God...divided the waters which were under the firmament from the waters which were above the firmament...' Also Psalms 148:4: '[the] waters that be above the heavens...'
25-30	Note the childlike humour here, a characteristic of the baroque.
43	*deaw*. Dew.
50-2	Balsam is an aromatic resin extracted from trees and used in medicines.
61-6	The tears are compared to the grape peeping from the vine. Crashaw's conceit is that Magdalen's tears will make better wine than the grape. The play upon wine and water in this and the next stanza recalls Christ's miracle in turning water into wine at the marriage feast at Cana (John 2:1-11).
70	Cf. Donne, 'Twicknam Garden': 'Hither, with cristal vials, lovers come,/And take my tears, which are love's wine'.
74	*Tagus*. A river in Spain, famous for its golden sands.
78	*then*. Than.
79-81	*May/April*. April is a rainy month in England, May represents the Spring.
89	*wit of loue!* See Hymn on 'The Name of Jesus', line 223 and note.
98	*bosom fires*. The fires of penitence that rage in Magdalen's breast and cause the outpouring of tears.
103	Christ is here compared to Cupid.
108	*lamb*. A sacrificial animal, and hence Christ.
110	*Galilean mountaines*. Galilee is the area where Christ lived and preached.
112-14	The images have been criticized as hyperbolical and absurd, but Martin cites many Latin and English analogues from contemporary literature. See also Jeremiah 9:1: 'Oh that...mine eyes [were] a fountain of tears.'
115-16	Magdalen is God's treasury ('store') wherein are stored rich, rare and expensive treasures.
118	*provoke*. Call forth.
121-2	Crashaw implies here that God has accepted Magdalen's penitence and decreed that His crown will henceforth be hers also.
140	*faith full*. Faithful.
140,143	*time, stop*. Technical terms from music.
141	*praire*. Prayer.
143-4	Magdalen's tears are here compared to the beads in a rosary.

160-2   Roses were said to sweat or yield their moisture when burnt in order to extract their essence. For Crashaw they weep. The heat of the till thus becomes, metaphorically, the heat of Magdalen's penitent suffering.

166   *tice*. Entice.

176   *Aurora*. The goddess of the dawn. The flowering of the rose and the violet in early morning suggests the image of these flowers being the darlings of Aurora's bed.

180   *want*. Lack.

181-4   Magdalen's tears say that least of all do they want to imitate ('trace') the fate of ordinary gems which have been chosen ('Preferr'd') to adorn the faces of proud women or the crown of dreaded kings.

186.   Cf. the ending of Marvell's 'The Coronet'.

ON MR. G. HERBERTS BOOKE INTITULED THE TEMPLE OF SACRED POEMS, SENT TO A GENTLEWOMAN

This poem is illustrative of Crashaw's interest in Herbert, whose imagery is recalled in the homely way of imagining angels. We also see Crashaw combining devotional sentiments with the gallantry of the courtier. Therefore his use of the tetrameter, common with Cavalier poets such as Thomas Carew, is appropriate.

On Mr. G. Herberts *booke intituled the Temple of Sacred Poems, sent to a Gentlewoman.*

Know you faire, on what you looke;
Divinest love lyes in this booke:
Expecting fire from your eyes,
To kindle this his sacrifice.
When your hands unty these strings,
Thinke you have an Angell by th' wings.
One that gladly will bee nigh,
To wait upon each morning sigh.
To flutter in the balmy aire,
Of your well perfumed prayer.   10
These white plumes of his heele lend you,
Which every day to heaven will send you:
To take acquaintance of the spheare,

And all the smooth faced kindred there.
And though *Herberts* name doe owe
These devotions, fairest; know
That while I lay them on the shrine
Of your white hand, they are mine.

NOTES

3-4   This conventional image comes from the Roman practice of offering
      burnt sacrifices. Herbert's book is the sacrifice which will be kindled
      by the fire of the mistress' eyes.
11   *beele*. He will.
13-14 *the spheare...there*. i.e. heaven and all its angelic inhabitants.

A HYMN TO THE NAME AND HONOR OF THE
ADMIRABLE SAINTE TERESA

St. Teresa's autobiography was translated into English under the title
The Flaming Heart in 1642. She describes a vision in which an angel,
diminutive but perfectly formed, pierced her heart with a spear
tipped with fire, causing her extreme agony which was also so
intensely pleasurable that she did not wish the experience to end.
The wound provided an entryway for God's love into her heart. This
passage became a favourite with baroque artists for its combination
of the sexual with the spiritual and forms the basis of the present
poem. Crashaw, in seeking to celebrate Teresa's vision, starts with
the conceit of Teresa as a young child wishing for martyrdom.
However, it is her fate not to experience a martyr's death or that of
a Christian who is killed on account of his faith, but to experience a
mystical death and thus be a martyr to God's love. Struck by the
agony of love, she will die many pleasing deaths while alive in order
to inherit the martyr's crown after she goes to heaven. In describing
the young child's ambition the poet adopts a playful tone, not
condescending but tender and truly childlike, and emphasizes the
humour of the situation through skipping tetrameters. Then the style
changes to one more suited to an evocation of mystical rapture as he
moves to an account of Teresa as a grown woman. This leads to the
third part of the poem where her reception in heaven is described.
The poem ends on a note of calm emphasized by the final epigram-
matic couplet.

A HYMN
TO
THE NAME AND HONOR
OF
THE ADMIRABLE
SAINTE
TERESA,
FOVNDRESSE
of the Reformation of the Discalced
CARMELITES, both
men & Women;
A
WOMAN
for Angelicall heigh of speculation, for
Masculine courage of performance,
more then a woman.
WHO
Yet a child, out ran maturity, and
durst plott a Martyrdome;

The Hymne.

Loue, thou art Absolute sole lord
Of LIFE & DEATH. To proue the word,
Wee'l now appeal to none of all
Those thy old Souldiers, Great & tall,
Ripe Men of Martyrdom, that could reach down
With strong armes, their triumphant crown;
Such as could with lusty breath
Speak lowd into the face of death
Their Great LORD's glorious name, to none
Of those whose spatious Bosomes spread a throne   10
For LOVE at larg to fill: spare blood & sweat;
And see him take a priuate seat,
Making his mansion in the mild
And milky soul of a soft child.
  Scarse has she learn't to lisp the name
Of Martyr; yet she thinks it shame
Life should so long play with that breath
Which spent can buy so braue a death.

She neuer vndertook to know
What death with loue should haue to doe;   20
Nor has she e're yet vnderstood
Why to show loue, she should shed blood
Yet though she cannot tell you why,
She can LOVE, & she can DY.
    Scarse has she Blood enough to make
A guilty sword blush for her sake;
Yet has she'a HEART dares hope to proue
How much lesse strong is DEATH then LOVE.
    Be loue but there; let poor six yeares
Be pos'd with the maturest yeares   30
Man trembles at, you straight shall find
Love knowes no nonage, nor the LIND.
'Tis LOVE, not YEARES or LIMBS that can
Make the Martyr, or the man.
    LOVE toucht her HEART, & lo it beates
High, & burnes with such braue heates;
Such thirsts to dy, as dares drink vp,
A thousand cold deaths in one cup.
Good reason. For she breathes All fire.
Her weake brest heaues with strong desire   40
Of what she may with fruitles wishes
Seek for amongst her MOTHER'S kisses:
    Since 'tis not to be had at home
She'l trauail to a Martyrdom.
No home for hers confesses she
But where she may a Martyr be.
    Sh'el to the Moores; And trade with them,
For this vnualued Diadem.
She'l offer them her dearest Breath,
With CHRIST'S Name in't, in change for death.   50
Sh'el bargain with them; & will giue
Them God; teach them how to liue
In him: or, if they this deny,
For him she'l teach them how to DY.
So shall she leaue amongst them sown
 Her LORD'S Blood; or at lest her own.
    FAREWEL then, all the world! Adieu.
TERESA is no more for you.
Farewell, all pleasures, sports, & ioyes,
(Neuer till now esteemed toyes)   60

Farewell what ever deare may bee,
MOTHER'S armes or FATHER'S knee
Farewell house, & farewell home !
SHE'S for the Moores, & MARTYRDOM.
   SWEET, not so fast ! lo thy fair Spouse
Whom thou seekst with so swift vowes,
Calls thee back, & bidds thee come
T'embrace a milder MARTYRDOM.
   Blest powres forbid, Thy tender life
Should bleed vpon a barborous knife;   70
Or some base hand haue power to race
Thy Brest's chast cabinet, & vncase
A soul kept there so sweet, o no;
Wise heaun will neuer haue it so
THOV art love's victime; & must dy
A death more mysticall & high.
Into loue's armes thou shalt let fall
A still-suruiuing funerall.
His is the DART must make the DEATH
Whose stroke shall tast thy hallow'd breath;   80
A Dart thrice dip't in that rich flame
Which writes thy spouse's radiant Name
Vpon the roof of Heau'n; where ay
It shines, & with a soueraign ray
Beates bright vpon the burning faces
Of soules which in that name's sweet graces
Find euerlasting smiles. So rare,
So spirituall, pure, & fair
Must be th'immortall instrument
Vpon whose choice point shall be sent   90
A life so lou'd; And that there be
Fitt executioners for Thee,
The fair'st & first-born sons of fire
Blest SERAPHIM, shall leaue their quire
And turn loue's souldiers, vpon THEE
To exercise their archerie.
   O how oft shalt thou complain
Of a sweet & subtle PAIN.
Of intolerable IOYES;
Of a DEATH, in which who dyes   100
Loues his death, and dyes again.
And would for euer so be slain.

And liues, & dyes; and knowes not why
To liue, But that he thus may neuer leaue to DY.
    How kindly will thy gentle HEART
Kisse the sweetly-killing DART!
And close in his embraces keep
Those delicious Wounds, that weep
Balsom to heal themselues with. Thus
When these thy DEATHS, so numerous,   110
Shall all at last dy into one,
And melt thy Soul's sweet mansion;
Like a soft lump of incense, hasted
By too hott a fire, & wasted
Into perfuming clouds, so fast
Shalt thou exhale to Heaun at last
In a resoluing SIGH, and then
O what? Ask not the Tongues of men.
Angells cannot tell, suffice,
Thy selfe shall feel thine own full ioyes   120
And hold them fast for euer. There
So soon as thou shalt first appear,
The MOON of maiden starrs, thy white
MISTRESSE, attended by such bright
Solues as thy shining self, shall come
And in her first rankes make thee room;
Where 'mongst her snowy family
Immortall wellcomes wait for thee.
    O what delight, when reueal'd LIFE shall stand
And teach thy lipps heau'n with his hand;   130
On which thou now maist to thy wishes
Heap vp thy consecrated kisses.
What ioyes shall seize thy soul, when she
Bending her blessed eyes on thee
(Those second Smiles of Heau'n) shall dart
Her mild rayes through thy melting heart!
    Angels, thy old freinds, there shall greet thee
Glad at their own home now to meet thee.
    All thy good WORKES which went before
And waited for thee, at the door,   140
Shall own thee there; and all in one
Weaue a constellation

Of CROWNS, with which the KING thy spouse
Shall build vp thy triumphant browes.
    All thy old woes shall now smile on thee
And thy paines sitt bright vpon thee
All thy sorrows here shall shine,
All thy SVFFRINGS be diuine.
TEARES shall take comfort, & turn gemms
And WRONGS repent to Diademms.   150
Eu'n thy DEATHS shall liue; & new
Dresse the soul that erst they slew.
Thy wounds shall blush to such bright scarres
As keep account of the LAMB's warres.
    Those rare WORKES where thou shalt leaue writt,
Loue's noble history, with witt
Taught thee by none but him, while here
They feed our soules, shall cloth THINE there.
Each heaunly word by whose hid flame
Our hard Hearts shall strike fire, the same   160
Shall flourish on thy browes, & be
Both fire to vs & flame to thee;
Whose light shall liue bright in thy FACE
By glory, in our hearts by grace.
    Thou shalt look round about, & see
Thousands of crown'd Soules throng to be
Themselues thy crown. Sons of thy vowes
The virgin-births with which thy soueraign spouse
Made fruitfull thy fair soul, goe now
And with them all about thee bow   170
To Him, put on (hee'I say) put on
(My rosy loue) That thy rich zone
Sparkling with the sacred flames
Of thousand soules, whose happy names
Heau'n keeps vpon thy score. (Thy bright
Life brought them first to kisse the light
That kindled them to starrs.) and so
Thou with the LAMB, thy lord, shalt goe;
And whereso'ere he setts his white
Stepps, walk with HIM those wayes of light   180
Which who in death would liue to see,
Must learn in life to dy like thee.

NOTES

4	*thy old Souldiers.* The other martyrs, representative of the Church Militant.
6	*crown.* Crown of martyrs.
10	i.e. their bosoms were large enough to serve as thrones for Love.
25-6	i.e. she has barely enough blood in her body to turn red the sword by which she would like to be slain.
30	*pos'd.* Balanced, compared.
32	i.e. love is always mature; it never experiences a state of childhood ('nonage').
47	*Sh'el.* She will.
48	*vnualued.* Unvalued, i.e. priceless.
71	*race.* Raze, despoil.
77-8	i.e. you will experience the living death of love.
79	Christ is here seen as a kind of divine Cupid.
90	*sent.* Executed.
99	*IOYES.* Joys.
108-9	i.e. the tears that the wounds cause are medicinal and cure the wounds.
112-17	The physical death of Teresa is compared to the melting of a lump of incense in the fire. In the poem's context the fire is not only death but also the fire of her passion for God.
118	ff. The reception of the virtuous soul in heaven was a common theme of baroque art.
123, 24	*MOON, MISTRESSE.* Virgin Mary.
129	*reueal'd LIFE.* Revealed Life, i.e. Christ.
133, 34	*she, her.* Either Virgin Mary, or more likely, a misprint for 'he', i.e. Christ.
139	*good WORKES.* The Catholics emphasized Justification by Works, as opposed to the Protestants who emphasized Justification by Faith.
143	*the KING thy spouse.* Christ, who is the true husband of Teresa. The idea that Christ is the spouse of the soul (or of the Church) is a common Christian idea.
148	*SVFFRINGS be diuine.* Sufferings be divine.
149-50	i.e. the tears that you wept when alive will turn into gems for your ornamentation, and the wrongs that you suffered will be expiated and be converted into crowns for you.
153-4	i.e. the wounds which the dart of love inflicted on you when you were alive will now shine brightly like the wounds of Christ on the cross. The Lamb is Christ.
155	*Those rare WORKES.* Your books.
163-4	Your books will shed glory on you in heaven, even as they bring grace into our lives here on earth.

167-9   Just as Mary, a virgin, bore Christ, so also the virgin Teresa, impreg-
         nated by the spirit of God, has given birth to many 'children'. The
         progeny consists of all the souls she has either converted to Christ
         through her books or influenced. These souls ('Sons of thy vowes'
         in line 167) will form the crown which Christ will put upon her
         head (lines 171-2).
171 ff. Christ's address to Teresa echoes the language of the love poetry
         of the Song of Songs. R.V. Young sees the poem as a sacred parody
         where Petrarchan conceits are used for religious purposes.

THE FLAMING HEART

Martz has argued that this poem refers to a painting by Gerhard
Seghers (1591-1651) entitled 'St. Teresa in Ecstasy' which now hangs
in a museum in Antwerp and that Crashaw saw it or a copy when in
Holland. Many of the poem's otherwise incomprehensible details
become clear when the poem is seen as a commentary on this
painting. 'The Flaming Heart' falls into three sections. In the first
(lines 1-58) the painter is criticized in a good-natured way and many
improvements in the painting are suggested through witty para-
doxes. In the second (lines 59-84) the nature of Teresa's impact on
other readers is described. In the final part the poet asks to share her
ecstasy of love's martyrdom. Crashaw's paradoxes and conceits in
this poem form an instructive contrast with Donne's. While the latter
uses them to explore a problem, Crashaw uses them as elaborations
on a basic theme. They enable him to look at the theme from a variety
of points of view and to celebrate it.

                              THE
                        FLAMING HEART
                      VPON THE BOOK AND
                    Picture of the seraphicall saint
                            TERESA,
            (As She Vsvally Expressed with a Seraphim biside her.)

Well meaning readers! you that come as freinds
And catch the pretious name this peice pretends;
Make not too much hast to' admire

That fair-cheek't fallacy of fire.
That is a SERAPHIM, they say
And this the great TERESIA.
Readers, be rul'd by me; & make
Here a well-plac't & wise mistake
You must transpose the picture quite,
And spell it wrong to read it right;   10
Read HIM for her, & her for him;
And call the SAINT the SERAPHIM.
    Painter, what didst thou vnderstand
To put her dart into his hand!
See, euen the yeares & size of him
Showes this the mother SERAPHIM.
This is the mistresse flame; & duteous he
Her happy fire-works, here, comes down to see.
O most poor-spirited of men!
Had thy cold Pencil kist her PEN   20
Thou couldst not so vnkindly err
To show vs This faint shade for HER
Why man, this speakes pure mortall frame;
And mockes with female FROST Loue's manly flame.
One would suspect thou meant'st to paint
Some weak, inferiour, woman saint.
But had thy pale-fac't purple took
Fire from the burning cheeks of that bright Booke
Thou wouldst on her haue heap't vp all
That could be found SERAPHICALL;   30
Whate're this youth of fire weares fair,
Rosy fingers, radiant hair,
Glowing cheek & glistering wings,
All those fair & flagrant things,
But before all, that fiery DART
Had fill'd the Hand of this great HEART.
    Doe then as equall right requires,
Since His the blushes be, & her's the fires,
Resume & rectify thy rude design;
Vndress thy Seraphim into MINE.   40
Redeem this iniury of thy art;
Giue HIM the vail, giue her the dart.
    Giue Him the vail; that he may couer
The Red cheeks of a riuall'd louer,

Asham'd that our world, now, can show
Nests of new Seraphims here below.
    Giue her the DART for it is she
(Fair youth) shootes both thy shaft & THEE
Say, all ye wise & well-peirc't hearts
That liue & dy amidst her darts,   50
What is't your tastfull spirits doe proue
In that rare life of Her, and loue?
Say & bear wittnes. Sends she not
A SERAPHIM at euery shott?
What magazins of immortall ARMES there shine!
Heaun's great artillery in each loue-spun line.
Giue then the dart to her who giues the flame;
Giue him the veil, who kindly takes the shame.
    But if it be the frequent fate
If all's praescription; & proud wrong
Hearkens not to an humble song;
For all the gallantry of him,
Giue me the suffring SERAPHIM.
His be the brauery of all those Bright things,
The glowing cheekes, the glistering wings;
The Rosy hand, the radiant DART;
Leaue HER alone THE FLAMING HEART.
    Leaue her that; & thou shalt leaue her
Not one loose shaft but loue's whole quiuer,   70
For in loue's feild was neuer found
A nobler weapon then a WOVND.
Loue's passiues are his actiu'st part.
The wounded is the wounding heart.
O HEART ! the aequall poise of lou'es both parts
Bigge alike with wounds & darts.
Liue in these conquering leaues, liue all the same;
And walk through all tongues one triumphant FLAME.
Liue here, great HEART; & loue and dy & kill;
And bleed & wound; and yeild & conquer still.   80
Let this immortall life wherere it comes
Walk in a crowd of loues & MARTYRDOMES.
    Let mystick DEATHS wait on't; & wise soules be
The loue-slain wittnesses of this life of thee.
O Sweet incendiary! shew here thy art,
Vpon this carcasse of a hard, cold, hart,

Let all thy scatter'd shafts of light, that play
Among the leaues of thy larg Books of day,
Combin'd against this BREST at once break in
And take away from me my self & sin,   90
This gratious Robbery shall thy bounty be;
And my best fortunes such fair spoiles of me.
O thou vndanted daughter of desires!
By all thy dowr of LIGHTS & FIRES;
By all the eagle in thee, all the doue;
By all thy liues & deaths of loue;
By thy larg draughts of intellectuall day,
And by thy thirsts of loue more large then they;
By all thy brim-fill'd Bowles of feirce desire
By thy last Morning's draught of liquid fire: 100
By the full kingdome of that finall kisse
That seiz'd thy parting Soul, & seal'd thee his;
By all the heau'ns thou hast in him
(Fair sister of the SERAPHIM)
By all of HIM we haue in THEE;
Leaue nothing of my SELF in me.
Let me so read thy life, that I
Vnto all life of mine may dy.

NOTES

Title.	See headnote to previous poem.
2	*this peice pretends*. This piece offers. 'This piece' refers to Crashaw's own poem, Teresa's autobiography, and Segher's painting.
4	This line refers to the angel with the dart portrayed in the painting. He is fair-cheeked and as a seraphim he is made up of fire. The following lines explain why his portrayal as an angel is fallacious.
15	*size*. In her autobiography Teresa desribed the angel as being small.
18	*fire-works*. Refers to Teresa's transports of love. The word picks up on 'flame' in the previous line and will lead to Teresa's 'artillery' in line 56, her being a 'sweet incendiary' in line 85, and 'draught of liquid fire' in line 100.
22	In Segher's painting Teresa is portrayed as pale faced. See also line 27 below.
28	*burning cheeks*. i.e. pages.

31   *youth*. The angel in the painting.
34   *flagrant*. Flaming, glowing.
49-54   These lines are addressed to Teresa's readers who have been shot
          or pierced by the darts sent from her autobiography.
59-60   i.e. something good often comes out of the worst things.
61   *If all's praescription*. If everything is determined by prescriptive
          conventions.
63   *For*. In exchange for.
64   *suffring SERAPHIM*. i.e. Teresa.
73-4   The paradox Crashaw exploits here and in line 76 is that the lover
          wounds and is wounded by love.
77   *leaues*. The pages of Teresa's book. The book is referred to also
          in the next line, where it is imagined as having been translated
          into many languages, and again in line 81.
79   The equation of love and death is common in the literature of
          mystical transport and was often used by baroque artists.
91   *gratious*. Gracious, kind.
93   *vndanted*. Undaunted.
94   *dowr*. Dower, i.e. wealth, possessions.
95   The eagle and the dove represent, respectively, strength and
          meekness. See Donne, 'The Canonization', line 22 and note.
97-100   The conceit here is that Teresa, in her spiritual thirst, drinks large
          quantities of light and liquid fire but cannot quench her thirst.
101-2   Crashaw imagines that when Teresa died physically, her last
          breath was caught by God in a kiss. That kiss was God's seal with
          which He claimed her as one of His saints.
103, 05   *him, HIM*. God.

A HYMN OF THE NATIVITY, SUNG BY THE SHEPHERDS

The hymn depicts simple shepherds celebrating the meaning of
Christ's birth. They see Christ as a bigger Sun than the sun they have
hitherto glorified. They offer Him typical shepherds' gifts but realize
that the greatest gift would be a gift of themselves. In the 1646 version
Crashaw made the poem a celebration of the Virgin and the infant
Christ. However, the 1652 version which is given here concentrates
on Christ, and the Virgin is celebrated only indirectly through Him.
This poem bears comparison with Milton's Nativity Ode with which
it is almost exactly contemporaneous. While Milton's epic sweep
spans the universe and history and dwells only briefly on the nativity
scene, Crashaw focuses almost exclusively on the scene in the

manger. The presence of two speakers and a chorus in the poem does not set up a dialectic between different views, as happens in Marvell's dialogue poems, but supplies different voices in a polyphonic song. The homely tone of the shepherds, and the fact that they are not, as was so often the case in the pastoral poetry of that period, courtiers masquerading as shepherds, their humorous chiding of the seraphim in lines 58 ff., and their criticism of court life in 91 ff.,identify this hymn with popular or folk traditions. These traditions, suitably purged of their anti-court sentiment, were sought to be revived by the Royalists but frowned on by the Puritans. Crashaw's use of them may therefore be seen as a political statement. For a more extended discussion of this point see Young, pp. 62-8.

IN

THE HOLY

NATIVITY

OF

OVR LORD GOD

A

HYMN

SVNG AS BY THE

SHEPHEARDS.

THE

HYMN.

CHORVS

Come we shepheards whose blest Sight
   Hath mett loue's Noon in Nature's night;
Come lift we vp our loftyer Song
   And wake the SVN that lyes too long.

To all our world of well-stoln joy
   He slept; and dream't of no such thing.
While we found out Heaun's fairer ey
   And Kis't the Cradle of our KING.
Tell him He rises now, too late
To show vs ought worth looking at.   10

Tell him we now can show Him more
    Then He e're show'd to mortall Sight;
Then he Himselfe e're saw before;
    Which to be seen needes not His light.
Tell him, Tityrus, where th'hast been
Tell him, Thyrsis, what th'hast seen.

Tityrus. Gloomy night embrac't the Place
    Where The Noble Infant lay.
The BABE look't vp & shew'd his Face;
    In spite of Darknes, it was DAY.   20
It was THY day, SWEET! & did rise
Not from the EAST, but from thine EYES.

      Chorus   It was THY day, Sweet

Thyrs. WINTER chidde aloud; & sent
    The angry North to wage his warres.
The North forgott his feirce Intent;
    And left perfumes in stead of scarres.
By those sweet eyes' persuasiue powrs
Where he mean't frost, he scatter'd flowrs.

      Chorus   By those sweet eyes'   30

Both. We saw thee in thy baulmy Nest,
    Young dawn of our aeternall DAY!
We saw thine eyes break from their EASTE
    And chase the trembling shades away.
We saw thee; & we blest the sight.
We saw thee by thine own sweet light.

Tity. Poor WORLD (said I.) what wilt thou doe
    To entertain this starry STRANGER?
Is this the best thou canst bestow?
    A cold, and not too cleanly, manger?   40
Contend, ye powres of heau'n & earth.
To fitt a bed for this huge birthe.

      Chorus   Contend ye powers

Thyr. Proud world, said I; cease your contest
    And let the MIGHTY BABE alone.
The Phaenix builds the Phaenix' nest.
    Love's architecture is his own.
The BABE whose birth embraues this morn,
Made his own bed e're he was born.

     Chorus   The BABE whose.   50

Tit. I saw the curl'd drops, soft & slow,
    Come houering o're the place's head;
Offring their whitest sheets of snow
    To furnish the fair INFANT'S bed
Forbear, said I; be not too bold.
Your fleece is white But t'is too cold.

     Chorus   Forbear, sayd I

Thyr. I saw the obsequious SERAPHIMS
    Their rosy fleece of fire bestow.
For well they now can spare their wings   60
    Since HEAVEN itself lyes here below.
Well done, said I: but are you sure
Your down so warm, will passe for pure?

     Chorus   Well done sayd I

Tit. No no. your KING'S not yet to seeke
    Where to repose his Royall HEAD
See see, how soon his new-bloom'd CHEEK
    Twixt's mother's brests is gone to bed.
Sweet choise, said we! no way but so
Not to ly cold, yet sleep in snow.   70

     Chorus   Sweet choise, said we.

Both. We saw thee in thy baulmy nest,
    Bright dawn of our aeternall Day!
We saw thine eyes break from their EAST
    And chase the trembling shades away.

We saw thee: & we blest the sight.
We saw thee, by thine own sweet light.

    Cho.   We saw thee, & c.

FVLL CHORVS.

Wellcome, all WONDERS in one sight!
    AEternity shutt in a span.   80
Sommer in Winter. Day in Night.
    Heauen in earth, & GOD in MAN.
Great little one! whose all-embracing birth
Lifts earth to heauen, stoopes heau'n to earth.

WELLCOME. Though nor to gold nor silk.
    To more then Caesar's birthright is;
Two sister-seas of Virgin-Milk,
    With many a rarely-temper'd kisse
That breathes at once both MAID & MOTHER,
Warmes in the one, cooles in the other.   90

WELCOME, though not to those gay flyes
    Guilded ith' Beames of earthly kings;
Slippery soules in smiling eyes;
    But to poor Shepheards, home-spun things:
Whose Wealth's their flock; whose witt, to be
    Well read in their simplicity.

Yet when young April's husband showrs
    Shall blesse the fruitfull Maja's bed
We'l bring the First-born of her flowrs
    To Kisse thy FEET & crown thy HEAD.   100
To thee, dread lamb! whose loue must keep
    The shepheards, more then they the sheep.

To THEE, meek Majesty! soft KING
    Of simple GRACES & sweet LOVES.
Each of vs his lamb will bring
    Each his pair of sylver Doues;
Till burnt at last in fire of Thy fair eyes,
    Our selues become our own best SACRIFICE.

NOTES

2   'Loue's Noon' is Christ whom the shepherds visited at night. See Luke
        20:8-20.
4   Note the humorous chiding of the late-sleeping sun, typical of
        popular art forms.
5   *well-stoln joy*. Because the joy was experienced away from the eyes
        of the sun. The shepherds humorously see themselves here as truant
        children.
7   *ey*. Eye. If the sun is the fair eye of heaven, Christ is the fairer eye.
24-5   The cold north wind blows in the winter. *Chidde* = chided.
31   *baulmy*. Perfumed. The phoenix, with which Christ is compared in
        line 46, was supposed to build its nest of perfumed twigs.
46   For Crashaw's use of the phoenix image, see Donne, 'The Canoniza-
        tion', line 23 and note.
48   *embraues*. Gives greater glory to. See Herbert's use of *brave* in
        'Virtue'.
49   i.e. it was Christ's decision to be born in a manger.
56,59   *fleece*. A word that shepherds would be expected to use. They use the
        same word for both the snow and the seraphs' fiery wings.
86   *then*. Than.
89-90   The dual response to the Virgin, both erotic and adoring, is charac-
        teristic of much baroque art and of the Spanish models who influ-
        enced Crashaw.
91   *gay flyes*. Contemptuous expression for courtiers.
92   *Guilded...Beames*. Gilt in the beams. To gild = to cover or plate with
        gold.
98   *Maja's bed*. Maia, the Roman goddess of fertility, here stands for the
        fecund earth.

TO THE NAME ABOVE EVERY NAME,
THE NAME OF JESUS. A HYMN

If this Hymn is baroque, it is so in a very different way from the
baroque of 'The Weeper'. The expanded epigrams inspired by
Marino's example have been replaced by a complex metrics, and the
long and sweeping sentences create an impression of the immense
and the sublime. While the metrical virtuosity and musical qualities
of this Hymn have always been admired, only recently have critics
begun to appreciate the theological content which gives it its struc-
ture. Martz studied its structure in relation to the meditative method
adumbrated in Joseph Hall's *Arte of Divine Meditation*. More

recently Young has argued that the Hymn should be read in light of
the poetry of the Spanish poet Lope de Vega and the theology of Fray
Luis. According to Luis, in Hebrew the name Jesus has all the letters
contained in God's name, with this difference: 'Jesus' can be pro-
nounced, but God's name is unpronounceable. Hence the name
represents a harmony of the earthly and divine and sums up Jesus'
dual nature as God and man. Young argues that Crashaw explores
this significance of Jesus' name in a poem which not only exploits the
concept of musical harmony but also creates a harmony of earthly
and heavenly images. Thus images of music, of light, of water, and of
perfumes are conjoined with the more abstract ones of the music of
the spheres and of angelic beings. The homely is conjoined to the
awesome. Further, Young finds a significance in the fact that accord-
ing to Luke 2:21 Christ was named on the day He was circumcised.
His ritualistic bleeding provides a justification for the introduction
into the poem of the bleeding of the martyrs, which early critics have
seen as a digression. Another seeming digression--the vision of
Judgement Day with which the poem closes--also becomes harmoni-
ously fused with the poem's theme when it is remembered that
Christ's bleeding at the time of the circumcision foreshadowed the
crucifixion, resurrection and final judgement.

TO
THE NAME
ABOVE EVERY NAME,
THE
NAME OF
IESVS
A HYMN.

I sing the NAME which None can say
But touch't with An interiour RAY:
The Name of our New Peace; our Good:
Our Blisse: & Supernaturall Blood:
The Name of All our Liues & Loues.
Hearken, And Help, ye holy Doues!
The high-born Brood of Day; you bright
Candidates of blissefull Light,
The HEIRS Elect of Loue; whose Names belong
Vnto The euerlasting life of Song;   10
All ye wise SOVLES, who in the wealthy Brest
Of this vnbounded NAME build your warm Nest.

Awake, My glory. SOVL, (if such thou be,
And That fair WORD at all referr to Thee)
   Awake & sing
   And be All Wing;
Bring hither thy whole SELF, & let me see
What of thy Parent HEAVN yet speakes in thee.
   O thou art Poore
   Of noble POWRES, I see,   20
And full of nothing else but empty ME,
Narrow, & low, & infinitely lesse
Then this GREAT mornings mighty Busynes.
   One little WORLD or two
   (Alas) will neuer doe.
   We must haue store.
Goe, SOVL, out of thy Self, & seek for More.
   Goe & request
Great NATVRE for the KEY of her huge Chest
Of Heauns, the self inuoluing Sett of Sphears   30
(Which dull mortality more Feeles then heares)
   Then rouse the nest
Of nimble ART, & trauerse round
The Aiery Shop of soul-appeasing Sound:
And beat a summons in the Same
   All-soueraign Name
To warn each seuerall kind
And shape of sweetnes, Be they such
   As sigh with supple wind
   Or answer Artfull Touch,   40
That they conuene & come away
To wait at the loue-crowned Doores of
   This Illustrious DAY.
Shall we dare This, my Soul? we'l doe't and bring
No Other note for't, but the Name we sing.
   Wake LVTE & HARP
   And euery sweet-lipp't Thing
   That talkes with tunefull string;
Start into life, And leap with me
Into a hasty Fitt-tun'd Harmony.   50
   Nor must you think it much
   T'obey my bolder touch;
I haue Authority in LOVE's name to take you
And to the worke of Loue this morning wake you

    Wake; In the Name
Of HIM who neuer sleeps, All Things that Are,
    Or, what's the same,
    Are Musicall;
    Answer my Call
    And come along;   60
Help me to meditate mine Immortall Song.
Come, ye soft ministers of sweet sad mirth,
Bring All your houshold stuffe of Heaun on earth;
O you, my Soul's most certain Wings,
Complaining Pipes, & prattling Strings,
    Bring All the store
Of SWEETS you haue; And murmur that you haue no more.
    Come, nere to part,
    NATVRE & ART!
    Come; & come strong,   70
To the conspiracy of our Spatious song.
    Bring All the Powres of Praise
Your Prouinces of well-vnited WORLDS can raise;
Bring All your LVTES & HARPS of HEAVN & EARTH,
    .t e're cooperates to The common mirthe
    Vessells of vocall Ioyes,
Or You, more noble Architects of Intellectuall Noise,
Cymballs of Heau'n, or Humane sphears,
Solliciters of SOVLES or EARES;
    And when you'are come, with All   80
That you can bring or we can call;
    O may you fix
    For euer here, & mix
    Your selues into the long
And euerlasting series of a deathlesse SONG;
Mix All your many WORLDS, Aboue,
And loose them into ONE of Loue.
    Chear thee my HEART!
    For Thou too hast thy Part
    And Place in the Great Throng   90
Of This vnbounded All-imbracing SONG.
    Powres of my Soul, be Proud!
    And speake lowd
To All the dear-bought Nations This Redeeming Name,
And in the wealth of one Rich WORD proclaim
New Similes to Nature.

May it be no wrong
Blest Heauns, to you, & your Superiour song,
That we, dark Sons of Dust & Sorrow,
   A while Dare borrow   100
The Name of Your Delights & our Desires,
And fitt it to so farr inferior LYRES.
Our Murmurs haue their Musick too,
Ye mighty ORBES, as well as you,
   Nor yeilds the noblest Nest
Of warbling SERAPHIM to the eares of Loue,
A choicer Lesson then the ioyfull BREST
   Of a poor panting Turtle-Doue.
And we, low Wormes haue leaue to doe
The Same bright Busynes (ye Third HEAVENS) with you. 110
Gentle SPIRITS, doe not complain.
   We will haue care
   To keep it fair,
And send it back to you again.
Come, louely NAME! Appeare from forth the Bright
   Regions of peacefull Light
Look from thine own illustrious Home,
Fair KING of NAMES, & come.
Leaue All thy natiue Glories in their Gorgeous Nest,
And giue thy SElf a while The gracious Guest   120
Of humble Soules, that seek to find
   The hidden Sweets
   Which man's heart meets
When Thou art Master of the Mind.
Come, louely Name; life of our hope!
Lo we hold our HEARTS wide ope!
Vnlock thy Cabinet of DAY
Dearest Sweet, & come away.
   Lo how the thirsty Lands
Gasp for thy Golden Showres! with long stretch't Hands 130
   Lo how the laboring EARTH
   That hopes to be
   All Heauen by THEE,
   Leapes at thy Birth.
The'attending WORLD, to wait thy Rise,
   First turn'd to eyes;
And then, not knowing what to doe;
Turn'd Them to TEARES, & spent Them too.

Come ROYALL Name, & pay the expence
Of All this Pretious Patience.   140
   O come away
And kill the DEATH of This Delay.
O see, so many WORLDS of barren yeares
Melted & measur'd out in Seas of TEARES.
O see, the WEARY liddes of wakefull Hope
(LOVE'S Eastern windowes) All wide ope
   With Curtains drawn,
To catch The Day-break of Thy DAWN.
O dawn, at last, long look't for Day!
Take thine own wings, & come away.   150
Lo, where Aloft it comes ! It comes, Among
The Conduct of Adoring SPIRITS, that throng
Like diligent Bees, And swarm about it.
   O they are wise;
And know what SWEETES are suck't from out it.
   It is the Hiue,
   By which they thriue,
Where All their Hoard of Hony lyes.
Lo where it comes, vpon The snowy DOVE'S
Soft Back; And brings a Bosom big with Loues.   160
WELCOME to our dark world, Thou
   Womb of Day!
Vnfold thy fair Conceptions; And display
The Birth of our Bright Ioyes.
   O thou compacted
Body of Blessings: spirit of Soules extracted !
O dissipate thy spicy Powres
(Clowd of condensed sweets) & break vpon vs
   In balmy showrs;
O fill our senses, And take from vs   170
All force of so Prophane a Fallacy
To think ought sweet but that which smells of Thee.
Fair, flowry Name; In none but Thee
And Thy Nectareall Fragrancy,
   Hourly there meetes
An vniuersall SYNOD of All sweets;
By whom it is defined Thus
   That no Perfume
   For euer shall presume
To passe for Odoriferous,   180

But such alone whose sacred Pedigree
Can proue it Self some kin (sweet name) to Thee.
SWEET NAME, in Thy each Syllable
A Thousand Blest ARABIAS dwell;
A Thousand Hills of Frankincense;
Mountains of myrrh, & Beds of spices,
And ten Thousand PARADISES
The soul that tasts thee takes from thence.
How many vnknown WORLDS there are
Of Comforts, which Thou hast in keeping!   190
How many Thousand Mercyes there
In Pitty's soft lap ly a sleeping!
Happy he who has the art
   To awake them,
   And to take them
Home, & lodge them in his HEART.
O that it were as it was wont to be!
When thy old Freinds of Fire, All full of Thee,
Fought against Frowns with smiles; gaue Glorious chase
To Persecutions; And against the Face   200
Of DEATH & feircest Dangers, durst with Braue
And sober pace march on to meet A GRAVE.
On their Bold BRESTS about the world they bore thee
And to the Teeth of Hell stood vp to teach thee,
In Center of their inmost Soules they wore thee,
Where Rackes & Torments striu'd, in vain, to reach thee,
   Little, alas, thought They
Who tore the Fair Brests of thy Freinds,
   Their Fury but made way
For Thee; And seru'd therein Thy glorious ends.   210
What did Their weapons but with wider pores
Inlarge thy flaming-brested Louers
   More freely to transpire
   That impatient Fire
The Heart that hides Thee hardly couers.
What did their Weapons but sett wide the Doores
For Thee: Fair, purple Doores, of loue's deuising;
The Ruby windowes which inrich't the EAST
Of Thy so oft repeated Rising.
Each wound of Theirs was Thy new Morning;   220
And reinthron'd thee in thy Rosy Nest,
With blush of thine own Blood thy day adorning,

It was the witt of loue o'reflowd the Bounds
Of WRATH, & made thee way through All Those WOVNDS.
Wellcome dear, All-Adored Name!
　　For sure there is no Knee
　　That knowes not THEE.
Or if there be such sonns of shame,
　　Alas what will they doe
　　When stubborn Rocks shall bow   230
And Hills hang down their Heaun-saluting Heads
　　To seek for humble Beds
Of Dust, where in the Bashfull shades of night
Next to their own low NOTHING they may ly,
And couch before the dazeling light of thy dread majesty.
They that by Loue's mild Dictate now
　　Will not adore thee,
Shall Then with Iust confusion, bow
　　And break before thee.

NOTES

Title.   Cf. Philippians 2:9-11: 'Wherefore God also hath highly exalted
　　　　　　him, and given him a name which is above every name: That at the
　　　　　　name of Jesus every knee should bow, of things in earth, and
　　　　　　things under the earth; and that every tongue should confess that
　　　　　　Jesus Christ is Lord...'

6-12   The invocation addresses the souls of the saints in heaven.

8   *Candidates.* From Latin *candidatus*, clothed in white robes.

21-30   The poet's soul, being single, is not enough to provide the song
　　　　　　that the occasion demands. Therefore it is asked to enlist the help
　　　　　　of all of Nature

26   *store.* Supply of abundance.

30-1   *the self inuoluing...beares.* The reference is to the Ptolemaic
　　　　　　theory of the universe according to which each sphere had its own
　　　　　　concentric circle ('self involving' = revolving within its own
　　　　　　circle) and the spheres made music as they revolved, though this
　　　　　　music was not audible to human ears.

50   *Fitt-tun'd.* A pun. Fit = suitable, appropriate. Fitt = part of a song
　　　　　　or strain of music.

56-8   For Crashaw, for a thing to exist is for it to be musical, since
　　　　　　existence presupposes order, pattern and coherence, which are
　　　　　　also the hallmarks of music.

62   *ministers...mirth.* Those who administer or provide sweet, sad
　　　　　　mirth, i.e. musicians.

62-7   Note the echoes of Herbert in words like 'mirth', 'houshold

	stuffe', 'prattling', 'store' and 'SWEETS'.
68	*nere.* Never.
71	*conspiracy.* Breathing together.
76	*Vessells...Ioyes.* The vessels of vocal joys are sweet singing voices.
78	*Cymballs of Heau'n.* Thunder.
87	*loose.* Lose.
94	*dear-bought.* A pun. Dear = costly; close to one's affections.
101	Jesus, who is the delight of the blessed spirits in heaven, is the object of human desire.
104	*ORBES.* Heavenly spheres. See note to lines 30-1 above.
107	*Lesson.* Here, music.
110	*Third HEAVENS.* Representing the outermost boundaries of the universe. Cf. 2 Corinthians 12:2: '...such an one caught up to the third heaven'.
123	*meets.* Experiences.
128	The language in which Christ is addressed is reminiscent of Elizabethan madrigals and the erotic poetry of the Song of Songs.
129	The image derives from Psalm 143:6: 'My soul thirsteth after thee as a thirsty land'.
130	*Golden Showres.* Martz thinks that the phrase recalls the classical story of Danae into whose lap Jupiter descended in a shower of gold.
143	*WORLDS...yeares.* Crashaw telescopes space and time here: mankind has awaited Christ's coming for a world of years.
144-8	Note that the images are highly concrete and abstract at the same time.
162-4	The newly born Christ is like a womb from which will emerge the scheme or plan of our future. 'Conceptions' in line 164 is a pun, meaning both the conception that takes place in the womb and Christ's plans for our salvation.
184	*ARABIAS.* Arabia was the home of perfumes. Cf. *Macbeth* 'Will not all the perfumes of Arabia sweeten this little hand?'
185-6	Frankincense and myrrh, the names of two costly perfumes, were among the gifts the Magi took to the infant Christ.
198ff.	These lines refer to early Christian martyrs who laid down their lives for their faith.
203	*On their...thee.* Crashaw imagines the wounds of the martyrs to have been like heraldic devices which the martyrs proudly displayed on their breasts.
216-20	The martyrs' wounds are compared here first to doors purple with the martyrs' blood and then to red coloured windows. Purple is associated with royalty and rubies with riches. Crashaw wittily says that the red and bleeding wounds of the martyrs are the red-tinged windows in which the sun is rising. This conceit plays upon the double meaning of sun/Son. Young points out that the violent

and grotesque imagery in these lines and in 211-12, the vivid coloration, and the association of love with blood are features of the baroque that Crashaw borrowed from the Spanish poet, Gongora.

222   This line, by suggesting that the blood of the martyrs was none other than that of Christ, makes the link between the passage on the martyrs and the rest of the poem clear. The martyrs shed blood because Christ did so on the cross. And because the crucifixion was prefigured in His circumcision, therefore a poem that celebrates the circumcision also becomes a celebration of the Church Triumphant as represented by the martyrs. See also headnote to the poem.

223   *the witt of loue*. The intellectual power of God who has ordained the intricate relationships, correspondences, and order in the whole universe, and who in this present instance has made the martyrs' wounds a door for His entry into their breasts. See also 'The Weeper', line 89.

226-7 See Biblical quotation in the note on title of the poem.

230-5 The images with which the Day of Judgement is conjured are based on Biblical sources like Revelation 8:8: 'a great mountain burning with fire was cast into the sea...' Luke 3:5 '... every mountain and hill shall be brought low...' and Psalm 18:7: 'Then the earth shook and trembled: the foundations also of the hills moved and were shaken...'

IN THE GLORIOUS EPIPHANIE OF OUR LORD GOD, A HYMN. SUNG AS BY THE THREE KINGS

The Feast of the Epiphany, observed on 6 January, marks the visit of the three Eastern kings or wise men (Magi) to the new-born Christ (see Matthew 2:1-12) and commemorates the 'showing forth' or manifestation of Christ to the non-Jewish world. Thus the Epiphany Hymn, together with the Nativity Hymn as sung by the shepherds and the hymn on Jesus' name, can be grouped as Crashaw's Christmastide poems. The intricate versification, the varied music of the short and long lines, and the fact that sometimes the kings sing solo while at other times they form a chorus, indicate that the poem can be seen as an oratorio or a dramatic composition written for voices and instruments to be performed in a church as part of a communal ritual. While the Hymn as sung by the shepherds may also lend itself to this kind of treatment, the differences between the two Hymns are just as important. The shepherds are simple people who bring simple gifts. But the kings represent an attempt to understand the meaning of the Nativity intellectually and mystically, and their vocabulary is full of such words as 'deliquium'. The whole poem revolves around the images of light and darkness. As eastern kings the singers had worshipped the sun, but in the presence of the Son they realize that their belief in the divinity of the sun was superstitious: while ostensibly worshipping light they were worshipping darkness. Christ is the true Light of the world, but His light is one that illumines the intellect and the spirit. The paradoxes of light and darkness lead naturally to the passage towards the end dealing with Dionysius, the Areopagite. Contemplating the crucifixion, which was attended by an eclipse of the natural sun, Dionysius asked how God's light could be kept alive in man. His answer was that if the world had rejected Christ, man should reject the world. Only by denying all senses and becoming dead to the world could he hope to experience God in his soul. Dionysius termed his mystic approach the via negativa or negative way, finding inner light through external darkness. Crashaw's kings arrive at a similar conclusion. And because their way can be the way only of the individual in mystic ecstasy and not that of a group of celebrants participating in a ritual, it may be said that Crashaw's Hymn combines the communal with the intensely personal. This feature renders the work unique in Crashaw's *oeuvre* and makes a redefinition of his baroque necessary. Baroque poems are usually vivid, concrete, full of ornamentation, public and celebratory. The Hymn, too, is detailed and elaborate. But instead of a physical palpability it possesses an intellectual quality, leading us to think of it as a new phenomenon: the baroque of the abstract.

IN
THE GLORIOVS
EPIPHANIE
OF OVR LORD GOD,
A HYMN.
SVNG AS BY THE
THREE KINGS
(I. *KINGE.*)

Bright BABE! Whose awfull beautyes make
  The morn incurr a sweet mistake;
(2) For whom the officious heauns deuise
To disinheritt the sun's rise,

(3) Delicately to displace
The Day, & plant it fairer in thy face;
[I] O thou born KING of loues,
   [2] Of lights,
   [3] Of ioyes!
(*Cho.*) Look vp, sweet BABE, look vp & see   10
   For loue of Thee
   Thus farr from home
   The EAST is come
To seek her self in thy sweet Eyes
(I) We, Who strangely went astray,
   Lost in a bright
   Meridian night,
(2) A Darkenes made of too much day,
   (3) Becken'd from farr
   By thy fair starr,   20
Lo at last haue found our way.
(*Cho.*) To THEE, thou DAY of night! thou east of west!
Lo we at last haue found the way.
To thee, the world's great vniuersal east.
The Generall & indifferent DAY.
(I) All-circling point. All centring sphear.
The world's one, round, AEternall year.
(2) Whose full & all-vnwrinkled face
Nòr sinks nor swells with time or place;
(3) But euery where & euery while   30
Is One Consistent solid smile;
   (I) Not vext & tost
   (2) 'Twixt spring & frost,
(3) Nor by alternate shredds of light
Sordidly shifting hands with shades & night.
(*Cho.*) O little all! in thy embrace
The world lyes warm, & likes his place.
Nor does his full Globe fail to be
Kist on Both his cheeks by Thee.
Time is too narrow for thy YEAR   40
Nor makes the whole WORLD thy half-sphear.
   (I) To Thee, to Thee
   From him we flee
(2) From HIM, whom by a more illustrious ly,
The blindnes of the world did call the eye;
(3) To HIM, who by These mortall clouds hast made

Thy self our sun, though thine own shade.
(I) Farewell, the world's false light.
   Farewell, the white
Aegypt! a long farewell to thee					50
Bright IDOL; black IDOLATRY.
   The dire face of inferior DARKNES, kis't
And courted in the pompous mask of a more specious mist.
   (2) Farewell, farewell
   The proud & misplac't gates of hell,
   Pertch't, in the morning's way
And double-guilded as the doores of DAY.
The deep hypocrisy of DEATH & NIGHT
More desperately dark, Because more bright.
   (3)Welcome, the world's sure Way!				60
   HEAVN'S wholsom ray.
   (*Cho.*) Wellcome to vs; and we
(SWEET) to our selues, in THEE.
(I) The deathles HEIR of all thy FATHER'S day!
   (2) Decently Born.
Embosom'd in a much more Rosy MORN,
The Blushes of thy All-vnblemish't mother.
   (3) No more that other
   Aurora shall sett ope
Her ruby casements, or hereafter hope				70
   From mortall eyes
To meet Religious welcomes at her rise.
(*Cho.*)We (Pretious ones!) in you haue won
A gentler MORN, a iuster sun.
(I) His superficiall Beames sun-burn't our skin;
   (2) But left within
(3) The night & winter still of death & sin.
(*Cho.*) Thy softer yet more certaine DARTS
Spare our eyes, but peirce our HARTS.
(I) Therefore with His proud persian spoiles			80
(2) We court thy more concerning smiles.
   (3) Therefore with his Disgrace
We guild the humble cheek of this chast place;
(*Cho.*) And at thy FEET powr forth his FACE.
(I) The doating nations now no more
Shall any day but THINE adore.
(2) Nor (much lesse) shall they leaue these eyes
For cheap Aegyptian Deityes.

(3) In whatsoe're more Sacred shape   90
Of Ram, He-goat, or reuerend ape,
Those beauteous rauishers opprest so sore
The too-hard-tempted nations.
   (I) Neuer more
By wanton heyfer shall be worn
(2) A Garland, or a guilded horn.
The altar-stall'd ox, fatt OSYRIS now
   With his fair sister cow,
(3) Shall kick the clouds no more; But lean & tame,
(*Cho.*) See his horn'd face, & dy for shame.   100
And MITHRA now shall be no name.
(I) No longer shall the immodest lust
Of Adulterous Godles dust
(2) Fly in the face of heau'n; As if it were
The poor world's Fault that he is fair.
(3) Nor with peruerse loues & Religious RAPES
Reuenge thy Bountyes in their beauteous shapes;
And punish Best Things worst; Because they stood
Guilty of being much for them too Good.
[I] Proud sons of death! that durst compell   110
Heau'n it self to find them hell;
[2] And by strange witt of madnes wrest
From this world's EAST the other's WEST.
[3] All-Idolizing wormes! that thus could crowd
And vrge Their sun into thy cloud;
Forcing his sometimes eclips'd face to be
A long deliquium to the light of thee.
[*Cho.*] Alas with how much heauyer shade
The shamefac't lamp hung down his head
   For that one eclipse he made   120
   Then all those he suffered!
[I] For this he look't so bigg; & euery morn
With a red face confes't this scorn.
Or hiding his vex't cheeks in a hir'd mist
Kept them from being so vnkindly kis't.
[2] It was for this the day did rise
   So oft with blubber'd eyes.
For this the euening wept; and we ne're knew
   But call'd it deaw.

[3] This dayly wrong   130
Silenc't the morning-sons, & damp't their song
[Cho.] Nor was't our deafnes, but our sins, that thus
Long made th'Harmonious orbes all mute to vs.
[1] Time has a day in store
    When this so proudly poor
And self-oppressed spark, that has so long
By the loue-sick world bin made
Not so much their sun as SHADE,
Weary of this Glorious wrong
From them & from himself shall flee   140
For shelter to the shadow of thy TREE;
[Cho.] Proud to haue gain'd this pretious losse
And chang'd his false crown for thy CROSSE.
[2] That dark Day's clear doom shall define
Whose is the Master FIRE, which sun should shine,
That sable Iudgment-seat shall by new lawes
Decide & settle the Great cause
    Of controuerted light,
[Cho.] And natur's wrongs rejoyce to doe thee Right.
[3] That forfeiture of noon to night shall pay   150
All the idolatrous thefts done by this night of day;
And the Great Penitent presse his own pale lipps
With an elaborate loue-eclipse
    To which the low world's lawes
    Shall lend no cause
[Cho.] Saue those domestick which he borrowes
From our sins & his own sorrowes.
[1] Three sad hour's sackcloth then shall show to vs
His penance, as our fault, conspicuous.
[2] And he more needfully & nobly proue   160
The nation's terror now then erst their loue.
[3] Their hated loues changd into wholsom feares,
[Cho.] The shutting of his eye shall open Theirs.
[1] As by a fair-ey'd fallacy of day
Miss-ledde before they lost their way,
So shall they, by the seasonable fright
Of an vnseasonable night,
Loosing it once again, stumble'on true LIGHT
[2] And as before his too-bright eye

Was Their more blind idolatry,   170
So his officious blindnes now shall be
Their black, but faithfull perspectiue of thee;
    [3] His new prodigious night,
Their new & admirable light;
The supernaturall DAWN of Thy pure day.
    While wondring they
(The happy conuerts now of him
Whom they compell'd before to be their sin)
    Shall henceforth see
To kisse him only as their rod   180
Whom they so long courted as GOD,
[*Cho.*] And their best vse of him they worship't be
To learn of Him at lest, to worship Thee.
[I] It was their Weaknes woo'd his beauty;
    But it shall be
Their wisdome now, as well as duty,
To injoy his Blott; & as a large black letter
Vse it to spell Thy beautyes better;
And make the night it self their torch to thee.
[2] By the oblique ambush of this close night   190
    Couch't in that conscious shade
The right-ey'd Areopagite
Shall with a vigorous guesse inuade
And catche thy quick reflex; and sharply see
    On this dark Ground
    To descant THEE.
[3] O prize of the rich SPIRIT! with what feirce chase
    Of his strong soul, shall he
    Leap at thy lofty FACE,
And seize the swift Flash, in rebound   200
From this obsequious cloud;
    Once call'd a sun;
    Till dearly thus vndone,
[*Cho.*] Till thus triumphantly tam'd (o ye, two
Twinne SVNNES!) & taught now to negotiate you.
[1] Thus shall that reuerend child of light,
[2] By being scholler first of that new night,
Come forth Great master of the mystick day;
[3] And teach obscure MANKIND a more close way

By the frugall negatiue light   210
Of a most wise & well-abused Night
To read more legible thine originall Ray,
[*Cho.*] And make our Darknes serue THY day;
Maintaining t'wixt thy world & ours
A commerce of contrary powres,
   A mutuall trade
   'Twixt sun & SHADE,
By confederat BLACK & WHITE
Borrowing day & lending night.
[1] Thus we, who when with all the noble powres   220
That (at thy cost) are call'd, not vainly, ours
   We vow to make braue way
Vpwards, & presse on for the pure intelligentiall Prey;
   [2] At lest to play
   The amorous Spyes
And peep & proffer at thy sparkling Throne;
[3] In stead of bringing in the blissfull PRIZE
   And fastening on Thine eyes,
   Forfeit our own
   And nothing gain   230
But more Ambitious losse, at lest of brain;
[*Cho.*] Now by abased liddes shall learn to be
Eagles; and shutt our eyes that we may see.

   The Close

Therfore to THEE & thine Auspitious ray
   (Dread Sweet!) lo thus
   At lest by vs,
The delegated EYE of DAY
Does first his Scepter, then HIMSELF in solemne Tribute pay.
   Thus he vndresses
   His sacred vnshorn tresses;   240
At thy adored FEET, thus, he layes down
   [1] His gorgeous tire
   Of flame & fire,
[2] His glittering ROBE, [3] his sparkling CROWN,
[1] His GOLD, [2] his MIRRH, [3] his FRANKINCENCE,
[*Cho.*] To which He now has no pretence.
For being show'd by this day's light, how farr

He is from sun enough to make THY starr,
His best ambition now, is but to be
Somthing a brighter SHADOW [sweet] of thee.   250
Or on heaun's azure forhead high to stand
Thy golden index; with a duteous Hand
Pointing vs Home to our own sun
The world's & his HYPERION.

NOTES

1	*awfull.* Aweful, awe-inspiring.
2	Seeing the infant Christ, the morning thinks that the sun has risen though it is still night.
4-6	The metaphor is that of a palace revolution. The heavens want to disinherit or displace the sun and appoint Christ in its place.
13	The kings play upon the paradox that they have come from the east to witness the rise of the sun (Christ).
15-18	In worshipping the sun the kings 'went astray' because such worship represents not the worship of light but paradoxically ('strangely') the height of darkness.
20	Refers to the star which guided the Eastern kings to Christ's manger (Matthew 2:2).
25	*indifferent.* Undiffering, unchanging.
26	The speaker's paradox recalls Hermes Trismegistus who said that God was a circle whose centre is everywhere and circumference nowhere.
28-9	The unchanging aspect of Christ is contrasted with the sun's changeableness in lines 32-5.
38-9	Unlike the sun's, the light of Christ shines on the eastern and western hemispheres at the same time.
44	*HIM.* The sun. *ly.* Lie.
46-7	By assuming a human body Christ has revealed Himself as the true sun of the world, even though He has thereby dulled His glory in the same way as the sun's glory is dimmed when it is clouded over. The body is here compared to clouds and God to the sun. Just as no one can look directly at the sun, so no one may view God's face. God has had to clothe Himself in human form in order to be visible to mankind.
50-3	Egypt stands for those lands which in their benightedness worshipped the earthly sun. In doing so they were worshipping not brightness but darkness disguised as light (line 53).
57	The contrast is between the sun, which is only gold-plated, as

against the genuine gold of Christ. People were misled by the bright appearance of the sun into thinking that it was truly God. There is a pun on *guilded* which means both gilded and guilty.

63   Here the kings identify themselves mystically with Christ: He is revealed to them, and they are seen to be in Him.

66-72   The Virgin Mary is compared to the dawn ('Aurora' in line 69) to the latter's detriment. The comparison prefigures the rout of pagan deities following Christ's birth that the poem will detail from line 89 ff.

80-4   Persia in line 80 stands for riches. The costly gifts which the kings brought for the infant Christ–gold, frankincense and myrhh (Matthew 2:11)– are seen by them as symbolic of the sun, so that in offering them to Christ they are offering the sun to him.

90-101 This passage bears comparison with Milton's account in his Nativity hymn of the expulsion of pagan gods and the silencing of their oracles that occurred when Christ was born. The Egyptians worshipped deities in the shape of animals such as rams, goats, heifers and oxen. Osiris, the Egyptian god of the sun, was worshipped in the form of a bull, Isis, another god, as a cow, and Mithra was a Persian sun-god.

106-9   Crashaw's references here are to Greek and Roman legends, such as those narrated in Ovid's *Metamorphoses*, of gods who pursued handsome boys or raped women. In their actions, says Crashaw, the gods showed themselves to be of lower moral calibre than the humans.

107   i.e. the pagan gods took revenge upon human beings because God in His bounty had given these humans beautiful shapes.

114-17 The sun is like a cloud for God. But the pagans took the sun to be their god. And because the sun is sometimes eclipsed, they thought that God's glory is also therefore sometimes dimmed.

117   *deliquium.* Absence, lack.

120   i.e. the time when the sun was truly eclipsed by the birth of Christ.

126-9   Morning rain and evening dew are compared to tears shed by the sun. Crashaw says that the sun used to cry because it knew that one day Christ would be born and its pretence to divinity would be exposed.

130-3   The sun's usurpation of divinity, or rather, mankind's sinful worship of natural phenomena instead of the true God, caused the spheres to stop singing to man.

134-89 This long passage anticipates the crucifixion during which the sun was eclipsed. Crashaw says that the sun's eclipse will prove that God is the master and the sun only His servant; it will also represent the sun's atonement for all those years when it usurped Godhead. If the light of the sun deceived men into thinking that it was a god, in the darkness of its eclipse their eyes will be opened

	to the truth.
134	*a day*. The day of the crucifixion.
136	*spark*. The sun. The word also carries a suggestion that the sun is a gallant and as such looks back to lines 106-9 where the loves and gallantries of pagan gods (of whom the sun is the chief symbol in this poem) are described.
138	Because men's worship of the sun has prevented them from worshipping the true God, it can be said that the light of the sun has acted as a shade or blind to hinder their sight.
141	*thy TREE*. The Cross.
150-1	On the day of Christ's crucifixion, the noon will pay a forfeiture to the night in that when the sun should be shining there will be an eclipse. Thus will be atoned the wrong done by the sun in making men erroneously believe that it was a god.
152	*Great Penitent*. The sun.
152-7	Martin suggests that the sun's compression of lips may signify its renunciation of the love or worship it had previously received. Or, again, its behaviour may be a gesture of self-effacement. People will try to explain the eclipse at the crucifixion but will find no physical reason. Therefore they will conjecture that it took place because the sun had some domestic cause to grieve or else because mankind's sins had become too much for it to bear.
158	*Three...sackcloth*. Sackcloth was worn as a sign of penance. Crashaw suggests that the sun's eclipse indicates that it is penitent. According to Matthew 27:45, Mark 15:33 and Luke 23:44 the eclipse at the crucifixion lasted three hours.
161	The terror that nations feel at the sun's eclipse on the occasion of the crucifixion will have more justification than the love they previously felt towards the sun.
162	*Their*. Pertaining to the nations', i.e. mankind's.
164-5	*fair-ey'd fallacy...Miss-ledde*. Men were misled by the fallacy that because the sun was bright and shone during the day therefore it must represent Godhead.
167	*vnseasonable*. Unexpected, occurring at the wrong time.
169	Martin quotes Gloucester from *King Lear*, IV. 1. 19: 'I stumbled when I saw'.
172	*black...thee*. The reference here is to Dionysius the Areopagite's 'via negativa'. See headnote to the poem.
177	*conuerts...of him*. Converts together with him.
180	i.e. the sun will henceforth be seen only as an agent of God's wrath ('rod') rather than as the Deity.
183	*at lest*. At least; or perhaps, at last.
187-8	i.e. the sun's eclipse ('Blott') will be as it were a letter in large black type which will help men to 'read' God more clearly.
190	*oblique ambush*. The phrase refers perhaps to the experience of

Dionysius who witnessed the eclipse at the time of the crucifixion from Heliopolis. He recorded that as the eclipse started the moon approached the sun, and at the lifting of the eclipse was once again 'placed back...into a line opposite the sun'.

191 *conscious shade.* Darkness which is witness or privy to the Areopagite's intentions.

193-6 The Areopagite will at once and through mystic intuition ('vigorous guesse') see the true nature of Christ ('catche..reflex'): the darkness of the eclipsed day will provide him with the background necessary to comprehend and discourse ('descant') on God.

200-1 i.e. in one leap the spirit of Dionysius the Areopagite will rebound away from sun worship and fasten on the true Light ('Flash') which is Christ.

205 *Twinne SVNNES.* Christ's eyes.

207 *new night.* i. e. the eclipse.

209 *obscure.* Lost in darkness.

210-11 *frugall negatiue...Night.* Refers to the via negativa as propounded by the Areopagite. 'Abused' (line 211) = used.

220-1 Though the powers of our intellect are paid for (i.e. granted to us: 'at thy cost' line 221) by God, we may without vanity also call them ours.

223-31 Two images are used here: the intellect as a hunter and the intellect as a spy. Crashaw says that through the intellect mankind wants to hunt out or spy upon the nature of God. But all it gets in return is a sense of blind (line 229) confusion.

232 *abased liddes.* Closed eyelids; i.e. through the kind of meditation recommended by Dionysius, the Areopagite.

233 *Eagles.* Eagles were supposed to be able to look at the sun without being blinded.

237 *delegated EYE of DAY.* At the end of the poem the sun is reduced from being a god to being merely a faithful performer of the duties delegated to him by God.

241-5 See note to lines 80-4 above.

248 i.e. far from being the sun, the sun is in reality only one of God's stars.

251-2 i.e. the sun wants to shine in the blue sky only in order that it may point us to heaven.

254 *HYPERION.* The god of the sun in ancient Greece and Rome. Crashaw implies that Christ is the true Hyperion, both for mankind and for the sun itself.

HENRY VAUGHAN

Henry Vaughan (1621/22-1695) was Welsh by birth and twin brother to Thomas, whose Hermetic philosophy was to influence Henry's poetry in later life. Henry Vaughan was educated in Wales and at Oxford, but did not take a degree. He studied law in London and in 1642, at the outset of the Civil War, returned to Wales where he probably saw military service in the King's cause. His first book, entitled *Poems*, was published in 1646. A second book of poems, *Olor Iscanus* (Latin for Swan of Isca or Usk, a river in Wales) was probably ready by 1649 but its publication was delayed and it did not appear till 1651. Around this time Vaughan began to call himself a Silurist, taking this name from that of an old British tribe that lived in Wales before the coming of the Saxons. He also came across the work of George Herbert, whose influence on Vaughan proved to be great. Indeed, Herbertian influences replaced all other earlier ones like those of Ben Jonson in Vaughan's work. The new quality of Vaughan's poetry, combined with some hints that Vaughan was later to give about a crisis in his life in the late 1640s, led some early biographers to conjecture that Vaughan underwent a religious conversion around 1648, but evidence for this is slight. More recent critics have questioned whether the religious poetry to which he now devoted himself was the outcome of a conversion and argued that it may have had other causes. This religious poetry is to be found in *Silex Scintillans*, the first part of which appeared in 1650, and which was reissued, with additions, as the second part in 1655. Vaughan's last book, *Thalia Rediviva* (1678), is a miscellany of prose and verse. While some poems are new, others would seem to be those that were, for one reason or another, not included in *Olor Iscanus*. The last years of Vaughan's life seem to have been spent in the practic of medicine, though he received no formal training as a physician.

Early critics regarded the poems in *Silex Scintillans*, especially the first part, as the best of Vaughan's work. Recent scholars, while agreeing with this estimate of *Silex*, have begun to find value in the earlier, secular poems as well. In particular, 'Charnel-house' and some of the verse epistles in the mode of Jonson and Carew from *Olor Iscanus* have come in for praise. Therefore I have included 'Charnel-house' in this anthology, but all other poems given here are from *Silex*, 'The Water-fall' and 'The Night' from Part Two and the others from Part One.

Silex Scintillans is a lyric sequence. Though it does not tell a story or have a beginning, a middle and an end, it does possess, as Thomas Calhoun has demonstrated, a supple and complex unity. Since this unity is inevitably destroyed in any selection from the work such as the present, its presence in the sequence as a whole may be emphasized here. In *Silex* themes are introduced, dropped and then reintroduced in different forms. They are wound and rewound in different ways with different themes. Images recur, but their altered contexts charge them with subtly changed meanings. Through all these meanderings the sequence of poems moves towards a goal: having the light of God shine upon the poet and restore the divine image in his heart. As Vaughan's spiritual malaise is healed and he becomes more aware of God, learns to hear His voice aright and experience Him in his heart, the poems also become more liturgical in nature. There are more such poems in Part Two of *Silex* than in Part One. By the end of Part One he has learned something about the meaning of the journey of life. In Part Two there is no further progression; instead, there are more meditations upon the nature of death and rebirth.

Vaughan's works were edited by L.C. Martin. Somewhat later French Fogle reexamined manuscripts in preparing his edition of Vaughan's poetry. The text given here is that in Fogle's edition, and the poems are printed in the same order as in Fogle.

Vaughan's title *Silex Scintillans* needs explanation. *Silex* in Latin means a stone whose touch was supposed to have the power of transmuting baser metals to gold. *Scintillans* means bright or shining. The title is connected to the emblem which formed the frontispiece of the first edition of this work. In the emblem a heart, in which one (or possibly two) human faces are discernible, is emitting flames and dripping blood. A hand (presumably God's) is reaching out from the clouds in order to strike the heart with an arrow. The heart being pierced by Cupid's arrow is a conventional enough motif in love poetry; Vaughan here gives the conceit a religious slant. The emblem seems to say that the human heart has been hardened by sin into stone or flint, and only when God's love pierces it can it turn human

again. When God strikes the heart and inflames it, man will again
resume the divine image in which he was made. God's love is like the
touch of the philosopher's stone: with it the base, worthless human
heart can be turned into a thing of value. These ideas are summed up
in the title and also adumbrated in a poem that accompanies the
emblem. *Silex Scintillans* is subtitled *Sacred Poems and Private
Ejaculations.* This was the subtitle that Herbert had given to *The
Temple,* and Vaughan's use of it not only affirms Herbert's influence
upon his poetry but also reminds us that the metaphor of the heart
as hard and flinty was common in Herbert and the conceit of asking
God to make the hard heart bleed is borrowed from *The Temple.*

THE CHARNEL-HOUSE

'The Charnel-house' recalls the 'strong-lined' style of Donne. The
poet shows an almost Hamlet-like obsession with death and corrup-
tion, and like Hamlet his attitude is marked also by mocking, at times
astringent satire. The power of the poem is apparent, but the reader
may be puzzled by the seeming pointlessness of Vaughan's gnomic
utterances on death if no attempt is made to root them in contempo-
rary politics. Without such an attempt the poem might appear to be
a memento mori, a series of epigrams intended to make the reader
aware that 'the paths of glory lead but to the grave'. However, as E.L.
Marilla has shown, together with being that, the work should also be
read as a denunciation of Parliamentarians; then it will be seen to
take on a more definite structure and sharper point. A political
interpretation will also make several lines, which might otherwise
appear obscure, meaningful and pertinent to the purposes of the
poem. The annotations that follow the poem are heavily indebted to
Marilla's commentary.

The Charnel-house.

Blesse me! what damps are here? how stiffe an aire?
Kelder of mists, a second *Fiats* care,
Frontspeece o'th' grave and darkness, a Display
Of ruin'd man, and the disease of day;
Leane, bloudless shamble, where I can descrie   5
Fragments of men, Rags of Anatomie;

Corruptions ward-robe, the transplantive bed
Of mankind, and th'Exchequer of the dead.
How thou arrests my sense? how with the sight
My *Winter'd* bloud growes stiffe to all delight?   10
Torpedo to the Eye! whose least glance can
Freeze our wild lusts, and rescue head-long man;
Eloquent silence! able to Immure
An *Atheists* thoughts, and blast an *Epicure.*
Were I a *Lucian,* Nature in this dresse   15
Would make me wish a Saviour, and Confesse.
 Where are you shoreless thoughts, vast tenter'd hope,
Ambitious dreams, *Aymes* of an Endless scope,
Whose stretch'd Excesse runs on a string too high
And on the rack of self-extension dye?   20
Chameleons of state, Aire-monging band,
Whose breath (like Gun-powder) blowes up a land,
Come see your dissolution, and weigh
What a loath'd nothing you shall be one day,
As th'Elements by Circulation passe   25
From one to th'other, and that which first was
Is so again, so 'tis with you; The grave
And Nature but Complott, what the one gave,
The other takes; Think then, that in this bed
There sleep the Reliques of as proud a head   30
As stern and subtill as your own, that hath
Perform'd or, fore'd as much, whose tempest-wrath
Hath levell'd Kings with slaves, and wisely then
Calme these high furies, and descend to men;
Thus *Cyrus* tam'd the *Macedon,* a tombe   35
Checkt him, who thought the world too straight a Room.
 Have I obey'd the *Powers* of a face,
A beauty able to undoe the Race
Of easie man? I look but here, and strait
I am Inform'd, the lovely Counterfeit   40
Was but a smoother Clay. That famish'd slave
Begger'd by wealth, who starves that he may save,
Brings hither but his sheet; Nay, th'*Ostrich-man*
That feeds on *steele* and *bullet,* he that can
Outswear his *Lordship,* and reply as tough   45
To a kind word, as if his tongue were *Buffe,*
Is *Chap*-faln here, wormes without wit, or fear

Defie him now, death hath disarm'd the *Bear*.
Thus could I run o'r all the pitteous score
Of erring men, and having done meet more,   50
Their shuffled *Wills*, abortive, vain *Intents*,
Phantastick *humours*, perillous *Ascents*,
False, empty *honours*, traiterous *delights*,
And whatsoe'r a blind Conceit Invites;
But these and more which the weak vermins swell,   55
Are Couch'd in this Accumulative Cell
Which I could scatter; But the grudging Sun
Calls home his beams, and warns me to be gone,
Day leaves me in a double night, and I
Must bid farewell to my sad library.   60
Yet with these notes. Henceforth with thought of thee
I'le season all succeeding Jollitie,
Yet damn not mirth, nor think too much is fit,
Excesse hath no *Religion,* nor Wit,
But should wild bloud swell to a lawless strain   65
One Check from thee shall *Channel* it again.

NOTES

1   *stiffe.* Heavy.
2   *Kelder.* Womb.
     Second Fiats care. In Genesis 1:3 God said, 'Fiat Lux' (Let there be
     light). Vaughan means that the darkness of the charnel house is so
     great that dispelling it will require (or need the 'care' of) a second Fiat
     Lux to be uttered by God.
3   *Frontspeece.* Frontispiece. The charnel house is an introduction to
     the grave and darkness.
5   *Shamble.* Place of destruction.
7   *Corruptions ward-robe.* Marilla explains that in the charnel house
     corruption puts on its 'dress' or makes its appearance.
7-8 *transplantive bed...mankind.* Flowers are *transplanted* in flower-
     beds; men are transplanted from life to death in the charnel house.
10   *Winter'd bloud.* Cold blood. The poet's blood runs cold at the sight
     of the corruption and decay in the charnel house.
11   *Torpedo.* A violent missile or projectile. The meaning is that the sight
     of the charnel house strikes the poet's eye forcefully. Marilla points
     out that the torpedo fish was supposed to be capable of emitting a
     paralyzing substance that could render fishermen immobile. The
     sense of paralyzing is carried over into the next line ('freeze...lusts').

12   *rescue...man.* The terrible sight pulls up short the man bent on pleasure or ambition.

13   *Immure.* Confine, limit, imprison. The idea is that the sights of the charnel house would convert an atheist to a belief in God.

15   *Lucian.* Greek satirist known for his attacks on old and revered institutions.

17   *shoreless.* Vast, boundless.
     vast tenter'd hope. 'Distended as upon a "tenter" or framework for stretching cloth' (Marilla). The image of stretching is continued in lines 19-20.

18   *Aymes...scope.* Limitless intentions.

17-18 Marilla says that the lines dealing with unlimited ambition are a satirical reference to the Parliamentarians who, in 1642, confidently advanced nineteen Propositions to the King in which they maintained that sovereignty rested not with him but with Parliament.

19-20 The lines continue the stretching image from line 17 above. The rack in line 20 was an instrument of torture on which prisoners were killed by being stretched. See Herbert 'The Temper I' line 9. Vaughan means that Parliamentarians' ambitions are so excessive and stretched out that their very excess will first torture and finally destroy them.

21   *Chameleons...band.* An air-monger, Marilla explains, is a foolish visionary. The term is here applied to Parliamentarians. They are also called chameleons because the chameleon was supposed to eat the air and because it was considered to be changeable and untrustworthy.

22   The reference here may be to the Gunpowder Plot or the Catholics' attempt to blow up Parliament.

25-9 *As th'Elements...takes.* The Aristotelian theory of the generation of elements held that the four elements of earth, air, water and fire were in a state of flux, each changing into the other three by turns and then back into its own form. The same is the case with human beings, for Nature and death plot together ('Complott' in line 28) to pass them from the hands of the former to those of the latter.

29-34 *Think then...men.* The thought that men have died in the years past who were just as proud or clever or ambitious as the Puritans should make the Puritans give up their 'high furies' and descend to the level of other men. Vaughan not only recommends a course of humility to the Puritans but also satirizes the zeal and bigotry of which they were often accused.

35-6 Alexander the Great of Macedonia, who is reputed to have cried because there were not enough worlds left for him to conquer, was deeply moved and saddened by thoughts of mortality when he came across the tomb of the Persian king Cyrus and read the inscription on it. Vaughan says that just as Cyrus' tomb made Alexander humble in the face of death, so the Puritans should think of mortality and learn humility instead of trying, in their anger, to level kings with slaves (line 33).

36   *straight.* Small of confining.

40-1 *lovely Counterfeit...clay.* The charnel house teaches that the beauty
      of the woman was not real but false ('counterfeit'), nothing more
      than a smoother clay than other human beings are made out of.

41-3 *famish'd slave...sheet.* The miser who is rich but lives like a beggar
      because he does not want to spend his wealth comes to the charnel
      house with none of his worldly goods but a shroud or a winding
      sheet. The destructive power of death over beautiful women, as also
      the figure of the miser, were stock themes in Elizabethan satire.

43-4 *Ostrich-man...bullet.* The ostrich was supposed to feed on metal.
      Here the 'ostrich-man' refers to the rude and aggressive Parliamen-
      tarians.

46   *Buffe.* A rough leather.

47   *chap-faln.* Decaying corpses were said to be chap-fallen because lips
      and cheeks had shrunk. The term was also applied in a derogatory
      fashion to Puritans to ridicule their severity and zeal which made
      their faces appear pinched.

51   *shuffled.* Inconstant.

52   *Phantastick humours.* Strange or eccentric desires..
      perillous Ascents. The dangers they courted in climbing up the
      ladder of success.

53   *traiterous delights.* Marilla sees this as a possible reference to the
      Puritan plan to impeach Queen Henrietta Maria and their thwarting
      of the king's attempts to arrest the five instigators of this scheme.

55   i.e. these and more dead people are devoured by vermin in the
      charnel house, causing the vermin to grow fat.

57   *which....scatter.* Because the dead people are now dust, I could
      scatter them with a breath.

57-8 *grudging Sun...beams.* i.e. the sun is about to set.

59   *double night.* The double darkness of night and depression.

60   *sad library.* The charnel house is the sad library where the poet has
      learned the lessons enumerated in the poem.

61   *thee.* Charnel house.

62-3 The idea is that the memories of the charnel house will prevent the
      poet in future from either being too jolly or giving up mirth alto-
      gether. These memories have taught him the lesson of moderation.

64   A satirical line directed against the Puritans whom Vaughan consid-
      ers guilty of excessive zeal in religion.

65-6 The metaphor is from lancing a boil. If an excess of blood causes an
      undesired swelling ('lawless strain' in line 65), then death will incise
      the boil and cause the blood to flow in the proper direction once
      again. The idea is that the Puritan uprising is as a tumour on the body
      politic, but the death of Puritans will heal the State. 'Channel' in line
      66 is a pun on 'charnel'.

REGENERATION

This poem, which deals with Vaughan's recognition of his sinfulness and with his gradual recovery of faith and hope of eventual salvation, is appropriately placed near the beginning of *Silex*. It starts off as an allegory in imitation of Herbert's 'The Pilgrimage', but ends very differently. It has been greatly admired by Vaughan's readers; but while the general meaning is clear, individual images and lines pose problems of interpretation.

Regeneration

A Ward, and still in bonds, one day
   I stole abroad,
It was high-spring, and all the way
   Primros'd, and hung with shade;
   Yet, was it frost within,   5
   And surly winds
Blasted my infant buds, and sinne
   Like Clouds ecclips'd my mind.

2

Storm'd thus; I straight perceiv'd my spring
   Meere stage, and show,   10
My walke a monstrous, mountain'd thing
   Rough-cast with Rocks, and snow;
   And as a Pilgrims Eye
   Far from reliefe,
Measures the melancholy skye   15
   Then drops, and rains for griefe,

3

So sigh'd I upwards still, at last
   'Twixt steps, and falls
I reach'd the pinacle, where plac'd
   I found a paire of scales,   20
   I tooke them up and layd
   In th'one late paines,
The other smoake, and pleasures weigh'd
   But prov'd the heavier graines;

4

With that, some cryed, *Away;* straight I   25
    Obey'd, and led
Full East, a faire, fresh field could spy
    Some call'd it, *Jacobs Bed;*
    A Virgin-soile, which no
    Rude feet ere trod,   30
Where (since he stept there,) only go
    Prophets, and friends of God.

5

Here, I repos'd; but scarse will set,
    A grove descryed
Of stately height, whose branches met   35
    And mixt on every side;
    I entred, and once in
    (Amaz'd to see't,)
Found all was chang'd, and a new spring
    Did all my senses greet;   40

6

The unthrift Sunne shot vitall gold
    A thousand peeces,
And heaven its azure did unfold
    Checqur'd with snowie fleeces,
    The aire was all in spice   45
    And every bush
A garland wore; Thus fed my Eyes
    But all the Eare lay hush.

7

Only a little Fountain lent
    Some use for Eares,   50
And on the dumbe shades language spent
    The Musick of her teares;
    I drew her neere, and found
    The Cisterne full
Of divers stones, some bright, and round   55
    Others ill-shap'd, and dull.

8

The first (pray marke,) as quick as light
   Danc'd through the floud,
But, th'last more heavy then the night
   Nail'd to the Center stood;   60
I wonder'd much, but tyr'd
   At last with thought,
My restless Eye that still desir'd
   As strange an object brought;

9

It was a banke of flowers, where I descried   65
   (Though 'twas mid-day,)
Some fast asleepe, others broad-eyed
   And taking in the Ray,
   Here musing long, I heard
   A rushing wind   70
Which still increas'd, but whence it stirr'd
   No where I could not find;

10

I turn'd me round, and to each shade
   Dispatch'd an Eye,
To see, if any leafe had made   75
   Least motion, or Reply,
   But while I listning sought
   My mind to ease
By knowing, where 'twas, or where not,
   It whisper'd; *Where I please.*   80

   Lord, then said I, *On me one breath,*
And let me dye before my death!

Cant. Cap. 5. ver. 17.
Arise, O North, and come thou South-wind, and blow upon
my garden that the spices thereof may flow out.

NOTES

1   *Ward...bonds.* A ward is a minor, and Pettet interprets the word this way. But if Vaughan is a minor, he can only be so in the guardianship of God, in which case it would be difficult to understand why he is also in 'bonds', i.e. in bondage. The puzzle disappears if 'ward' is understood in the now rare sense of 'the condition of being a prisoner' (*OED* sense 3). Vaughan is a prisoner in sin's bondage. However, the sense of being a minor is not entirely absent, for the poem depicts the growth of a spiritual consciousness from the infantile to maturity. The sense that the poet is yet a child spiritually is present in line 7 also.

3-8   The contrast between the outward beauty of Nature and the wintry storms of the spirit indicates the poet's sense of dissatisfaction with his life of sin and suggests that the process of spiritual recovery has already begun, since though he can perceive the attractiveness of a sinful life (symbolized here by the beauty of the Spring), he does not find enjoyment in it.

4   *Primros'd.* Covered with primroses which bloom in late Spring. The word suggests the poet's youth, but it also carries suggestions of destruction, as in the phrase 'the primrose path of destruction.'

7   *infant buds.* A continuation of the flower metaphor. The buds would be the awakening spiritual sense which the mind's agitation nipped.

9   *Storm'd.* Used both literally to mean overwhelmed by the storm, and figuratively as a military metaphor to mean overcome by a sense of sinfulness.

10   *stage and show.* 'Show' echoes Psalm 39:6: 'Surely every man walketh in a vain show.' The 'stage' is the stage in the theatre where 'shows' are performed. The sense behind the two words is that the Spring (i.e. the pleasures of sinfulness) was illusory.

11   *mountain'd.* Mountains had not come to be regarded, as they would be in the late eighteenth century and in Wordsworth, as sublimely beautiful. In Vaughan they carry the connotation of something fearful and monstrous. The notion that a journey towards spiritual salvation requires a movement upwards is conventional.

15   *Measures.* Takes measure of, looks at.

16   *rains for griefe.* Sheds tears of grief.

20   *a paire of scales.* The image of scales is common in the Bible and was often used in contemporary emblem books. Vaughan is probably not referring to any specific Biblical passage or emblem.

21-4   The sense here is obscure because it is not clear what Vaughan considers to be heavier than what. It is obvious that in the scales he weighs the sufferings he has undergone in the course of his journey ('late pains') against the pleasures (earlier symbolized by the beauty of the Spring) which he has rejected. But are the pleasures, which now appear to be as insubstantial as 'smoke', lighter or heavier than his sufferings? Common sense would suggest that the sufferings are heavier. But Vaughan may be implying that paradoxically the pleasures may prove to be heavier than the sufferings, for whereas his sufferings may take him upwards to salvation, the pleasures would drag him down to hell.

25   The voice mentioned in this line is obviously that of an angel, but Vaughan does not identify it further.

26-7   *led...East.* The voice leads the poet to the East. The East, where the light dawns, was also the direction from which it was believed that mankind would receive the knowledge of God.

28   *Jacobs Bed.* Refers to Genesis 28:11 ff. where Jacob dreamt of a ladder on which angels were ascending and descending and at the top of which stood God. God told Jacob that the land where he was sleeping would be his. The field which Vaughan sees is obviously the land given to Jacob, and therefore the land of the elect.

32   *friends of God.* Refers to the Patriarchs. Cf. James 2:23: 'Abraham believed God... and he was called the Friend of God.'

33-5   Though groves were associated with pagan worship, the grove in Vaughan recalls a church. L.C. Martin quotes the following passage from Thomas Vaughan's *Lumen de Lumine* as a possible source for his twin Henry's image: 'Being thus troubled to no purpose, and wearied with long endeavours, I resolved to rest myself... I had not long continued in this humour, but I could hear the whispers of a soft wind that travelled towards me, and suddenly it was in the leaves of the trees, so I concluded myself to be in some wood, or wilderness.' Later he adds: 'I found myself in a grove of bays.'

39   The *new spring* of spiritual regeneration, brought about through worship in the church, is to be distinguished from the Spring of sinfulness and infancy with which the poem begins.

41   *The unthrift Sunne...gold.* The line may simply describe the bright, golden, life-giving ('vital') rays of the sun. But it probably also refers to Divine Illumination. Pettet sees the line as referring to the belief that precious metals in the earth were formed as a consequence of the heat of the sun. The notion of transformation from the baser to the more valuable squares well with that of spiritual regeneration in this poem.

44   According to Pettet, the line was almost certainly inspired by *Song of Songs* 4:16: 'Arise O North, and come thou South-wind, and blow upon my garden, that the spices thereof may flow out.'

47-8   Here the power of the eye is not rejected, but the idea is that the sight is not enough. The power of hearing needs to be stimulated also, for only through the ear can God's word be apprehended. As these lines suggest, the poet's eye has been taught to see aright, but his auditory powers are still dormant.

49   *Fountain.* A symbol of Christ. Cf. Psalms 36:9: 'For with thee is the fountain of life.' The water image contained in *fountain* is traditionally associated with life-giving powers, and the water in these lines is also the water of baptism.

51-2 The lines may be glossed thus: The sweet music of the water drops was, as it were, the language of the fountain. However, the fountain's words were uttered in vain ('spent') to the unresponsive dumb shades; this failure made the fountain shed tears. The image of the fountain's water as tears is common enough; what is difficult to interpret is the phrase 'dumb shades.' Pettet thinks that the line may be corrupt. Could the expression refer to unregenerate humanity? It could be argued that fallen mankind is dumb because it is deaf to the voice of God, and sin has reduced it to a shadow. But this interpretation may represent an unwarranted stretching of the meaning.

55-60 R.A. Durr says that the two types of stone in the fountain's basin represent the regenerate who have been quickened by the waters of grace and those who remain insensitive to Christ and are therefore nailed to the 'centre' (in the sense of earth and, ultimately, hell, which was sometimes located in the centre of the globe.)

66   *mid-day.* Suggestive of the full, clear light of God.

67-8 The two types of flowers, like the two types of stone earlier, are representative of unregenerate and regenerate mankind respectively. The flower image here and in line 75 recalls the earlier flower image in the poem; but whereas earlier the flowers were symbolical of sin, now they stand for the souls of men. 'Ray' in line 68 is the life-giving grace of God earlier referred to in line 41.

70   The 'rushing wind' is the breath of God. Vaughan's sources are John 3:8: 'The wind bloweth where it listeth, and thou hearest the sound thereof, but canst not tell whence it cometh, and whither it goeth...' and Acts 2:2: 'And suddenly there came a sound from heaven as of a rushing mighty wind, and it filled all the house...'

81-2 The poet at last and in a flash recognizes the significance of his journey and the nature of the wind. This is in contrast to the bafflement he felt at various places in the poem, e.g. in lines 8, 38 and 69. His desire in the last line of the poem to die before his death represents a desire to let the old Adam die in him so that he can be born in the spirit.

THE RETREATE

Thomas Calhoun points out that this poem is based upon a passage of Boethius' *De Consolatione* which Vaughan had earlier translated into verse. Vaughan uses the Boethian idea of a happy childhood but transforms it to his own uses. 'The Retreate' has invited comparisons with Wordsworth's *Ode to the Intimations of Immortality*. But though both Vaughan and Wordsworth see childhood as a state of purity and innocence when memories of the soul's stay in heaven are still present, Vaughan is interested not so much in presenting a philosophy of childhood as in recreating a vision of purity. He expresses a contrast between the state of disorder which characterizes adulthood and the state of innocence experienced as a child, and he 'forces us to contemplate both states simultaneously.' (Simmonds). The forward motion of the poet in time leads to sin, the backward motion to innocence. Thus the forward motion in time becomes, paradoxically, a morally backward motion, and a backward motion in time a morally forward one.

The Retreate

Happy those early dayes! when I
Shin'd in my Angell-infancy.
Before I understood this place
Appointed for my second race,
Or taught my soul to fancy ought   5
But a white, Celestiall thought,
When yet I had not walkt above
A mile, or two, from my first love,
And looking back (at that short space,)
Could see a glimpse of his bright-face;   10
When on some *gilded Cloud*, or *flowre*
My gazing soul would dwell an houre
And in those weaker glories spy
Some shadows of eternity;
Before I taught my tongue to wound   15
My Conscience with a sinfull sound,
Or had the black art to dispence
A sev'rall sinne to ev'ry sence,
But felt through all this fleshly dresse
Bright *shootes* of everlastingness.   20
    O how I long to travell back
And tread again that ancient track!
That I might once more reach that plaine,

Where first I left my glorious traine,
From whence th'Inlightned spirit sees   25
That shady City of Palme trees;
But (ah!) my soul with too much stay
Is drunk, and staggers in the way.
Some men a forward motion love,
But I by backward steps would move,   30
And when this dust falls to the urn
In that state I came return.

NOTES

2   *Angell-infancy.* Infancy when I was pure as an angel.

3   *this place.* The world.

4   *second race.* The first stage of the soul's existence or journey (race) takes place in heaven, the second on earth.

6   Cf. Marvell's 'The Garden': 'Green thought in a green shade.'

7-8   'My first love' is heaven. Since I was a child, my soul had just come to this world from heaven and so I could not be said to be very far from there. 'Above' in line 7 means more than.

10   *his.* God's.

13   *those weaker glories.* The beauty of natural objects was only a faint reflection of the glories of heaven, but in it I was able to perceive those glories. The idea that natural objects are reflections or shadows of eternal Types is Platonic. Cf. 'I walkt the other day', line 50 and note.

18   *A sev'rall sinne.* Different sins.

20   Commentators have pointed out that this line is a quotation from Feltham's *Resolves: Divine, Political and Moral* (1631).

21-2 The poet wishes to retrace his steps to the past when he was a child.

25-6 From the top of Pisgah, Moses viewed the valley of Jericho which God had promised to the Israelites. Deuteronomy 34:3 describes it as 'the city of palm trees.' The vantage point from which Vaughan hopes to have a vision of heaven is the earliest years of his childhood.

27-8 *too much...drunk.* My soul is intoxicated by having stayed too long in this world and therefore staggers in its attempts to trace the steps back to my childhood.

30   *move.* The suggestion is that a movement back to childhood would also be a spiritual progression.

31-2 Death will free me from my 'fleshly dresse' (line 19) and then my soul will regain the state it was in when it came down to the earth. In that state it will return once again to heaven.

PEACE

Nothing in the vision of heaven offered in this delicate lyric is non-traditional, but the poem makes a strong impact by characterizing heaven as a place of remoteness and peace. Worth noting also in the first part is the paradox that there is peace in heaven because Christ is the perfect soldier and general.

Peace

My Soul, there is a Countrie
   Far beyond the stars,
Where stands a winged Centrie
   All skilfull in the wars,
There above noise, and danger   5
   Sweet peace sits crown'd with smiles,
And one born in a Manger
   Commands the Beauteous files,
He is thy gracious friend,
   And (O my Soul awake!)   10
Did in pure love descend
   To die here for thy sake,
If thou canst get but thither,
   There growes the flowre of peace,
The Rose that cannot wither,   15
   Thy fortresse, and thy ease;
Leave then thy foolish ranges;
   For none can thee secure,
But one, who never changes,
   Thy God, thy life, thy Cure.   20

NOTES

3   *Centrie.* Sentry. The reference is to Christ, or possibly the Archangel Michael.
7   Christ was born in a manger.
8   *Files.* Ranks, Armies.
17   *Ranges.* Movements, wanderings.
18   *Secure.* save.

THE WORLD

This remarkable poem draws its vigour as much from its dazzling
opening where a mystical vision is presented as from the bold, hard-
hitting satire that follows and gives substance to John Aubrey's
comment that with his enemies Vaughan could be 'proud and
humorous.' It has been suggested that the figure of the 'darksome
States-man' at the beginning of the second stanza is Cromwell, but
this is mere conjecture. The victims of the poet's satire are probably
just types rather than particular individuals. After showing how
completely worldly concerns have divorced men from heaven, the
poet exhorts sinners to follow the way which 'leads up to God.' But
as happens in so much satirical writing, a contemplation of evil has
so tainted the satirist himself that he realizes at the end of the poem
that he cannot follow his own advice and that the vision with which
the poem opened is not for him.

The World

I Saw Eternity the other night
Like a great *Ring* of pure and endless light,
   All calm, as it was bright,
And round beneath it, Time in hours, days, years
     Driv'n by the spheres   5
Like a vast shadow mov'd, In which the world
   And all her train were hurl'd;
The doting Lover in his queintest strain
     Did their Complain,
Neer him, his Lute, his fancy, and his flights,   10
     Wits sour delights,
With gloves, and knots the silly snares of pleasure
     Yet his dear Treasure
All scatter'd lay, while he his eys did pour
     Upon a flowr.   15

2

The darksome States-man hung with weights and woe
Like a thick midnight-fog mov'd there so slow
   He did nor stay, nor go;

Condemning thoughts (like sad Ecclipses) scowl
    Upon his soul,   20
And Clouds of crying witnesses without
    Pursued him with one shout.
Yet dig'd the Mole, and lest his ways be found
    Workt under ground,
Where he did Clutch his prey, but one did see   25
    That policie,
Churches and altars fed him, Perjuries
    Were gnats and flies,
It rain'd about him bloud and tears, but he
    Drank them as free.   30

3

The fearfull miser on a heap of rust
Sate pining all his life there, did scarce trust
    His own hands with the dust,
Yet would not place one peece above, but lives
    In feare of theeves.   35
Thousands there were as frantick as himself
    And hug'd each one his pelf,
The down-right Epicure plac'd heav'n in sense
    And scornd pretence
While others slipt into a wide Excesse   40
    Said little lesse;
The weaker sort slight, triviall wares Inslave
    Who think them brave,
And poor, despised truth sate Counting by
    Their victory.   45

4

Yet some, who all this while did weep and sing,
And sing, and weep, soar'd up into the *Ring*,
    But most would use no wing.
O fools (said I,) thus to prefer dark night   50
    Before true light,
To live in grots, and caves, and hate the day
    Because it shews the way,

The way which from this dead and dark abode
    Leads up to God,
A way where you might tread the Sun, and be   55
    More bright than he.
But as I did their madnes so discusse
    One whisper'd thus,
This Ring the Bride-groome did for none provide
    But for his bride.   60

John Cap. 2. ver. 16, 17.
All that is in the world, the lust of the flesh, the lust of the Eys, and the pride of life is not of the father, but is of the world.

And the world passeth away, and the lusts thereof, but he that doth the will of God abideth for ever.

NOTES

2   *Ring.* Rings and circles are symbols of perfection. At the end of the poem the ring will also become the wedding ring with which Christ weds His bride, the Church.

4-7   Note the contrast between the stillness of the ring of eternity and the vigorous movement ('hurl'd' in line 7) that takes place underneath it. The commonplace medieval notion that time was created by the movement of the eight spheres is given a dramatic and unusual representation in lines 4 and 5: the spheres are like a charioteer driving the chariot of time as represented by 'hours, days, years' (line 4). Time is also a 'vast shadow' (line 6) because it was held by Platonists to be a shadow or reflection of Reality. Vaughan establishes a link between time and all the activities of the world. The personages and their activities which he satirizes are caught up in time, and their frantic rush (which corresponds with and results from the hurtling movement of the chariot of time) prevents them from having a vision of the stillness of eternity.

8   *queintest strain.* Quaintest, most affected manner.
9   *their.* There.
10-15 The medley of objects that surround the lover not only suggests his disordered mind but also indicates that he is a conventional courtly lover such as had by now passed into a figure of fun.
10-11 *fancy...delights.* The lover's fancy, his flights of imagination, which once delighted him had now turned sour.
12   *knots...pleasure.* Lovers' knots were meant to symbolize a tying together of hearts. Vaughan dismisses them with good-humoured contempt as 'silly'.

16-17 The 'weights and woe' that hang over the statesman like a 'thick midnight-fog' are presumably the cares of office; as line 18 suggests, they immobilize him.

19   *Condemning thoughts.* Thoughts of his guilt, or his moral scruples and conscience.

21   The 'crying witnesses' or accusers whose shouts of denunciation surround the statesman match his inner thoughts described in lines 19-20.

23-6 The mole is a rodent that burrows underground. The secret schemings of the statesman make this an apt comparison. Vaughan suggests (lines 25-6) that though the statesman makes attempts to keep his corrupt policies secret, they are visible. 'One' in line 15 may refer to the poet himself, who possesses a vision from which the statesman's intentions cannot remain hidden. Or it may refer to mankind generally.

27   *Churches...him.* If the passage refers to Cromwell, the reference here could be to his ban on the Church of England in Wales.

27-8 *Perjuries...flies.* This probably means that the statesman's lies were as common as flies. The Puritans removed the poet's twin brother Thomas from his position as Rector of the parish church in Llansantffraed in Wales on trumped-up charges of drunkenness and whoring.

32-5 The miser is so scared of being robbed that he hardly dares to touch his gold with his own hands lest he should commit the robbery.

37   *pelf.* Wealth, possessions.

38-9 The epicure, scorning any pretence of religious belief, thinks that heaven is synonymous with a gratification of the senses.

40-1 Other people who were guilty of different kinds of excesses, as great as the epicure's, concurred with him.

42-3 May be paraphrased: Trivial wares or objects enslaved the weaker sort, who regarded these trivialities as wonderful.

44   *sate.* Sat.
      Counting. Reckoning, considering. Since the whole stanza describes attachment to, or counting of, worldly wealth, truth is said to be counting too: despised and poor, she sits neglected by lovers of the world and observes ('counts') them counting their wealth.

46-7 According to Hermetic notions, 'those who have escaped the world by ascending through the seven spheres and have attained the eighth sphere sing...before entering into God' (Fogle). Fogle adds that Vaughan may have associated these ascending souls with the great multitude from whose eyes 'God shall wipe away all tears' (Revelation 21:4), and this association might have given him the notion that the souls were weeping as well as singing.

59-60 See headnote to the poem. Though Vaughan believes that some souls are on their way to salvation, he is not one of them though he has been vouchsafed a vision of eternity and of souls ascending to God.

I WALKT THE OTHER DAY (TO SPEND MY HOUR)

'I walkt the other day' may be read as a pastoral elegy on the death
of a friend or relative who is mentioned in the last lines. The dead
person may be seen to be symbolized by the 'gallant' flower, and we
may take the poem as an attempt on the poet's part to understand the
meaning of his friend's death, which leads eventually to an under-
standing of the meaning of his own life. But the poem is more than
a conventional elegy. Starting off as a description of a natural phe-
nomenon, it proceeds to turn this phenomenon into a moral and
religious emblem. The flower in the poem is both flower and symbol,
both a physical and a metaphysical entity (not to mention its role as
symbol of the poet's dead friend). The notion of the flowerbed as
both a grave and a bed enables the poet to see the flower as the
harbinger of his own mortality and also as conveying the hopeful
message of resurrection. Through this multiple use of the flower
image the poet succeeds in recognizing the ineluctable fact of death,
and yet perceiving that in a larger scheme of things death is not final
but only the prelude to a new life.

Thomas Calhoun points out that the poet's balancing act, which
saves him from either treating the flower totally realistically or from
transcending its physical reality altogether, is part of that larger
design which enables him to hold the past, the present and the future
in suspension. The poem takes place in the present, but the past is
recalled so vividly that it becomes part of the present also. The
present itself is sought to be transformed into a more desirable
future, which, however, by the end of the poem remains an ideal as
yet unachieved. Thus by taking a stance which is not quite in the past
or present or future the poet is able to combine these three in the
same way as he combines symbol with reality, invisible God with
visible Nature, and death with regeneration and a new life.

I walkt the other day

I walkt the other day (to spend my hour,)
    Into a field
Where I sometimes had seen the soil to yield
    A gallant flowre,
But Winter now had ruffled all the bowre   5
    And curious store
  I knew there heretofore.

3

Yet I whose search lov'd not to peep and peer
    I'th' face of things
Thought with my self, there might be other springs   10
    Besides this here
Which, like cold friends, sees us but once a year,
    And so the flowre
    Might have some other bowre.

Then taking up what I could neerest spie   15
    I digg'd about
That place where I had seen him to grow out,
    And by and by
I saw the warm Recluse alone to lie
    Where fresh and green   20
    He lived of us unseen.

4

Many a question Intricate and rare
    Did I there strow,
But all I could extort was, that he now
    Did there repair   25
Such losses as befel him in this air
    And would e'r long
    Come forth most fair and young.

5

This past, I threw the Clothes quite o'r his head,
    And stung with fear   30
Of my own frailty dropt down many a tear
    Upon his bed,
Then sighing whisper'd, *Happy are the dead!*
    What peace doth now
    Rock him asleep below?   35

6

And yet, how few believe such doctrine springs
    From a poor root

Which all the Winter sleeps here under foot
    And hath no wings
To raise it to the truth and light of things,   40
    But is stil trod
  By ev'ry wandring clod.

7

O thou! whose spirit did at first inflame
    And warm the dead,
And by a sacred Incubation fed   45
    With life this frame
Which once had neither being, forme, nor name,
    Grant I may so
  Thy steps track here below,

8

That in these Masques and shadows I may see   50
    Thy sacred way,
And by those hid ascents climb to that day
    Which breaks from thee
Who art in all things, though invisibly;
    Shew me thy peace,   55
  Thy mercy, love, and ease,

9

And from this Care, where dreams and sorrows raign
    Lead me above
Where Light, Joy, Leisure, and true Comforts move
    Without all pain,   60
There, hid in thee, shew me his life again
    At whose dumbe urn
  Thus all the year I mourn.

NOTES

4   *Gallant flowre*. According to the *OED* the gallant is an English
     garden flower of Levantine origin.
5   *bowre*. Bower, or the place where the flower was growing.

6   *curious store*. 'Curious' is used in the common seventeenth-century
       sense of fine, delicate, choice or intricate. 'Store' refers to all the ap-
       purtenances, accessories and belongings of the flower, in a word,
       everything related to it.

8-9   i.e. not content with peeping and peering into the face of things, I
       wanted to investigate deeper.

10-14 Though the meaning is simple, it is expressed rather awkwardly. The
       poet means: I thought that there must be other places ('springs' in
       line 10 = places of rising or issuing from the ground) besides this
       garden which the flower visits. Indeed, maybe it visits this garden
       only infrequently, just as cold or distant friends visit us infrequently;
       be that as it may, perhaps it has gone somewhere else.

16   *digg'd*. Dug.

19   *Recluse*. The flower, like a hermit, has withdrawn into its under-
       ground solitude and made itself comfortable there. The withdrawal
       underground refers, of course, to the fact that while the stem of the
       flower has withered, the vital spirit or sap has retreated to the root.

25-6   The flower has withdrawn underground to repair the damages that
       befell it while it was growing above ground. The notion is that death
       is a restorative for the ills of life and a preparation for a new life. How-
       ever, as the next stanza suggests, the poet does not understand this
       lesson right away. Instead, he thinks of death as final. It is only from
       stanza 6 and, even more, from 7 that the poet becomes aware of this
       larger meaning.

29   The word *Clothes* here refers to the soil which the poet had dug in
       order to get to the root. He buries the root again; and in doing so is
       reminded that he, too, will be buried one day. This thought leads to
       the expression in the rest of the stanza of the fear and sorrow of death.
       But though the poet is not aware of it as yet, the word *Clothes* suggests
       also the bedclothes that cover a sleeper. In this sense the poet's act
       of throwing the clothes over the sleeper indicates that death is but a
       sleep from which there will be a reawakening. The poet will reach an
       awareness of this latter meaning later in the poem, whereupon the
       elegiac lament over death, which we find in stanza 5, will be trans-
       muted to a prayer for being absorbed in God on the other side of the
       grave.

37   *poor root*. Though, in terms of the larger moral and religious
       meanings that Vaughan is about to draw from his experience, the
       flower may appear little more than a poor root, this term does not in
       any way negate or transcend the pastoral-elegiac experience of the
       earlier part of the poem. The flower is both a 'gallant' flower and a
       poor root trodden upon by everybody.

39-40 Unlike the root, the poet is able to raise himself to the 'truth and light
       of things.' Thus the flower is not an emblem of the poet's own life in

every way, but it is the foundation for his understanding of the nature of life and death.

Stanza 7. Pettet points out that the imagery associated here with God's creation of man ('inflame', 'Incubation') is borrowed from Hermetic philosophy. In this stanza Vaughan says that the spark of life in human beings was kindled from the spirit of God.

48-9   Vaughan means that all natural objects on earth are, as it were, God's footsteps, and it is possible for man to climb up to God by following these footsteps. That is, man can reach God by learning to read and understand Nature correctly. The poem is an example of how this can be done: meditation on the nature of the flower has led Vaughan to God.

50   *Masques and shadows.* Though the metaphor is changed, the idea here is the same as in line 49 above. Natural objects are seen here as Plato saw them: as unreal and insubstantial reflections of God's reality, but capable of leading man to an apprehension of God. Cf. 'The Retreate' lines 11-14 and note.

57   *raign.* Reign.

61-2   *his life...urn.* The person to whose death the poet refers here has not been identified. The last lines suggest that the poem is to be read retrospectively as an elegy in which Vaughan mourns the death of a loved one and, at the end, arrives at the hope that after his own death and resurrection in God he will be able to meet his loved one again and understand his death aright. Seen thus, the 'gallant flower' of the poem becomes a symbol not only of death and rebirth but also of the person who is being mourned here.

THE NIGHT

Given its content, the placement of 'The Night' towards the end of the second part of *Silex* is appropriate. The poem is based upon the story of Nicodemus's encounter with Christ, not, as Vaughan says, in John 2:3 but in John 3:2. The story goes that Nicodemus, a Pharisee, met Christ at night and heard from Him what man needs to do in order to be saved. Neither Augustine, nor Chrysostom, nor Luther, nor Calvin believed that Nicodemus understood what Christ told him about the need to be born again in the spirit. However, Vaughan exalts Nicodemus to the status of a 'most blest believer', possibly because he wants to suggest a similarity between Nicodemus and himself and also the extent to which his own age is less propitious than when Christ performed His ministry. Like the Pharisee he, too, is living in an age of ignorance. If Nicodemus lived in a 'land of darkness and blinde eyes', the Puritan interregnum in which Vaughan is writing is equally dark since the Anglican Church has been proscribed. Therefore he is forced to seek Christ in the dark. But Nicodemus was doing so at the beginning of the Christian era, whereas Vaughan believes that he is doing so at the end. For a brief moment he is able to perform a Nicodemus-like miracle of seeing the sun at midnight, but at the end of the poem he returns to the world of discord. The ideal union which Nicodemus experienced may be possible, but only briefly, in these degenerate times.

Commentators often point out that in this poem Vaughan does not employ his standard imagery of brightness, morning and light. The idea that God's voice can be heard only in the dark of the night, when the hubbub of the world is stilled, is traditional enough. But Jonathan Post also points out that for Vaughan it is more important than ever to hear God's voice in the dark, for the darkness in this poem symbolizes the darkness that Vaughan believes fell over Britain with the success of Puritanism. Post sees the poem as allegorical of the poet's vision of the end of this world and the coming of the Millenium; as such it looks forward to a time when Puritanism will be undone.

The Night.
John 2.3

    Through that pure *Virgin -Shrine,*
That sacred vail drawn o'r thy glorious noon
That men might look and live as Glo-worms shine,
      And face the Moon:
    Wise *Nicodemus* saw such light   5
    As made him know his God by night.

    Most blest believer he!
Who in that land of darkness and blinde eyes
Thy long expected healing wings could see,
      When thou didst rise,   10
    And what can never more be done,
    Did at mid-night speak with the Sun!

    O who will tell me, where
He found thee at that dead and silent hour!

What hallow'd solitary ground did bear   15
    So rare a flower,
  Within whose sacred leafs did lie
  The fulness of the Deity.

  No mercy-seat of gold,
No dead and dusty *Cherub,* nor carv'd stone,   20
But his own living works did my Lord hold
    And lodge alone;
  Where *trees* and *herbs* did watch and peep
  And wonder, while the *Jews* did sleep.

  Dear night! this worlds defeat;   25
The stop to busie fools; cares check and curb;
The day of Spirits; my souls calm retreat
    Which none disturb!
  Christs progress, and his prayer time;
  The hours to which high Heaven doth chime.   30

  Gods silent, searching flight:
When my Lords head is fill'd with dew, and all
His locks are wet with the clear drops of night;
    His still, soft call;
  His knocking time; The souls dumb watch,   35
  When Spirits their fair kinred catch.

  Were all my loud, evil days
Calm and unhaunted as is thy dark Tent,
Whose peace but by some *Angels* wing or voice
    Is seldom rent;   40
  Then I in Heaven all the long year
  Would keep, and never wander here.

  But living where the Sun
Doth all things wake, and where all mix and tyre
Themselves and others, I consent and run   45
    To ev'ry myre,
  And by this worlds ill-guiding light,
  Erre more then I can do by night.

There is in God (some say)
A deep, but dazling darkness; As men here   50
Say it is late and dusky, because they
    See not all clear;
O for that night! where I in him
Might live invisible and dim.

NOTES

1-4   *Virgin-shrine...Moon.* The lines are packed with allusions and none
too clear. Thomas Calhoun says that 'Virgin-shrine' may mean the
Virgin Mary. Christ is like the bright light of the noon which dazzles
any human eye that dares to look at it. However, men may study and
contemplate Him by regarding his countenance in and through
Mary, who is, as it were, a veil ('vail' in line 2) which shades His light
and makes it bearable to the human eye. In this respect Mary can be
compared to the moon which reflects the light of the sun and makes
it accessible to the viewer. Men, then, would be like glow-worms. For
glow-worms shine only because they face the moon and reflect its
light in the same way as Mary reflects Christ's life. If the lines are
interpreted this way, the identification of the Virgin Mary with the
moon would take on special significance since in Greek mythology
Diana, the moon goddess, was also the goddess of chastity; similarly
the comparison of mankind with glow-worms would suggest its
inferior and dependent status. Pettet reads the lines differently. He
quotes Exodus 33:20, where God said, 'Thou canst not see my face:
for there shall no man see me, and live.' He also quotes Hebrews
10:20, which describes the Christian way as a 'new and living way,
which he [Christ] hath consecrated to us, through the veil, that is to
say, his flesh.' On the basis of these two quotations he interprets
'Virgin-shrine' as a reference to the incarnation of God as man in a
human body. Men can look on God only because He is clothed
(veiled) in the human body. The advantage in accepting Pettet's
reading is that it provides a more logical transition than does
Calhoun's to lines 5 and 6 of the poem. For what Vaughan is saying
there is that though Nicodemus met the human Christ at night, he
recognized Him immediately as the source of all light.

8   Nicodemus's age was characterized by 'darkness and blinde eyes' be-
cause his fellow Jews failed to recognize Christ's divinity.

9   *long expected healing wings.* Cf. Malachi 4:2: 'But unto you that fear
my name shall the Sun of righteousness arise with healing in his
wings.' From this line on the poet addresses Christ directly.

12   *mid-night...Sun.* Nicodemus did something which is now impossible
      since Christ does not walk physically in our midst any more. 'Sun' is,
      of course, a pun on 'Son.'

15   *hallow'd solitary ground.* According to Pettet, Vaughan imagines
      that Nicodemus met Christ in some solitary place like the Mount of
      Olives where Christ often retreated for prayer and meditation.

17   *leafs.* Leaves or petals.

19-22 Vaughan contemptuously contrasts the splendours of richly wrought
      temples to the simple environment in which Christ chose to work.
      Lines 19 and 20 are an echo of Exodus 25:17-18 'And thou shalt make
      a mercy seat of pure gold...And thou shalt make two cherubims of
      gold...' In a poem where darkness, not light, is a thing of value, the
      gold of the temple represents a less desirable quality than the silence
      and solitude which surround Christ in the previous stanza.

21   *hold.* Occupy. The sense of this line is that Christ is not to be found
      in splendid temples but may be encountered in His works.

23-4 The lines create a vivid sense of all of creation intently focused upon
      Christ at midnight while mankind sleeps oblivious of His existence.

25-8 In the vehement and scornful rejection of the activities of the day may
      be read Vaughan's denunciation of the activities of the Puritans.

26   Night puts a stop to the activities of busy fools and acts as a check and
      curb to all cares. But the line may also mean that night puts a stop to
      the efforts of those Puritan fools and zealots who would intrude upon
      him and allays his fears (or cares) that they will continue to be
      importunate.

27   *The day of Spirits.* According to Paracelsus the night is the working
      time of spirits.

29   In the 1655 edition of *Silex*, Vaughan indicated that the source of this
      line was Luke 21:37: '[A]nd at night he [Christ] went out, and abode
      in the mount that is called the mount of Olives'. 'The phrase 'Christ's
      progress' may refer to His visitation of man's soul when he is asleep
      at night. Cf. Job 33:14-16: 'For God speaketh once, yea twice, yet man
      perceiveth it not. In a dream, in a vision of the night, when deep sleep
      falleth upon men...he openeth the ears of men, and sealeth their in-
      struction.'

32-3 These lines are a quotation from Song of Solomon 5:2: 'I sleep, but
      my heart waketh: it is the voice of my beloved that knocketh, saying,
      Open to me, my sister, my love, my dove, my undefiled: for my head
      is filled with dew, and my locks with the drops of the night.' The 'dew'
      which covers Christ's head probably symbolizes grace.

34-5 Line 34 echoes the Biblical phrase 'a still small voice' in 1 Kings 19:12.
      The first part of line 35 recalls Revelation 3:20: 'Behold, I stand at the
      door, and knock: if any man hear my voice, and open the door, I will
      come into him, and will sup with him, and he with me.'

36   *kinred.* Kindred. The night is the time when spirits respond to one another, man's to God's and God's to man's.

38   *unhaunted.* Undisturbed, not only by the press of business but also by Puritan clamour.

38-40 *dark Tent...rent.* The dark night is the tent underneath which God shelters. Its peace is seldom disturbed except perhaps by the sound of an occasional angel's wing or voice.

41-2 *Heaven...keep.* I would always live ('keep') a heavenly kind of life.

43   The sun here represents daylight. The meaning of the line makes it clear that the sun-Son pun is far from Vaughan's mind.

44,46 *tyre/myre.* Tire/mire.

44   *all...tyre.* All things lose their purity by being blended indiscriminately. Pettet sees in 'tyre' a probable reference 'to the hermetic belief in the destructive wearing down of the Creation towards its final end.'

49-50 *There is...darkness.* L.C. Martin suggests that Vaughan may here be referring to Dionysius, the Areopagite who described the Divine Intelligence as a Divine Darkness. See Crashaw's 'Epiphany...sung as by the Three Kings,' lines 190 ff.

50-2 *As men...clear.* These are obscure and rather weak lines. Commentators usually gloss them as meaning that when men cannot see clearly they say that it is growing late and dark. Similarly some people say that there is a dazzling darkness in God.

53-4 *night...dim.* Here night represents not only the 'dazzling darkness' of God but also the end of the world. Vaughan looks forward to the end of the world when he will be absorbed in God. At the same time the poem's last line suggests that his notion of man's resurrection is that though being absorbed, he will also retain a dim consciousness of his earthly existence.

THE WATER-FALL

Like so many of his other nature poems, Vaughan's 'The Water-fall' is both naturalistic and religious. Without ever losing its specificity as a natural object, the waterfall also provides the poet with an occasion for a meditation on life and death and becomes, in fact, a symbol of the human condition. Because Vaughan says that the waterfall is one by which he has often sat, some critics have tried to identify it, but the poet could have had any one of a number of waterfalls in mind when he wrote the poem, or even no particular one. The first stanza, with its skilful weaving of pentameters and dimeters, enacts the slow movement of the water as it reaches the edge of the cliff, the

rapid cascading down the fall, and the roar as the water hits the
bottom and the spray rises up to the top. The later stanzas, where the
poet moralizes, are in octosyllabic couplets and perhaps less suc-
cessful. These stanzas show that the influence of Herbert, so strong
in the first part of *Silex,* had begun to wane by the time the second
part, from which this poem is taken, was written.

The Water-fall.

With what deep murmurs through times silent stealth
Doth thy transparent, cool and watry wealth
    Here flowing fall,
    And chide, and call,
As if his liquid, loose Retinue staid   5
Lingring, and were of this steep place afraid,
    The common pass
    Where, clear as glass,
    All must descend
    Not to an end.   10
But quickned by this deep and rocky grave,
Rise to a longer course more bright and brave.

    Dear stream! dear bank, where often I
    Have sate, and pleas'd my pensive eye,
    Why, since each drop of thy quick store   15
    Runs thither, whence it flow'd before,
    Should poor souls fear a shade or night,
    Who came (sure) from a sea of light?
    Or since those drops are all sent back
    So sure to thee, that none doth lack,   20
    Why should frail flesh doubt any more
    That what God takes, hee'l not restore?
    O useful Element and clear!
    My sacred wash and cleanser here,
    My first consigner unto those   25
    Fountains of life, where the Lamb goes?
    What sublime truths, and wholesome themes,
    Lodge in thy mystical, deep streams!
    Such as dull man can never finde

Unless that Spirit lead his minde,   30
Which first upon thy face did move,
And hatch'd all with his quickning love.
As this loud brooks incessant fall
In streaming rings restagnates all,
Which reach by course the bank, and then   35
Are no more seen, just so pass men.
O my invisible estate,
My glorious liberty, still late!
Though art the Channel my soul seeks,
Not this with Cataracts and Creeks.   40

NOTES

1   *times silent stealth.* Time steals by silently; in the same way the stream
    of water flows by the poet silently, almost imperceptibly, and inces-
    santly.
2   *thy.* The stream's.
4-6 As the leading edge of the stream reaches the cliff from where it will
    descend in the form of the waterfall, it starts making a noise. To the
    poet this noise suggests that the leading edge is chiding the body of
    the water which is behind it ('liquid, loose retinue' in line 5) for
    hesitating with fright at the moment of descent.
5   *staid.* Stayed.
7-12 *common pass...brave.* The cliff over which the water cascades is
    analogous to a gate or a 'pass' through which all men must go;
    however, this passage does not spell the end of their lives. The gate
    or pass is, of course, death, which the poet sees as an opening into a
    new life.
12 *brave.* Shining, splendid.
14 *sate.* Sat.
15-18 Each waterdrop follows the others, though it knows that the others
    have tumbled down the cliff in the form of the waterfall. Since
    waterdrops are not afraid to fall, why should men be afraid to die,
    especially as they know that so many men before them have died?
15 *quick.* Living and moving.
17 *shade or night.* The darkness of the grave.
18 *sea of light.* A Hermetic concept that souls originated in the light of
    heaven and will return there after the body's death.
19 The poet imagines that when the water hits the bottom of the fall, the
    spray that rises sends the water back up to the river again. Thus a
    never-ending cycle of falling and rising is created which is symboli-
    cal of birth, death and rebirth.

22   *bee'l*. He will.
23. *useful Element*. Pettet points out that Hermetic philosophy assigned a special importance to water in the cosmic process.
24   The line refers to baptism: water is the element in which men are baptized.
25-6 The water of the stream is the poet's 'first consigner' (i.e. prefiguration) of the water of life to which the Lamb of God will lead him after his death. The reference is to Revelation 7:17: 'the Lamb...shall lead them unto living fountains of waters.'
31   The reference is to Genesis 1:2: 'And the spirit of god moved upon the face of the waters.'
32   The idea that the world was 'hatched' by the Holy Spirit is Hermetical. Cf. 'I Walkt the other day (to spend my hour), line 45.
34   *restagnates all*. Makes all the waterdrops stagnant. The idea is that as the waterfall hits the bottom, a ring of spray rises. Because the water falls incessantly, this ring is permanently present.
35-6 Although the ring of spray (line 34 above) is permanent, each drop of water in the spray, once it has rejoined the stream, loses its separateness and can never again be identified. Similarly once men die they can never again be found. Vaughan does not mean that after death the souls of men are lost--to say that would be to contradict the whole poem--but rather that death causes the soul to be absorbed in God. He regards his eventual absorption as 'glorious liberty' (line 38). See 'The Night' lines 53-4.
39-40 The 'Channel' or stream that Vaughan seeks is not the physical one which is described in the poem but rather the Stream of God. Up to now the physical stream has been used as an analogue for the Stream of God, but now the poet distinguishes between the two. He expresses a preference for the mystical Stream and rejects the physical.

ANDREW MARVELL

Andrew Marvell (1621-1678) was born in Yorkshire and grew up in Hull. He entered Trinity College, Cambridge, in 1633, and in 1637 published Greek and Latin poems addressed to the king and queen. He left Cambridge in 1640 on the death of his father and, after being employed in a business house for two years, travelled in France and Italy from about 1642 to 1646, thus missing most of the Civil War years in England. In 1649 he addressed a poem to the Royalist poet, Sir Richard Lovelace, and the following year wrote 'An Horatian Ode upon Cromwell's Return from Ireland'. From 1650 to 1653 he lived at Appleton House, Yorkshire, as tutor to Mary, the daughter of Lord Fairfax, Britain's Commander in Chief, who, having disagreed with Cromwell about the need to invade Scotland, had retired to his estate. To these years belong most of Marvell's pastoral and lyric poems as well as the long *Upon Appleton House*. Failing in 1653 to obtain a government position for which Milton had recommended him, he became tutor to Cromwell's ward who was then studying at Eton. In 1655 he addressed 'The First Anniversary of the Government under His Highness the Lord Protector' to Cromwell, and in 1657 was appointed Latin Secretary, the other person holding this position being Milton. 1658 saw Marvell's poem on 'The Death of his Late Highness, the Lord Protector'. The following year he became M.P. for Hull and held the position till his death. As M.P. he helped to save Milton from execution after the Restoration and was active in state affairs. He satirized England's conduct of the war against Holland in 'The Second Advice to a Painter' (1655), travelled *incognito* to Holland as a spy, and wrote two prose tracts, *The Rehearsal Transpros'd* (1672) and *The Growth of Popery and Arbitrary Government* (1677), in which he criticized England's alliance with Catholic France against Protestant Holland, attacked what he saw as the growing tendency towards dictatorship in England, and argued the need in public affairs for men who were committed to principles rather than parties. Perhaps his last poem was written in 1674 to serve as a preface to the second edition of *Paradise Lost*.

Like the other poets anthologized here Marvell published only a few 'public' poems in his lifetime. His collected poems were published in 1681 by an imposter calling herself Mary Marvell and claiming to be his wife. Though she did this out of a hope for monetary gain, her text is generally sound. H.M. Margoliouth used it for his 1927 edition of *The Poems and Letters of Andrew Marvell*, though he supplemented it with manuscript material. The text in the present anthology is that contained in Margoliouth as revised and corrected for the third edition in 1971 by Pierre Legouis with the help of E.E. Duncan-Jones

There is agreement among Marvell scholars that his earlier poems are superior to those written after he entered public service. The favoured metre for the earlier poems was the tetrameter couplet, which he handled more effectively than the pentameter in which the later poems are written. The irony of the earlier poems is open-ended, exploratory and inconclusive; that used in the post-Restoration poems is directed against deviations from well-established norms. The earlier lyrics have haunting, recessive, elusive resonances against which the meaning of the later poems seems more definite and limited. While these perceptions recognize the artistic forfeit that Marvell paid when he made his commitment to public service, and incidentally reveal a bias for the 'Metaphysical' over the Restoration mode of writing poetry, they ignore the fact that Marvell himself did not consider the price too high: for him commitment was indispensable in fostering a private contemplation and exploration of the soul. The later poems are important for an all-round understanding of a man of many facets; and this belief has led me to include Marvell's poem on Milton in this anthology, the others being too long for a book like the present.

A DIALOGUE, BETWEEN THE RESOLVED SOUL, AND CREATED PLEASURE

Debate poems such as this were very popular through the Middle Ages and into the Renaissance. But though Marvell uses a traditional form, he gives it a quite unique twist. The poem has three speakers, Created Pleasure, the Resolved Soul, and the Chorus. Though we are meant to hear the poet's own voice in the Chorus's initial encouragement to the Soul and his joy in the final triumph, there is a danger in making too easy an identification between the Soul's attitudes and those of the poet. Consideration has to be given, too, to the courtesy with which Pleasure speaks thoughout and its evocation of the sensuous beauty of the physical whose dismissal by the Soul is curt, almost churlish at times. The tone in which the Soul speaks renders less effectual the irony which it directs at Pleasure's temptations.

A Dialogue, Between
The Resolved Soul, and Created Pleasure

Courage my Soul, now learn to wield
The Weight of thine immortal Shield.
Close on thy Head thy Helmet bright.
Ballance thy Sword against the Fight.
See where an Army, strong as fair,
With silken Banners spreads the air.
Now, if thou bee'st that thing Divine,
In this day's Combat let it shine:
And shew that Nature wants an Art
To conquer one resolved Heart.   10

Pleasure

Welcome the Creations Guest,
Lord of Earth, and Heavens Heir.
Lay aside that Warlike Crest,
And of Nature's banquet share:
Where the Souls of fruits and flow'rs
Stand prepar'd to heighten yours.

Soul

I sup above, and cannot stay
To bait so long upon the way.

Pleasure

On these downy Pillows lye,
Whose soft Plumes will thither fly:
On these Roses strow'd so plain   20
Lest one Leaf thy Side should strain.

Soul

My gentler Rest is on a Thought,
Conscious of doing what I ought.

Pleasure

If thou bee'st with Perfumes pleas'd,
Such as oft the Gods appeas'd,
Thou in fragrant Clouds shalt show
Like another God below.

Soul

A Soul that knowes not to presume
Is Heaven's and its own perfume.   30

Pleasure

Every thing does seem to vie
Which should first attract thine Eye:
But since none deserves that grace,
In this Crystal view *tby* face.

Soul

When the Creator's skill is priz'd,
The rest is all but Earth disguis'd.

Pleasure

Heark how Musick then prepares
For thy Stay these charming Aires;
Which the posting Winds recall,
And suspend the Rivers Fall.   40

Soul

Had I but any time to lose,
On this I would it all dispose.
Cease Tempter. None can chain a mind
Whom this sweet Chordage cannot bind.

Chorus

Earth cannot shew so brave a Sight
As when a single Soul does fence
The Batteries of alluring Sense,
And Heaven views it with delight.
    Then persevere: for still new Charges sound:
    And if thou overcom'st thou shalt be crown'd   50

Pleasure

All this fair, and soft, and sweet,
   Which scatteringly doth shine,
Shall within one Beauty meet,
   And she be only thine.

Soul

If things of Sight such Heavens be,
What Heavens are those we cannot see?

Pleasure

Where so e're thy Foot shall go
   The minted Gold shall lie;
Till thou purchase all below,
   And want new Worlds to buy.   60

Soul

Wer't not a price who'ld value Gold?
And that's worth nought that can be sold.

Pleasure

Wilt thou all the Glory have
   That War or Peace commend?
Half the World shall be thy Slave
   The other half thy Friend.

Soul

What Friends, if to my self untrue?
What Slaves, unless I captive you?

Pleasure

Thou shalt know each hidden Cause;
    And see the future Time: 70
Try what depth the Centre draws;
    And then to Heaven climb.

Soul

None thither mounts by the degree
Of Knowledge, but Humility.

Chorus

Triumph, triumph, victorious Soul;
The World has not one Pleasure more:
The rest does lie beyond the Pole,
And is thine everlasting Store.

NOTES

1-4   The first two lines indicate that the Soul is being tried for the first
      time. The soul's arming recalls Ephesians 6: 14-16 where Paul advises
      the Christian to put on the armour of truth, righteousness and faith;
      at the same time, the playful tone throughout the poem suggests that
      the combat between Pleasure and the Soul is going to be a friendly
      duel rather than a fight unto death.

7   *if thou bee'st.* The note of doubt undercuts the poet's commitment
      to the cause of the Soul.

9   *Nature....Art.* The Nature-Art antithesis is common in the Renais-
      sance. While exploiting it, Marvell also bridges it through the sugges-
      tion here that all arts are natural.

11-16 Pleasure is subtle enough to recognize that the Soul is creation's
      'guest,' not its permanent inhabitant. The temptations it offers are
      those which, while antithetical to the Soul's aspirations, are also
      subtly in consonance with its nature. Hence it is not fruits and flowers
      that are offered to the Soul but rather their spiritual essence.

18   *bait.* To feed while upon a journey.

20   *thither.* To heaven. Instead of trying to divert the Soul's flight to
      heaven, Pleasure offers temptations which, it claims, will make the
      journey smoother.

21   *plain.* Smooth, even.

23-4 While Pleasure proffers temptations which may be said to represent the physical at its most spiritual, the Soul's interests are purely abstract but expressed in language apprehensible to the senses, as here.

29-30 Part of the drama of the poem lies in the way the Soul disentangles various levels of meaning in Pleasure's speeches and turns the tempter's speeches against itself. In these lines the Soul does not exhibit a puritanical rejection of pleasures. It acknowledges the beauty of perfumes, but insists that the sweetest of them are not external aids but rather self-generated rewards of virtue.

39-40 Pleasure means that music has the power to make winds, which are hurrying on errands ('posting'), to tarry and the waterfall to be suspended: Art is capable of controlling Nature. Since Pleasure has hitherto represented the principle of Nature, not Art, these lines are also supposed to indicate its shifting, infirm nature.

44 *Chordage.* A pun: cordage = fetters; chordage = pertaining to musical chords.

46-7 *fence...Sense.* Ward off the attacks of the five senses. Pleasure has tempted the soul with taste (lines 11-16), touch (19-22), smell (25-28), sight (31-34) and sound (37-40).

51-68 Having overcome sensuous temptations the Soul's strategy undergoes a change. Now every time a temptation is proferred, it asks Pleasure a rhetorical question which Pleasure is unable to answer, till finally in line 68 the roles of the protagonists are reversed. Now it is the Soul which wishes to captivate Pleasure, thus showing their mutual interdependence.

71 *Centre.* The centre of the earth.

77 *beyond the Pole.* i.e. in heaven.

ON A DROP OF DEW

A beautiful natural object becomes, in this poem, the occasion for religious meditation and ultimately the rejection of the physical in favour of a spiritual world. Even as the physical is rejected, the poet's careful and detailed observation makes it real and palpable, and the description of the dewdrop possesses the qualities of a finely wrought still-life painting. The cool self-sufficiency of the dewdrop may be compared to that of the Soul in the previous poem. The metaphor of the soul's descent from and ascent to heaven was commonplace.

On a Drop of Dew

See how the Orient Dew,
Shed from the Bosom of the Morn
   Into the blowing Roses,
Yet careless of its Mansion new;
For the clear Region where 'twas born
   Round in its self incloses:
And in its little Globes Extent,
Frames as it can its native Element.
   How it the purple flow'r does slight,
     Scarce touching where it lyes,   10
   But gazing back upon the Skies,
     Shines with a mournful Light;
       Like its own Tear,
Because so long divided from the Sphear.
     Restless it roules and unsecure,
      Trembling lest it grow impure:
     Till the warm Sun pitty it's Pain,
And to the Skies exhale it back again.
     So the Soul, that Drop, that Ray
Of the clear Fountain of Eternal Day,   20
Could it within the humane flow'r be seen,
     Remembring still its former height,
     Shuns the sweat leaves and blossoms green;
     And, recollecting its own Light,
Does, in its pure and circling thoughts, express
The greater Heaven in an Heaven less.
     In how coy a Figure wound,
     Every way it turns away:
     So the World excluding round,
     Yet receiving in the Day   /   30
     Dark beneath, but bright above:
     Here disdaining, there in Love.
   How loose and easie hence to go:
   How girt and ready to ascend.
   Moving but on a point below,
   It all about does upwards bend.
Such did the Manna's sacred Dew destil;
White, and intire, though congeal'd and chill.
Congeal'd on Earth: but does, dissolving, run
Into the Glories of th' Almighty Sun.   40

NOTES

1   *Orient.* Legouis points out that the word means both pearl-like and
        born at sunrise.
4   *careless of.* Unconcerned about.
5-6   Because of the region where it was born (heaven) it encloses its self
        within itself.
7   *Globes.* The roundness or circular shape suggested by this word is a
        common symbol of perfection. See below, *circling* in line 25.
8   *native Element.* i.e. the life or animating principle it has brought with
        it from heaven.
14   *Sphear.* Sky, heaven.
21   *humane flow'r.* Human flower, i.e. the body.
23   *sweat.* Sweet.
24   *Recollecting.* A pun: remembering (line 22) and collecting or gather-
        ing within itself.
27   *coy.* The dewdrop may be coy about admitting any contact with this
        world, but it is open to the light of the spiritual day.
37-40 Cf. Exodus 16:21: 'and they gathered it [manna] morning by
        morning...and when the sun waxed hot, it melted'. Manna was the
        dewlike food dropped from heaven for the Israelites on their way
        from Egypt through the desert to the Chosen Land.

THE CORONET

'The Coronet' is a pastoral poem that questions the sincerity of the
genre, a skilfully constructed work of art that denies the value of art,
a religious poem that expresses the inadequacy of religious poems.
The intricate rhyme structure and varying line length are integral to
its total meaning and effect. Throughout, the metaphor of flowers
braided into a garland is developed, examined, rejected, and finally
reaffirmed in a totally unexpected manner.

The Coronet

When for the Thorns with which I long, too long,
    With many a piercing wound,
    My Saviours head have crown'd,
I seek with Garlands to redress that Wrong:
    Through every Garden, every Mead,

I gather flow'rs (my fruits are only flow'rs)
  Dismantling all the fragrant Towers
That once adorn'd my Shepherdesses head.
And now when I have summ'd up all my store,
  Thinking (so I my self deceive)   10
  So rich a Chaplet thence to weave
As never yet the king of Glory wore:
  Alas I find the Serpent old
  That, twining in his speckled breast,
  About the flow'rs disguis'd does fold,
  With wreaths of Fame and Interest.
Ah, foolish Man, that would'st debase with them,
And mortal Glory, Heavens Diadem!
But thou who only could'st the Serpent tame,
  Either his slipp'ry knots at once untie,   20
And disintangle all his winding Snare:
Or shatter too with him my curious frame:
And let these wither, so that he may die,
Though set with Skill and chosen out with Care.
That they, while Thou on both their Spoils dost tread,
May crown thy Feet, that could not crown thy Head.

NOTES

1-3   The poet implicates himself—and all of mankind—in the tortures
       inflicted on Christ on the cross.

7-8   *Towers....bead.* 'Towers' are high head-dresses worn by women. The
       poet's mistresses are shepherdesses because the poet is writing a
       pastoral poem in which the fiction of the poet as a shepherd is
       sustained. The lines imply a rejection of love poetry in favour of
       religious verse. The use of the pastoral genre for Christian purposes
       was common in the Renaissance.

13-16 The literal meaning of the passage is that the serpent, being speckled,
       could not be distinguished from the flowers, and was therefore
       mistakenly used to thread them together in the garland. Metaphori-
       cally, since the Serpent is Satan, Marvell is saying that his good
       intentions of praising God are brought to nought by the devil who
       inseparably entwines such base motives as self-praise and self-interest
       (line 16) with the poet's religious feelings. In so far as the poem is
       itself the coronet that Marvell is weaving—the long and intricate

sentences that crisscross one another suggest the intricacy of the
garland—the lines imply that no religious poetry can be free of the
poet's pride in composing it, just as no garland can be held together
without a thread.

19   *thou.* Christ. Marvell may be referring in this line to the medieval
      belief that between the time of his crucifixion and resurrection
      Christ descended to harrow hell; or the reference may be to Revela-
      tion 12:9 and 20:2 where the casting out of Satan by Christ is
      described.

20-1 The images of slipperiness and winding snares are indicative of
      Satan's wily nature.

22   *my curious frame.* My elaborately wrought coronet. The words are
      equally descriptive of the poem.

23   *these.* i.e. the flowers I have culled for you. They are the subject of the
      next line.

25   *Spoils.* A pun: ruins or remnants; also, booty captured in war.

EYES AND TEARS

There is the same ingenious elaboration of the weeping image in this
poem as in Donne's 'A Valediction: Forbidding Weeping' and Crashaw's
'The Weeper'; yet its differences from those poems are as important
as the similarities. Donne uses the extended weeping image as part
of a larger argument, while for Marvell the argument has to be found
through an understanding of the image itself. While Crashaw's poem
is characterized by exaggerated conceits, Marvell maintains a cool
detachment throughout. Each image in his poem remains separate,
sharply defined and emblematic, yet they all contribute to the devel-
opment of a theme which may be stated to be that of 'These weeping
Eyes, those seeing Tears'. At the beginning of the poem eyes and
tears are conjoined, but this conjunction soon breaks down as tears
come to be valued above eyes and Marvell realizes that eyes may see
but tears possess insight. In the meantime the eyes, which contained
only two tears when the poem opened, begin to overflow. This flood
once again establishes a conjunction between eyes and tears.

Eyes and Tears

                    I

How wisely Nature did decree,
With the same Eyes to weep and see!

That, having view'd the object vain,
They might be ready to complain.

II

And, since the Self-deluding Sight,
In a false Angle takes each hight;
These Tears which better measure all,
Like wat'ry Lines and Plummets fall.

III

Two Tears, which Sorrow long did weigh
Within the Scales of either Eye,   10
And then paid out in equal Poise,
Are the true price of all my Joyes.

IV

What in the World most fair appears,
Yea even Laughter, turns to Tears:
And all the Jewels which we prize,
Melt in these Pendants of the Eyes.

V

I have through every Garden been,
Amongst the Red, the White, the Green;
And yet, from all the flow'rs I saw,
No Hony, but these Tears could draw.   20

VI

So the all-seeing Sun each day
Distills the World with Chymick Ray;
But finds the Essence only Showers,
Which straight in pity back he powers.

VII

Yet happy they whom Grief doth bless,
That weep the more, and see the less:
And, to preserve their Sight more true,
Bath still their Eyes in their own Dew.

VIII

So *Magdalen,* in Tears more wise
Dissolv'd those captivating Eyes,   30
Whose liquid Chaines could flowing meet
To fetter her Redeemers feet.

IX

Not full sailes hasting loaden home,
Not the chast Ladies pregnant Womb,
Nor *Cyntbia* Teeming show's so fair,
As two Eyes swoln with weeping are.

X

The sparkling Glance that shoots Desire,
Drench'd in these Waves, does lose it fire.
Yea oft the Thund'rer pitty takes
And here the hissing Lightning slakes.   40

XI

The Incense was to Heaven dear,
Not as a Perfume, but a Tear.
And Stars shew lovely in the Night,
But as they seem the Tears of Light.

XII

Ope then mine Eyes your double Sluice,
And practise so your noblest Use.
For others too can see, or sleep;
But only humane Eyes can weep.

XIII

Now like two Clouds dissolving, drop,
And at each Tear in distance stop: 50
Now like two Fountains trickle down:
Now like two floods o'return and drown.

XIV

Thus let your Streams o'reflow your Springs,
Till Eyes and Tears be the same things: 50
And each the other's difference bears;
These weeping Eyes, those seeing Tears.

NOTES

3   *vain*. Worthless.
5-8   The stanza may be paraphrased: Eyes do not perceive reality accu-
       rately nor can they gauge the height of objects correctly because the
       rays of light that come from these objects strike the eyes at an angle.
       On the other hand, tears provide a better method of measurement
       because they fall perpendicularly, like the lines or plummets that
       sailors drop into the ocean to measure its depth. For Marvell's view
       that the power of visual perception is dependent upon beams from
       object striking the eyes, see Donne, 'The Ecstasy' lines 7-8 and notes.
       Lines and *plummets* are nautical terms. Part of the 'wit' in this stanza
       consists of regarding tears as the liquid *lines* which help to judge the
       depth of water.
9-10   Eyes are here compared to the two pans of a pair of scales in which
       one tear is being weighed against the other.
11   *paid out*. i.e. shed.
       Poise. Balance or weight.
12   *price*. The word develops the metaphor of making a payment used in
       line 11.
16   *Pendants*. A pendant is a piece of jewellery which hangs from some
       part of the body. Both the sense of hanging and that of precious or
       beautiful jewellery are contained in the description of tears as the
       eyes' pendants.
19-20 These tears are the only honey I was able to gather from the flowers.
21-4   Like an alchemist the sun heats the earth in order to distill its essence,
       but upon finding that this essence is only water, it pours (*powers* in
       line 24) the water back upon the earth in the form of rain. The image
       suggests that the sun, which is the eye of the day, is weeping.
29-32 *Magdalen*. Mary Magdalen washed Christ's feet with her tears and
       dried them with her hair. Marvell says that in thus dissolving her eyes
       in tears she proved the superiority of tears over eyes. They formed a
       liquid chain which bound Christ's feet, whereas her eyes, however
       captivating, would never have succeeded in this endeavour. Note the
       pun in line 32 on *fetter....feet*. Cp. with the end of Crashaw's 'The
       Weeper'.

34   *chast*. The word chaste does not mean a virgin but a woman faithful in marriage.

35   *Cynthia Teeming*. Cynthia is the Greek goddess of the moon. The phrase therefore refers to the full moon.

39   *Thund'rer*. Refers to the passionate lover who shoots sparkling glances of desire mentioned in line 37-38. The general sense of these lines is that tears quench the ardours of desire.

49-52 The poet's tears get progressively more voluminous. First they are like slowly falling raindrops between which some distance is maintained, then they turn into a trickle, and finally into a flood.

55   i.e till each begins to possess the distinguishing qualities of the other.

A DIALOGUE BETWEEN THE SOUL AND BODY

Another of the 'debate' poems of which Marvell wrote so many, this poem bears contrast with 'A Dialogue between The Resolved Soul, and Created Pleasure'. Rosalie Colie remarks that in this poem Marvell criticizes the inadequacy of the medieval genre of the debate poem. Neither the body nor the soul wins the sympathy of the reader to whom both address their case; instead, they seem to be 'whining complainers' who are neither independent of each other nor willing to recognize their interdependence. The poem remains open-ended and in the conclusion nothing is concluded. The puns, word play and irony are characterized by a sharp precision which is at the same time highly abstract.

A Dialogue between the Soul and Body

Soul

O who shall, from this Dungeon, raise
A Soul inslav'd so many wayes?
With bolts of Bones, that fetter'd stands
In Feet; and manacled in Hands.
Here blinded with an Eye; and there
Deaf with the drumming of an Ear.
A Soul hung up, as 'twere, in Chains
Of Nerves, and Arteries, and Veins.
Tortur'd, besides each other part,
In a vain Head, and double Heart.   10

Body

O who shall me deliver whole,
From bonds of this Tyrannic Soul?
Which, stretcht upright, impales me so,
That mine own Precipice I go;
And warms and moves this needless Frame:
(A Fever could but do the same).
And, wanting where its spight to try,
Has made me live to let me dye.
A Body that could never rest,
Since this ill Spirit it possest.   20

Soul

What Magick could me thus confine
Within anothers Grief to pine?
Where whatsoever it complain,
I feel, that cannot feel, the pain.
And all my Care its self employes,
That to preserve, which me destroys:
Constrain'd not only to indure
Diseases, but, whats worse, the Cure:
And ready oft the Port to gain,
Am Shipwrackt into Health again.   30

Body

But Physick yet could never reach
The Maladies Thou me dost teach;
Whom first the Cramp of Hope does Tear:
And then the Palsie Shakes of Fear.
The Pestilence of Love does heat:
Or Hatred's hidden Ulcer eat.
Joy's chearful Madness does perplex:
Or Sorrow's other Madness vex.
Which Knowledge forces me to know;
And Memory will not foregoe.   40
What but a Soul could have the wit
To build me up for Sin so fit?
So Architects do square and hew,
Green Trees that in the Forest grew.

NOTES

3-4   *fetter'd....Hands.* Fetters are applied to feet and manacles to hands
      (from Old Aryan *fed* = foot and Latin *manus* = hand). The Soul wittily
      implies that the body's feet are its fetters and the body's hands its
      manacles.

5-6   Cf. Donne, 'The Second Anniversary' 296-7: 'Thou shalt not peep
      through lattices of eyes,/Nor hear through labyrinths of ears...' The
      Soul paradoxically affirms that its 'senses' are rendered ineffectual by
      being embodied in the body's organs of perception.

7   *hung up.* Hanging or stringing up a prisoner was a form of torture.

10   The body's head is *vain* or useless for the soul because the soul can
      exercise its intelligence independently of the human brain. *Vain* also
      carries the sense of being proud. *Double* implies treachery, but this
      epithet may also have been applied to the heart because Renaissance
      anatomists mistakenly thought of the heart as being two-chambered.

13-14 The soul, being upright, makes the body literally stand straight so that
      the eyes, looking down to the feet, seem to be contemplating a
      precipice. Impaling was a form of torture where the prisoner had a
      stake thrust vertically through his body.

15   *needless.* Having no need. The body claims that it would not have any
      motion or sense but for the soul.

19-20 Either that the soul, like an evil spirit, has possessed the body, or that
      the body possesses the soul.

24   The soul, being insensate, cannot feel pain its own.

25-6 The body uses the intelligence ('Care') which only the soul could
      provide in order to stay alive; but so long as the body is alive the soul
      is trapped in it and cannot do what it would most like—escape to
      heaven. In this sense the body's health is the soul's shipwreck, while
      the body's death would enable the soul to reach its destination (lines
      29-30).

35   *Pestilence...heat.* The plague was thought to be caused by excessively
      hot weather.

42   The body is right in that according to the Christian doctrine it is not
      the body by itself but the soul that sins. However, Marvell probably
      wants us to realize too that the soul is capable of sinning only because
      it has been embodied.

TO HIS COY MISTRESS

This justly admired poem combines the theme of seduction with the
carpe diem theme. While maintaining a rigorously dialectical argu-

ment ('if...then. But since....therefore') it uses images that are as hard
to define precisely as they are striking. The conventions of celebrat-
ing the lady and addressing her courteously are fully preserved, but
they are also undercut by a constant reminder of the inexorable
passage of time. At the heart of the poem lies a sense of emptiness, of
the 'desarts of vast eternity' against which love making may prove to
be an anodyne but which it cannot conquer. As B. Rajan remarks, 'To
actively "devour" [time] rather than to passively "languish" [in its
power] is not to escape the end but to accelerate its arrival...[The
strength of the poem] is that having turned against itself [at the
beginning of the second stanza], it then turns against its own internal
objections, leaving us with the desert that is the poem's centre'. We
may note, too, the variety of emotional and tonal ranges that it
exhibits from the languorous to the ironic , the hyperbolical to the
desperate, to the violent, the macabre, and frankly sexual.

To his Coy Mistress

Had we but World enough, and Time,
This coyness Lady were no crime.
We would sit down, and think which way
To walk, and pass our long Loves Day.
Thou by the *Indian Ganges* side
Should'st Rubies find: I by the Tide
Of *Humber* would complain. I would
Love you ten years before the Flood:
And you should if you please refuse
Till the Conversion of the *Jews*.   10
My vegetable Love should grow
Vaster then Empires, and more slow.
An hundred years should go to praise
Thine Eyes, and on thy Forehead Gaze.
Two hundred to adore each Breast:
But thirty thousand to the rest.
An Age at least to every part,
And the last Age should show your Heart.
For Lady you deserve this State;
Nor would I love at lower rate.   20

But at my back I alwaies hear
Times winged Charriot hurrying near:
And yonder all before us lye
Desarts of vast Eternity.
Thy Beauty shall no more be found;
Nor, in thy marble Vault, shall sound
My ecchoing Song: then Worms shall try
That long preserv'd Virginity:
And your quaint Honour turn to dust;
And into ashes all my Lust.   30
The Grave's a fine and private place,
    But none I think do there embrace.
Now therefore, while the youthful hew
Sits on thy skin like morning dew,
And while thy willing Soul transpires
At every pore with instant Fires,
Now let us sport us while we may;
And now, like am'rous birds of prey,
Rather at once our Time devour,
Than languish in his slow-chapt pow'r.   40
Let us roll all our Strength, and all
Our sweetness, up into one Ball:
And tear our Pleasures with rough strife,
Thorough the Iron gates of Life.
Thus, though we cannot make our Sun
Stand still, yet we will make him run.

NOTES

6-7   *Tide of Humber.* The Humber flows through Hull in Yorkshire where
      Marvell grew up. His father was drowned in the Humber. The
      juxtaposition of the Humber with the Ganga suggests that of the
      homely and familiar with the remote and exotic.

7-10 It was believed that Noah's Flood occurred 1656 years after the
      creation of the world, and that Jews would be converted to Christi-
      anity in 1656 A.D. Marvell may have had this parallelism in mind when
      writing these lines; if so, the poem must predate 1656. It is not clear
      what the phrase 'ten years before the Flood' means. Margoliouth
      suggests that it may refer to 1646. But in what sense would the poet
      continue to love till a date which is already in the past?

11   *vegetable Love.* A difficult phrase. It may refer to the Aristotelian
      notion of the three souls of man, the vegetative, the animal and the
      rational. Or the adjective may mean 'living and growing as a plant or
      organism endowed with the lowest form of life' (OED). Some readers
      see a phallic reference here.

13-18 The allocation of segments of time to different portions of the
      mistress's anatomy shows the poet examining the 'official premises'
      of the poem: as Rosalie Colie points out, 'Time threatens love, so the
      poet takes a long look at all time...made "endless" in the literary
      hyperbole of compliment.'

18   *last Age.* The millenium, marked by the second coming of Christ,
      after which the world and time will cease.

29   *quaint.* Dainty, fastidious; perhaps also carrying the now obsolete
      sense of proud or haughty. Margoliouth reminds us that the word
      also meant the vagina, although the last recorded use in this sense is
      1598.
      Honour. Margoliouth points out that a secondary meaning of the
      word is the vagina.

33   *hew.* Hue, complexion.

34   *dew.* This is the reading in the Margoliouth text. However, George de
      F. Lord has made a plausible case for emending *dew* to *glew*, a
      northern English dialectal variation of *glow*, with which Marvell, as
      a Yorkshireman, would have been familiar. If Lord's reading is
      accepted, '[t]he youthful *hue* of the lady' will be compared to 'the
      tints of the sky at dawn'.

40   *slow-chapt pow'r.* 'The power of his slowly-devouring jaws' (Margo-
      liouth).

42   *Ball.* Margoliouth says that the image is that of a pomander (a mixture
      of aromatic substances compressed into a ball); only, here the
      pomander is made up of strength and sweetness, male and female.
      Berthoff notes other interpretations, 'including the ashes gathered
      by the phoenix "into a compact mass" and a cannonball' and adds,
      perhaps ironically, that a 'case could be made...for its being a *pellet*
      (a little ball, esp. of food which a bird of prey devours).'

44   *Thorough.* Through.
      Iron gates of Life. Another much discussed phrase. In a sense, this is
      a commonplace metaphor implying the soul's imprisonment in the
      body and the exit the soul takes at the moment of death. But then,
      what lies on the other side of these gates is presumably the 'desarts
      of vast eternity'. Does this mean that the violent intensity of the
      lovers' lovemaking, engaged in as a response to the swift flight of
      time, will lead them the more certainly to death? The last two lines of
      the poem suggest that this is indeed the case; however, their actions
      will have made their time on earth meaningful.

THE FAIR SINGER

This madrigal-like poem develops the musical-military metaphor, thus exhibiting an elaboration of the phrase 'sweet chordage' used in 'The Resolved Soul, and Created Pleasure': The cool detachment, the conventional metaphors of love as warfare, and the Petrarchan language suggest that it grew not out of passionate commitment to a lady but out of a desire to pay a formal compliment; yet Marvell's deep love for music and his talent in exploiting the musical potentialities of the language are real, and the poem is so well poised, its artifice so perfect, that it makes an impact far transcending that of merely formal poetry. Scholars have pointed to Marvell's remarkable closeness here to Marino's sonnet 'Bella Sonatrice'.

The Fair Singer

I

To make a final conquest of all me,
Love did compose so sweet an Enemy,
In whom both Beauties to my death agree,
Joyning themselves in fatal Harmony;
That while she with her Eyes my Heart does bind,
She with her Voice might captivate my Mind.

II

I could have fled from One but singly fair:
My dis-intangled Soul it self might save,
Breaking the curled trammels of her hair.
But how should I avoid to be her Slave,   10
Whose subtile Art invisibly can wreath
My Fetters of the very Air I breath?

III

It had been easie fighting in some plain,
Where Victory might hang in equal choice,
But all resistance against her is vain,
Who has th' advantage both of Eyes and Voice,
And all my Forces needs must be undone,
She having gained both the Wind and Sun.

NOTES

2,4   *compose, Harmony.* Besides carrying their ordinary meanings both
      words are technical musical terms.
3   *both Beauties.* i.e. beautiful eyes (or looks) and a beautiful voice.
7   *singly fair.* Having only one attribute of beauty.
8-9   i.e. my soul could have disentangled itself from the net ('trammels')
      she has created with her curly hair.
11-12 The *art* refers to her singing, but it is also imaged as an invisible net
      made out of the air. *Air* is a pun, meaning both the wind and songs.
18   *Wind and Sun.* In warfare the army that gained the wind and sun (i.e.
      positioned itself so that they were at its back) had an advantage. The
      singer has gained wind and sun by being both a beautiful singer and
      beautiful to look at.

THE DEFINITION OF LOVE

Though many of the words that Marvell uses in this poem–'Love,'
'Despair,' 'Hope,' 'Fate,' 'Tyrannick pow'r,' 'Heaven'–come from
conventional love poetry, 'The Definition of Love' is unique by any
standard. It shows the utter impossibility of defining anything except
in the terms in which it is defined–which is to say, the utter
impossibility of all definitions–for there is no way in which Marvell's
'definition' can be paraphrased. The poem recalls the Platonic no-
tion of the Ideal. In its spareness, its cold logic as well as the source
and abstract accuracy of some of its imagery it is closely allied with
geometry. It is not so much about what love means as about the
concept of absence which alone can make for presence and which
undergirds it by never being there. These qualities make 'The
Definition of Love' a truly remarkable metaphysical poem.

The Definition of Love

I

My Love is of a birth as rare
As 'tis for object strange and high:
It was begotten by despair
Upon Impossibility.

II

Magnanimous Despair alone
Could show me so divine a thing,
Where feeble Hope could ne'r have flown
But vainly flapt its Tinsel Wing.

III

And yet I quickly might arrive
Where my extended Soul is fixt,   10
But Fate does Iron wedges drive,
And alwaies crouds it self betwixt.

IV

For Fate with jealous Eye does see
Two perfect Loves; nor lets them close:
Their union would her ruine be,
And her Tyrannick pow'r depose.

V

And therefore her Decrees of Steel
Us as the distant Poles have plac'd,
(Though Loves whole World on us doth wheel)
Not by themselves to be embrac'd.   20

VI

Unless the giddy Heaven fall,
And Earth some new Convulsion tear;
And, us to joyn, the World should all
Be cramp'd into a *Planisphere.*

VII

As Lines so Loves *oblique* may well
Themselves in every Angle greet:
But ours so truly *Paralel,*
Though infinite can never meet.

VIII

Therefore the Love which us doth bind,
But Fate so enviously debarrs,   30
Is the Conjunction of the Mind,
And Opposition of the Stars.

NOTES

3   *begotten.* Fathered by. The only union that takes place in this poem
      is the present one of despair and Impossibility; yet the poet's tone
      remains exultant rather than despairing.

5   *Magnanimous.* Perhaps a pun on the normal meaning of the word
      and *magnus animus* = great-souled. Despair is magnanimous
      because it discourages hope (line 7).

10   *extended Soul is fixt.* Descartes argued that only matter was capable
      of extension; Marvell's application of the word to the soul is therefore
      paradoxical. 'Fixed,' according to the *OED*, means intently directed
      towards an object. The line may be paraphrased: My soul extends or
      stretches towards the object on which it is focused.

11   *wedges.* A wedge is a tool for prising, parting or keeping apart, often
      used by carpenters. But as Isabel MacCaffrey and Kitty Datta have
      argued, a wedge is also the axle that both separates and at the same
      time binds the wheels of a cart. This interpretation of Marvell's image
      suggests that if fate keeps the lovers apart, it also provides an inextri-
      cable bond between them. Margoliouth quotes an anonymous critic:
      'Fate is symbolized by the products of one of the industries which
      were transforming rural Britain'.

21-5 Since we are the poles on which the earth rotates (lines 18-19), the
      only way we could be united is if the earth were flattened into a
      planisphere either as a result of the sky falling on top of it, or through
      some other natural calamity. A planisphere was 'an astrolabe, a round
      plate on which the two sides showed the two hemispheres and the
      poles were consequently brought together' (Gardner).

27-8 In Euclidean geometry parallel lines meet at infinity. The parallel
      lines of the poet's love are like the latitudes, and they are contrasted
      with the oblique or longitudinal lines of other lovers. Longitudes
      meet at the poles. *Oblique* means at an angle, but the word also
      carries a pejorative moral connotation as contrasted with the infinity
      of the poet's love.

31,32 *Conjunction, Opposition.* Both words are taken from astrology. Our
      love may be star-crossed; but for it to be so, the stars themselves,
      which are opposed to us, have to be in a certain conjunction. Once
      again the idea of unity-in-separation, already explored through the
      wedge and poles images, is emphasized.

THE PICTURE OF LITTLE *T.C.* IN A PROSPECT OF FLOWERS

Gardens and the pastoral theme are traditionally associated with love poetry. However, Marvell dissociates this pastoral poem from love's passion by making the heroine a young, sexually immature girl. Love, we are told, will come, but only in the future and not in the world of the garden but in the world beyond its walls. The girl's role will then be not that of the beloved but rather that of the scourge of love. Meanwhile, walled in within the security of the garden she is like an innocent Eve giving names to flowers and, through her superior moral nature born as much of her innocence as of her beauty and symbolic role, improving Nature. A gatherer of flowers, she is herself seen as the loveliest of flowers. But even as the poem celebrates a virtuous life within the safe confines of the garden, it subjects its vision to ironic scrutiny. Violence is implicit in the world of the garden in that T.C.'s 'taming' of the 'wilder flowers' is emblematic of her later martial role as the enemy of love. Besides, the girl cannot confer attributes to flowers which Nature has denied. By the end of the poem the protection that the pastoral world was seen to afford threatens to collapse in Marvell' exhortation to his heroine to spare the buds lest death should pluck her while she is still in the bud of her life.

The Picture of little T.C. in a Prospect of Flowers

I

See with what simplicity
This Nimph begins her golden daies!
In the green Grass she loves to lie,
And there with her fair Aspect tames
The Wilder flow'rs, and gives them names:
But only with the Roses playes;
    And them does tell
What Colour best becomes them, and what Smell.

II

Who can foretel for what high cause
This Darling of the Gods was born!   10

Yet this is She whose chaster Laws
The wanton Love shall one day fear,
And, under her command severe,
See his Bow broke and Ensigns torn.
　　　Happy, who can
Appease this virtuous Enemy of Man!

III

O then let me in time compound,
And parly with those conquering Eyes;
Ere they have try'd their force to wound,
Ere, with their glancing wheels, they drive   20
In Triumph over Hearts that strive,
And them that yield but more despise.
　　　Let me be laid,
Where I may see thy Glories from some shade.

IV

Mean time, whilst every verdant thing
It self does at thy Beauty charm,
Reform the errours of the Spring;
Make that the Tulips may have share
Of sweetness, seeing they are fair;
And Roses of their thorns disarm: 30
　　　But most procure
That Violets may a longer Age endure.

V

But O young beauty of the Woods,
Whom Nature courts with fruits and flow'rs,
Gather the Flow'rs, but spare the Buds;
Lest *Flora* angry at thy crime,
To kill her Infants in their prime,
Do quickly make th'Example Yours;
　　　And, ere we see,
Nip in the blossome all our hopes and Thee.   40

NOTES

Title. T.C. is Theophila Cornewall, born September 1644. Her younger
   sister of the same name had died the second day after birth; perhaps
   this fact leads Marvell to warn his T.C. not to court an early death.
1 *simplicity.* Perhaps there is more to this word than meets the eye.
   'Simples' refers to herbs and flowers with curative powers. 'Simple'
   also means naive. Both meanings would be appropriate, the former
   in the context of the poem's pastoralism and the latter as a reference
   to the girl's innocence, her attempt to improve upon Nature, and the
   danger of her unwittingly angering Flora (stanza 5).
11-12 i.e. sexual love will be awed by her strength and sternness, the result
   of her chastity.
14 *Bow broke.* Cupid, the god of love, traditionally carries a bow. The
   victor in battle imposed the humiliation upon the defeated enemy of
   having his weapons broken and ensign or banner torn.
17-18 *compound, And parly.* Negotiate peace terms. Both words are from
   warfare.
20 *glancing wheels.* Berthoff points out the pun on the Nymph's glance
   and the murderous barbs of her chariot's wheels.
23-4 Berthoff suggests that by the time the young girl is old enough to fight
   against Love, the poet himself will be dead ('laid' = buried) and will
   therefore watch her triumph from his grave in some shady spot.
28-9 Tulips have no scent.
35 'Gather the flowers' is a common piece of advice given by the *carpe
   diem* poet to his mistress. Marvell tempers this advice here with the
   admonition not to gather the buds.
36 *Flora.* The goddess of vegetation.

THE MOWER TO THE GLO-WORMS

Marvell has four Mower poems. Critics have disagreed on whether
Damon, their hero, remains the same figure throughout or repre-
sents different attitudes in different poems. He may owe something
to the hardworking herdsmen of Virgil's Eclogues, though parallels
have also been found in French poetry. He is a countryman, a farmer,
a singer-poet, a paradisiacal figure who is at one with Nature. He can
be courteous and refined, a 'natural' man and at times a satirist who
lashes out against the artifice, corruption and luxury of the world
outside his fields. And in his role as mower of grass he represents
death. Death is not seen in these poems as anything fearsome but
rather as part of the process of Nature, a natural and necessary

extinction. Therefore the troubles that Damon bemoans are not the
consequence either of a sense of alienation from Paradise or of the
awareness of mortality; rather, he has fallen in love and this distracts
him from his true pursuits, even causing him, in a fit of revenge, to
round upon Nature and try to lay it waste.

The present poem laments Damon's lack of direction resulting
from his having fallen in love. The speaker seems to stand midway at
a point between complete concordance with Nature and a severance
from it. The poem states that Nature will not enable him to regain his
old equilibrium, but his address to Nature indicates his hope for a
saving grace from it.

The Mower to the Glo-Worms

I

Ye living Lamps, by whose dear light
The Nightingale does sit so late,
And studying all the Summer-night,
Her matchless Songs does meditate;

II

Ye Country Comets, that portend
No War, nor Princes funeral,
Shining unto no higher end
Then to presage the Grasses fall;

III

Ye Glo-worms, whose officious Flame
To wandring Mowers shows the way,   10
That in the Night have lost their aim,
And after foolish Fires do stray;

IV

Your courteous Lights in vain you wast,
Since *Juliana* here is come,
For She my Mind hath so displac'd
That I shall never find my home.

NOTES

1   *living Lamps.* The phrase is literally applicable to glow worms. Kitty Datta has shown that glow worms were a common subject of Caroline court poetry.

5   *Country Comets.* According to Pliny glow worms were a substitute for stars, provided by Nature so that farmers could work at night. The appearance of comets presaged great disasters. Marvell here says that the only disaster that glow worms presage is the fall of the grass.

9   *officious.* Zealous, attentive (Margoliouth).

12   The reference is to naturally occurring phosphorescence which was wrongly attributed to mischievous spirits like Jack o'Lantern who, it was believed, shone their lights over bogs and other treacherous places in order to mislead benighted travellers. Damon implies that glow worms may lead the traveller safely home, but they will not be able to help him who is misled by the false light of love.

15   *displac'd.* Distracted. The word also carries the suggestion that something has been lost by being misplaced; this sense is picked up in the word *find* in the next line.

THE GARDEN

For Marvell the garden is 'a quiet retreat; a lover's delight; the paradise of the temporally bound soul; man's earthly heaven, his second Eden' (Berthoff). It is the product of art, but an art which contains and improves on Nature. A place for contemplation that enables man to transcend the temporal and natural, in it the principle of temporality is not absent but only sweetened. All these ways of regarding the garden are germane to an understanding of this poem, which has been read as a philosophical lyric, a poem of contemplation and meditation, an ironic satire, a political statement, and a retelling of the Fall myth. Marvell's skill lies in combining these heterogeneous elements into a unified whole. Equally remarkable is his ability to convey these, and other meanings, in a highly polished, terse, epigrammatic style which is, at the same time, resonant of earlier literature, full of puns, unexpected elaborations, teasing abstractions and concrete details.

The Garden

I

How vainly men themselves amaze
To win the Palm, the Oke, or Bayes;
And their uncessant Labours see
Crown'd from some single Herb or Tree.
Whose short and narrow verged Shade
Does prudently their Toyles upbraid;
While all Flow'rs and all Trees do close
To weave the Garlands of repose.

II

Fair quiet, have I found thee here,
And Innocence thy Sister dear!   10
Mistaken long, I sought you then
In busie Companies of Men.
Your sacred Plants, if here below,
Only among the Plants will grow.
Society is all but rude,
To this delicious Solitude.

III

No white nor red was ever seen
So am'rous as this lovely green.
Fond Lovers, cruel as their Flame,
Cut in these Trees their Mistress name.   20
Little, Alas, they know, or heed,
How far these Beauties Hers exceed!
Fair Trees! where s'eer your barkes I wound,
No Name shall but your own be found.

IV

When we have run our Passions heat,
Love hither makes his best retreat.
The *Gods,* that mortal Beauty chase,
Still in a Tree did end their race.
Apollo hunted *Daphne* so,

Only that She might Laurel grow.   30
And *Pan* did after *Syrinx* speed,
Not as a Nymph, but for a Reed.

V

What wound'rous Life in this I lead!
Ripe Apples drop about my head;
The Luscious Clusters of the Vine
Upon my Mouth do crush their Wine;
The Nectaren, and curious Peach,
Into my hands themselves do reach;
Stumbling on Melons, as I pass,
Insnar'd with Flow'rs, I fall on Grass.   40

VI

Mean while the Mind, from pleasure less,
Withdraws into its happiness:
The Mind, that Ocean where each kind
Does streight its own resemblance find;
Yet it creates, transcending these,
Far other Worlds, and other Seas;
Annihilating all that's made
To a green Thought in a green Shade.

VII

Here at the Fountains sliding foot,
Or at some Fruit-trees mossy root,   50
Casting the Bodies Vest aside,
My Soul into the boughs does glide:
There like a Bird it sits, and sings,
Then whets, and combs its silver Wings;
And, till prepar'd for longer flight,
Waves in its Plumes the various Light.

VIII

Such was that happy Garden-state,
While Man there walk'd without a Mate:
After a Place so pure, and sweet,
What other Help could yet be meet!   60

But 'twas beyond a Mortal's share
To wander solitary there:
Two Paradises 'twere in one
To live in Paradise alone.

IX

How well the skilful Gardner drew
Of flow'rs and herbes this Dial new;
Where from above the milder Sun
Does through a fragrant Zodiack run;
And, as it works, th' industrious Bee
Computes its time as well as we.   70
How could such sweet and wholsome Hours
Be reckon'd but with herbs and flow'rs!

NOTES

1   *vainly.* A pun: uselessly; proudly.
        amaze. Another pun: stupify themselves; lose themselves as in a
        maze or labyrinth.
2   The palm leaf was traditionally awarded to the victor in battle, the
        oak leaf for civic distinction, and the bay or laurel leaf to outstand-
        ing poets.
6   By its narrowness the shade of the tree wisely ('prudently') chastises
        ('upbraids') men who labour hard ('toyle') only to win a leaf when
        they could have the whole garden for their repose. However, as
        critics have pointed out, the line can be read differently: The short
        and narrow verge of shade is emblematic of the economy ('pru-
        dently') with which the trees weave ('upbraid') the snares ('toyles')
        in which labouring men will be 'amazed'. This is to be contrasted
        with the generosity with which the whole garden contributes to
        man's repose. Marvell may here be criticizing the Puritan ethic with
        its emphasis on restraint and economy (narrowness produces
        snares and toils) as against the courtly or Cavalier tradition of
        exuberance. If so, later in the poem (e.g. stanza 5) he will direct his
        irony at the Cavalier ethic. He may also be suggesting in these lines
        that men 'amaze' themselves to win leaves when it is the trees, in
        fact, that create mazes for men. This latter reading would make trees
        the agents, not objects, of men's destiny, allowing the rest of the
        poem to explore this paradox.
7-8   *close....repose.* The flowers and trees are so abundant that they
        join together to form not just a wreath out of leaves but a whole

garland to crown with repose the man who rejects the world's pursuits in favour of the garden.

9-10   Together with Solitude, Quiet and Innocence form the three Graces of Marvell's garden.

12   Either, I sought you in the company of busy men; or, I sought you in busy groups.

15   The inversion of sense is witty, since traditionally the city is associated with civility (the two words share the same root) while rudeness is supposed to thrive in rustic solitude.

17-18   Lovely, which is the interpretation Margoliouth favours for *am'rous*, is sanctioned by the *OED*, though it records this usage as obsolete. But the current sense of 'amorous' as pertaining to love is also present here, for Marvell rejects love in line 17. White and red are the conventional colours associated with the mistress; and in preferring the green of plants Marvell may also be expressing a rejection of anything which is double in favour of the integrity suggested by the number one.

19   *Fond*. A common Elizabethan and seventeenth-century pun: (1) loving, amorous; (2) foolish.
        Flame. The word refers both to the heat of love the lovers feel and to their mistresses. Cf. line 25 below.

23-4   As so often in this poem, here the poet modulates into a stance which invites irony at his expense and thus provides a critique of the positions he is upholding.

25   *run...beat*. Either, when we have exhausted the heat of our passion; or, when we have finished running the heat (a race before the final contest).

27-8   There is irony in the fact that the gods chased the women only so that they might be turned into trees which cannot run.

29-32   Marvell's two examples come from Ovid's *Metamorphoses*. They are part of the process that has been going on in the poem of retreating from the world of action into the garden. But they raise some questions also. If the purpose of the chase was to turn the women into trees in the garden, how is it that these trees have come to represent art which flourishes in the world outside the garden? (The laurel represents poetry, of which Apollo is god, and the reed the pastoral with which Pan is associated: see line 2). Furthermore, is the chase viewed as a necessary precondition for a retreat into the garden? The word *When* in line 25 suggests that, desirable though the retreat is, it is possible only after we have exhausted ourselves in worldly affairs, and the value of contemplation cannot be understood by one who has not experienced action.
        Stanzas 5, 6 and 7. They describe, respectively, the retreat of the body, the mind and the soul. In stanza 5 the exaggerations of

Nature's bounty probably have a comic intention which is not absent from the conceits in stanzas 3 and 4 and signal that a critical scrutiny of the ideal is going on even as the ideal is being presented and upheld. See lines 39-40 and note below.

37 *curious.* Exquisite.

39-40 *Stumbling...Insnar'd...fall.* The garden is not free from dangers and snares, though they do not cause the poet any hurt. *Insnared* recalls the 'toyles' that the trees braid in line 6 and raises the question whether the garden is a trap for the unwary enthusiast rather than a paradisiacal state of being. *Fall* suggests the fall from the Garden of Eden.

41 *from pleasures less.* Either, the inferior pleasures of the body described above; or, as a consequence of the lessening or palling of these pleasures.

43-4 Sir Thomas Browne in *Vulgar Errors*, 3.24 discusses the popular misconception 'that all animals of the Land are in their kind in the Sea' (Margoliouth). If the ocean reflects the reality of the material world, and the mind is an ocean reflecting that reflection, the images of the mind can be said to be twice removed from material reality. But here it is these images of images which are upheld as the truly real, suggesting a Platonic emphasis upon the Ideal as opposed to the material. 'The Garden' possesses many Platonic and neo-Platonic ideas which Marvell may have acquired while at Cambridge, a great centre of Platonic thought in the early years of the century.

45-8 A multi-step process is described here. First, the mind withdraws from a contemplation of the external world to a contemplation of the images of that world which it finds in itself. These images are then transcended by others of its own making, till finally they are all cancelled in favour of one image which bears no relation to physical reality.

47-8 These lines have been much commented on. Line 47 suggests that meditation in its highest form involves more than creation and, in reaching it, multitudinousness gives way to a certain intense singleness. The singular *Thought* in the next line is to be contrasted with the plural images which it replaces. *Green* may symbolize perfection (cf. line 18 above) as well as being naturally associated with the garden where the reverie is taking place.

49-50 In meditative trance external objects lose their distinguishing features. The gliding or flowing waters of the fountain take on the attributes of the roots of a tree.

51 *Vest.* Clothes. The body clothes the soul.

52 *glide.* The word recalls the *slide* of the fountain in line 49, suggesting that the soul, the tree and the fountain partake of the same nature.

53   Critics have seen a parallel to Yeats's bird in 'Sailing to Byzantium'. Just as Yeats's bird, though out of Nature, can only sing of what is in Nature, so Marvell's bird, while waiting to fly to heaven, waves its wings in the variegated ('various') light of the world (line 56). The mind may annihilate the world, but while man is alive the soul cannot remain unaffected by it.

57-8   The reference here is to Adam in the Garden of Eden before the creation of Eve.

60   Marvell plays upon God's words regarding the reason for Eve's creation in Genesis 2:18: 'I will make him an help meet for him' (meet = suitable).

65   *Gardner.* If the poem was written while Marvell was in Fairfax's employ at Appleton, the word could refer to Fairfax who was a keen gardener. The capitalization may indicate that the skilful *Gardner* is God.

66-8   *Dial...Zodiac.* The reference is to a flower clock where the flowers were planted to resemble a clock's dial. As different flower beds began to receive the sunlight their flowers would open. Marvell compares the flower clock with its beds of different flowers to the different signs of the Zodiac through which the sun moves in the sky and says that the sun that moves through the 'fragrant Zodiac' of the flowers is milder than that which shines elsewhere.

69   *industrious Bee.* The bee possesses the quality of industriousness prized by the Puritans. The introduction of time and the bee's labour in the garden shows that if the garden is, for Marvell, a retreat from the world and an antithesis to it, it is also the world's image made more perfect. In moments of meditation which the garden makes possible the world may be annihilated but, in the final analysis, the garden exists in the world and the world in the garden.

70   *computes its time.* Tells time; but the phrase also connotes an awareness of impending mortality. Time, too, may be a pun since thyme was frequently grown in seventeenth-century gardens.

AN HORATIAN *ODE UPON* CROMWEL'S *RETURN FROM* IRELAND

'Horatian' in the title suggests not only that the poem is a regular ode as opposed to the Pindaric or irregular ode but also the way it is to be read. Horace's ode on Cleopatra's defeat at Actium and subsequent suicide (*Carmina* 1.37) starts as a panegyric to Caesar but slides into a celebration of the vanquished queen. In like manner Marvell starts by praising Cromwell, who returned victorious from his Irish campaign in 1650, but modulates into a tribute to Charles I, who was executed the previous year. As Charles is elevated to a tragic hero, Cromwell, the ostensible hero of the poem, comes under critical scrutiny. Thus the poem maintains an equidistance between the two figures and Marvell is able to steer clear of the intense partisanship that characterized both the Royalists and the Republicans in that period. The question that he asks at the beginning is whether a life of retirement and contemplation is possible in moments·of great crisis. The answer is that both the poet and the great man can best preserve the values of retirement (such as those described in 'The Garden') if they are willing to take part in the making of history. Indeed, only a man who knows the value of retirement can be a hero in action: Cromwell's success stems from his both ;knowing and acting, possessing both virtue and *virtu*. It is this combination that makes him a providential hero, an invincible natural force. But the celebration of such a force should not blind us to the destruction it inevitably causes of things that were truly beautiful or to the fact that once unleashed it can maintain its momentum only through further destruction.

An Horatian *Ode upon* Cromwel's *Return from* Ireland

The forward Youth that would appear
Must now forsake his *Muses* dear,
    Nor in the Shadows sing
    His Numbers languishing.
'Tis time to leave the Books in dust,
And oyl th'unused Armours rust;
    Removing from the Wall
    The Corslet of the Hall.
So restless *Cromwel* could not cease
In the inglorious Arts of Peace,   10
    But through adventrous War
    Urged his active Star.
And, like the three-fork'd Lightning, first
Breaking the Clouds where it was nurst,
    Did thorough his own Side
    His fiery way divide.
For 'tis all one to Courage high
The Emulous or Enemy;
    And with such to inclose

Is more then to oppose.   20
Then burning through the Air he went,
And Pallaces and Temples rent:
    And *Caesars* head at last
    Did through his Laurels blast.
'Tis Madness to resist or blame
The force of angry Heavens flame
    And, if we would speak true,
    Much to the Man is due.
Who, from his private Gardens, where
He liv'd reserved and austere,   30
    As if his highest plot
    To plant the Bergamot,
Could by industrious Valour climbe
To ruine the great Work of Time,
    And cast the Kingdome old
    Into another Mold.
Though Justice against Fate complain,
And plead the antient Rights in vain:
    But those do hold or break
    As Men are strong or weak.   40
Nature that hateth emptiness,
Allows of penetration less:
    And therefore must make room
    Where greater Spirits come.
What Field of all the Civil Wars,
Where his were not the deepest Scars?
    And *Hampton* shows what part
    He had of wiser Art.
Where, twining subtile fears with hope,
He wove a Net of such a scope,   50
    That *Charles* himself might chase
    To *Caresbrooks* narrow case.
That thence the *Royal Actor* born
The *Tragick Scaffold* might adorn:
    While round the armed Bands
    Did clap their bloody hands.
He nothing common did or mean
Upon that memorable Scene:
    But with his keener Eye
    The Axes edge did try: 60

Nor call'd the *Gods* with vulgar spight
To vindicate his helpless Right,
   But bow'd his comely Head,
   Down as upon a Bed.
This was that memorable Hour
Which first assur'd the forced Pow'r.
   So when they did design
   The *Capitols* first Line,
A bleeding Head where they begun,
Did fright the Architects to run;   70
   And yet in that the *State*
   Foresaw it's happy Fate.
And now the *Irish* are asham'd
To see themselves in one Year tam'd:
   So much one Man can do,
   That does both act and know.
They can affirm his Praises best,
And have, though overcome, confest
   How good he is, how just,
   And fit for highest Trust: 80
Nor yet grown stiffer with Command,
But still in the *Republick's* hand:
   How fit he is to sway
   That can so well obey.
He to the *Commons Feet* presents
A *Kingdome*, for his first years rents:
   And, what he may, forbears
   His Fame to make it theirs:
And has his Sword and Spoyls ungirt,
To lay them at the *Publick's* skirt.   90
   So when the Falcon high
   Falls heavy from the Sky,
She, having kill'd, no more does search,
But on the next green Bow to pearch;
   Where, when he first does lure,
   The Falckner has her sure.
What may not then our *Isle* presume
While Victory his Crest does plume!
   What may not others fear
   If thus he crown each Year!   100
A *Caesar* he ere long to *Gaul*,

To *Italy* an *Hannibal*,
   And to all States not free
   Shall *Clymacterick* be.
The *Pict* no shelter now shall find
Within his party-colour'd Mind;
   But from this Valour sad
   Shrink underneath the Plad:
Happy if in the tufted brake
The *English Hunter* him mistake;   110
   Nor lay his Hounds in near
   The *Caledonian* Deer.
But thou the Wars and Fortunes Son
March indefatigably on;
   And for the last effect
   Still keep thy Sword erect:
Besides the force it has to fright
The Spirits of the shady Night,
   The same *Arts* that did *gain*
   A *Pow'r* must it *maintain*.   120

NOTES

1   *forward.* Ambitious.

2   *Muses dear.* Used generally to mean studies, though the sense of a
        poetic vocation is not absent, the nine Muses being the presiding
        deities of the arts.

9   *cease* From Latin *cessare* = to rest.

12   *active Star.* The star under which he was born, i.e. his fate.

13-16 Lightning was believed to be born by tearing through the side of its
        own body, which was the cloud. Comparing Cromwell with three-
        pronged lightning identifies him as a violent force of Nature armed
        with a trident and not subject to conventional moral judgements;
        he will not only destroy the enemy but also members of his own
        party ('side').

17-20 These lines further develop the ideas of lines 13-16. To 'inclose' (i.e.
        surround or be on the same side as) a man like Cromwell is to invite
        destruction even more surely than by opposing him, for to such a
        man there is no difference between supporters who want to be like
        him ('emulous') and enemies.

23   *Caesars.* Lord points out that the title, applied here to Charles I, is
        transferred to Cromwell in line 101.

24   The laurel was supposed to be immune to lightning. In 'The Garden' the laurel wreath is associated with poetry, here with kingship.

31-2   The bergamot is a type of pear. The word 'plot' suggests that, though at present innocent, Cromwell is capable of Machiavellian intrigue.

34   *great Work of Time.* The British monarchy.

37-40   Marvell suggests here that justice and tradition ('ancient Rights') were on the king's side, but they could not withstand Cromwell's superior force.

41-2   Nature, which abhors a vacuum, abhors even more two bodies occupying the space meant for one. Cromwell and Charles could not have coexisted.

47-52   Charles, having fled from Hampton Court to Carisbrooke Castle on the Isle of Wight in 1647, received rumours that Cromwell was planning to attack him, whereupon he tried to escape through a narrow window ('case', line 52) and was apprehended. Marvell suggests that the rumours were floated by Cromwell to achieve precisely this result: they were the net he wove out of Charles' fears and hope. Cromwell comes across here as a scheming politician.

53-6   Marvell likens the king ascending the scaffold to a tragic hero appearing on the stage, and the jeers of his bloody murderers are transformed into applause for a fine performance.

59-60   The king glanced at the executioner's axe in order to see how sharp it was. So collected was his demeanour that it could be said that his eye was sharper than the axe.

67-72   Pliny 'relates how a human head was found in laying the foundations of the [Roman] Capitol and how the most celebrated priest...interpreted the head as a favourable omen' (Lord).

81   *yet grown stiffer.* The implication is that, in the future, Cromwell may become imperious and uncontrollable by Parliament.

85   *Commons.* Parliament. The House of Lords was abolished by the Republicans.

87-8   i.e. although he may take credit for the victories, he forbears to do so, instead allowing the glory to shine on Parliament.

92   *falls heavy.* Swoops down. The falcon image suggests Cromwell's predatory nature, that he is, like birds, beyond moral categorization, and that so far he is controllable.

96   *Falckner.* Falconer.

101-2   Caesar defeated France and Hannibal, Italy.

104   *Clymacterick.* 'Critical, epoch-making' (Lord).

105-6   The *Pict* is the Scot. Cromwell assumed command of the Scottish campaign after Fairfax's refusal to attack Scotland without provocation. *Party-colour'd* (multi-coloured, and therefore changeable, fickle) is a pun on 'Pict', which is derived from the Latin *pingere* = to paint.

107   *sad.* Steadfast.

108   *Plad.* Obsolete form of 'plaid', a woollen garment worn by the Scots.

109   *brake.* Bracken, a plant common in the Scottish Highlands.

112   *Caledonian.* Scottish, from Caledonia, the old name for Scotland.

116   Holding the sword erect by its blade was considered a charm for warding off evil spirits. Here the phrase also means: 'Always be prepared for battle'.

119-20 Marvell implies that having gained power through war and aggression, Cromwell must continue in that path.

ON *MR.* MILTON'S *PARADISE LOST*

This poem was prefixed to the second edition of *Paradise Lost* (1674). Its praise is the more genuine for exhibiting in full measure the doubts that Marvell had about Milton's project when he first sat down to read him. In its 'public' theme, the directness of its utterance, its use of rhymed decasyllabic couplets, and its clearly expressed meaning, the poem is closer to the achievement of Restoration poetry than to his own earlier work. Marvell apologizes humorously for using rhyme to praise a poem which had rejected rhyme in favour of blank verse; there is also satire directed against Dryden who turned *Paradise Lost* into an opera entitled *The State of Innocence.*

On Mr. Milton's *Paradise lost*

When I beheld the Poet blind, yet bold,
In slender Book his vast Design unfold,
Messiah Crown'd, *Gods* Reconcil'd Decree,
Rebelling *Angels,* the Forbidden Tree,
Heav'n, Hell, Earth, Chaos, All; the Argument
Held me a while misdoubting his Intent,
That he would ruine (for I saw him strong)
The sacred Truths to Fable and old Song,
(*So Sampson* groap'd the Temples Posts in spight)
The World o'rewhelming to revenge his Sight.   10
    Yet as I read, soon growing less severe,
I lik'd his Project, the success did fear;

Through that wide Field how he his way should find
O're which lame Faith leads Understanding blind;
Lest he perplext the things he would explain,
And what was easie he should render vain.
    Or if a Work so infinite he spann'd,
Jealous I was that some less skilful hand
(Such as disquiet alwayes what is well
And by ill imitating would excell)   20
Might hence presume the whole Creations day
To change in Scenes, and show it in a Play.
    Pardon me, *mighty Poet,* nor despise
My causeless, yet not impious, surmise.
But I am now convinc'd, and none will dare
Within thy Labours to pretend a Share.
Thou hast not miss'd one thought that could be fit,
And all that was improper dost omit:
So that no room is here for Writers left,
But to detect their Ignorance or Theft.   30
    That Majesty which through thy Work doth Reign
Draws the Devout, deterring the Profane.
And things divine thou treatst of in such state
As them preserves, and Thee inviolate.
At once delight and horrour on us seize,
Thou singst with so much gravity and ease;
And above humane flight dost soar aloft,
With Plume so strong, so equal, and so soft.
The *Bird* nam'd from that *Paradise* you sing
So never Flags, but alwaies keeps on Wing.   40
    Where couldst thou Words of such a compass find?
Whence furnish such a vast expense of Mind?
Just Heav'n Thee, like *Tiresias,* to requite,
Rewards with *Prophesie* thy loss of Sight.
    Well mightst thou scorn thy Readers to allure
With tinkling Rhime, of thy own Sense secure;
While the *Town-Bays* writes all the while and spells,
And like a Pack-Horse tires without his Bells.
Their Fancies like our bushy Points appear,
The Poets tag them; we for fashion wear.   50
I too transported by the *Mode* offend,
And while I meant to *Praise* thee, must Commend.
Thy verse created like thy *Theme* sublime,
In Number, Weight, and Measure, needs not *Rhime.*

NOTES

5   *Argument.* Subject.
6   *misdoubting...Intent.* i.e. I had doubts about his intentions.
8   Marvell was afraid that Milton would ruin his sacred Christian theme
      by putting it into a pagan epic form ('old Song') and through the use
      of pagan or Greek myths ('Fable').
9   *Samson Agonistes,* in which the hero destroys himself when he pulls
      down the temple of the Philistines to avenge his blindness and impris-
      onment, was published in 1671.
14   The subjects that Milton deals with, like God's providence, His fore-
      knowledge, and man's free will, cannot be properly understood but
      have to be accepted as an act of faith.
15   *perplext.* Confused.
18-22 The reference to the 'less skilful hand' is to Dryden who turned
      Milton's epic into an opera, though it was never produced. Marvell's
      opposition to Dryden stemmed from the fact that they had both
      entered service under Cromwell, but at the Restoration Dryden
      became a firm Royalist while Marvell continued to maintain his
      independence. Dryden was to satirize Marvell in *Religio Laici* (1682)
      as 'Martin Marprelate, The Marvel of those times...'
19   *disquiet.* Spoil, ruin.
30   *detect.* Expose.
33-4 You treat of divine things in such a way that they remain divine and
      your poetic reputation is not sullied.
37-8 Cf. *Paradise Lost* I. 13-14: '...my adventurous song/That with no
      middle flight intends to soar...'
39-40 i.e., So that bird, named after the paradise about which you sing,
      never ceases its flight. Birds of paradise were thought to have no feet,
      and therefore to be constantly in the air.
42   *expense.* Expanse.
43-4 Cf. *Paradise Lost,* III. 33-36:
      Those other two equal'd with me in fate,
      So were I equal'd with them in renown,
      Blind *Thamyris* and blind *Maeonides,*
      And *Tiresias* and *Phineus,* Prophets old...
      Tiresias was a blind Greek prophet.
47   *Town-Bays.* Dryden, nicknamed Mr. Bays by his enemies.
48   A pack-horse, or plodding beast of burden, would tire if he did not
      have bells on; similarly, a bad poet would not be able to write without
      the help of rhyme. The image is suggested by the use of the word
      'tinkling' to describe rhymed verse in line 46.

49-50 The inferior poet's rhymes are like bushy points, or tasselled laces for tying stockings: the poet tags them on to all his poems, and we submit to them because they are regarded as fashionable. When Dryden asked Milton for permission to turn *Paradise Lost* into an opera, Milton is reported to have replied that Dryden had his permission 'to tag his verses'.

52 Marvell means: 'I, too, have been affected by the fashion for rhyme. I wanted to say "I praise you", but because the word "praise" does not rhyme, I have instead to say "I commend".'

INDEX OF FIRST LINES